This book examines the life, times, and legacy  dictator and president during most of the pei Levine's chief concern is how Vargas's legacy what extent his social legislation affected people's lives. Vargas ignored individual rights, working for state-regulated citizenship without disharmony, without the right to dissent. His revolution was partial, one in which new constituencies and rules were grafted onto traditional political practices. Vargas devoted as much effort to manipulating workers as he did to benefiting them. By the end of his long tenure in power, some things had hardly changed at all: the readiness of the armed forces to intervene; the elite's tenacious hold on privilege; and the historical predominance of the Center-South. Brazil's distribution of income remained among the least equable in the world, but Vargas did not perceive this as a problem that needed to be solved. That Vargas promised more than he delivered did not diminish the adulation that Brazilians held for him. Ordinary people would shrug and say: O presidente sempre lembrou da gente ("the president always remembered us").

FATHER OF THE POOR?

NEW APPROACHES TO THE AMERICAS

Edited by Stuart Schwartz, Yale University

ALSO PUBLISHED IN THE SERIES:

Noble David Cook, *Born to Die: Disease and New World Conquest, 1492–1650*

FORTHCOMING IN THE SERIES:

Alberto Flores Galindo (translated by Carlos Aguirre and Charles Walker), *In Search of an Inca*

Sandra Lauderdale Graham, *Slavery in Nineteenth-Century Brazil*

Gilbert Joseph and Patricia Pessar, *Rethinking Rural Protest in Latin America*

Herbert Klein, *A History of the Atlantic Slave Trade*

John McNeill, *Epidemics and Geopolitics in the American Tropics*

Susan Socolow, *Women in Colonial Latin America*

Eric Van Young, *Popular Rebellion in Mexico, 1810–1821*

FATHER

OF THE POOR?

VARGAS AND HIS ERA

ROBERT M. LEVINE
University of Miami,
Coral Gables

CAMBRIDGE
UNIVERSITY PRESS

PUBLISHED BY THE PRESS SYNDICATE OF THE UNIVERSITY OF CAMBRIDGE
The Pitt Building, Trumpington Street, Cambridge, CB2 1RP, United Kingdom

CAMBRIDGE UNIVERSITY PRESS
The Edinburgh Building, Cambridge CB2 2RU, United Kingdom
40 West 20th Street, New York, NY 10011-4211, USA
10 Stamford Road, Oakleigh, Melbourne 3166, Australia

First published 1998

Printed in the United States of America

Typeset in Goudy

Library of Congress Cataloging-in-Publication Data
Levine, Robert M.
Father of the poor? : Vargas and his era / Robert M. Levine.
p. cm.
Includes bibliographical references (p.   ) and index.
ISBN 0-521-58515-5. – ISBN 0-521-58528-7 (pb)
1. Vargas, Getúlio, 1883–1954. 2. Brazil – Politics and
government – 1930–1945. 3. Brazil – Politics and
government – 1945–1954. 4. Brazil – Economic policy. 5. Brazil –
Social policy. I. Title.
F2538.L48 1997
981.06'1'092 – dc21   97-11309
CIP

A catalog record for this book is available from
the British Library.

ISBN 0 521 58515 5 hardback
ISBN 0 521 58528 7 paperback

For Peggy

Contents

Acknowledgments

Much has changed since I went to Brazil to begin my dissertation research in May 1964, less than two months after the military coup that overthrew Brazil's constitutional government. I intended to study the Vargas period, not knowing at the time that the military regime, wary of the late president's popularity, would make Getúlio Vargas a "nonperson." In fact, Vargas's daughter Alzira may have granted me permission to use her father's archive because she felt that Brazilian historians were reluctant to write about the Vargas era. After 1968, the dictatorship turned repressive. When my book on the Vargas regime was published by Columbia University Press in 1970, several Brazilian publishers contacted me for publication rights, but two different translation drafts were rejected by police censors. The book finally appeared in Brazil ten years later, when briefly it became a best seller, perhaps because readers saw parallels between the post-1964 military regime still in power and the authoritarian Vargas years that I had analyzed.

After the military government yielded to civilian rule during the mid-1980s, interest in Vargas rekindled. CPDOC, a Rio de Janeiro research center established at the Getúlio Vargas Foundation, put teams of staff members to work collecting and cataloging documents and taking depositions from Vargas-era elites. Books and theses began to appear, but few concentrated on Vargas himself or on the impact of his social and nationalist programs. It is telling that there still is no updated, full-scale biography of Vargas; nor is there a detailed analysis of the Estado Novo, the 1946 Constitution, Vargas's relations with the military, his foreign policy, or his final term. Equally important, we have no studies addressing the lives of ordinary people during the Vargas era. Vargas's personal journal covering the years between 1930 and 1942 has now been edited by his granddaughter, forty-one years after his death, but the diary entries for the most part are dry and sketchy. Vargas never revealed his reactions or motives, even to himself.

This book, an interpretive synthesis based on many years of studying Vargas and modern Brazil, considers a series of fundamental questions. How did Vargas influence the evolution of the Brazilian state? How did Brazil change from 1930 to 1954? What was Vargas's political legacy? How far did Vargas's reforms change day-to-day life, not only in the major cities but throughout the vast country? And why did millions of Brazilians come to revere him if he acted, as wags claimed, not only as "father of the poor" but "mother to the rich"?

Funds for the study came from a collaborative research grant from the National Endowment for the Humanities supplemented by resources from the University of Miami. Matching support was provided by the Brazilian-American Chamber of Commerce of Florida, the Americas Foundation, Bank Cafeeiro, the Embraer Corporation, Varig Airlines, Robert J. Duffy, and Michael Bander.

I am, of course, responsible for the final result. I wish to give special thanks to the beleaguered National Endowment for the Humanities, which was willing to consider my grant application even though my computer (and our house) had been knocked out by Hurricane Andrew in August 1992. Some of the pages of the grant application, in fact, mailed right before the deadline, were water-stained. I appreciate the NEH staff's understanding during those difficult days. I am deeply appreciative of everything the NEH has done to assist scholarship in this country, and hope that the U.S. Congress will come to its senses and increase this agency's budget in the years ahead.

Persons who helped included Nancy Naro; Michael La Rosa; Ann D. Witte; Mai Lai; and Carmen Fernández; Ángela de Castro Gomes and Marieta de Morais Ferreira (CPDOC); Juliano Spyer, Eric Vanden Bussche (USP); Andréa Casa Nova Maia (Belo Horizonte); Cristina Mehrtens, John J. Crocitti, Bill Smith, and Quélia Quaresma (University of Miami); and Maria da Graça Salgado and Sérgio Murilo D. Zarro (Rio de Janeiro). More than anyone else, José Carlos Sebe Bom Meihy aided every stage of this project. He is an indefatigable colleague and a sensitive and empathetic friend as well.

CHAPTER ONE

INTRODUCTION:

VARGAS AS ENIGMA

Getúlio Dornelles Vargas, the most influential Brazilian of the twentieth century, held the posts of state legislator, federal congressman, cabinet minister, governor, revolutionary chief of state, interim president, dictator, senator, and popularly elected president. The simplicity of his private life contrasted distinctively with the careers of many of his contemporaries, although he was more earthy and colorful than people suspected. His calculating nature enabled him to rationalize contradictions that would have brought down lesser politicians. He cultivated an image as a homespun family man but he also could be cold-blooded and heartless. Although the explanation is insufficient, it was popular to attribute Vargas's character to his origins in Rio Grande do Sul and a *gaúcho* heritage characterized by a tenacious independence. *Gaúchos* were proud of their tradition. "If it had been all Portuguese who came [to our state]," one of its governors remarked later, revealing his nationalistic arrogance, "we'd have been as backward as Uruguay."

A realist and master at hiding his intentions, Vargas was difficult to decipher, even by his friends. To mask his personal earthiness, he cultivated blandness. He disliked to respond immediately, claiming that he preferred to think things out. As a result, people learned not to trust him. During every stage in his career, he remained a mysterious figure, enigmatic and inscrutable, a man who represented different things to different people. Yet he understood power and always dreamed, perhaps quixotically, of propelling his nation forward until it could control its own destiny.

Vargas displayed a morose side, as well. "How many times have I longed for death to solve the problems of my life," he wrote describing his guilt at having to send, soon after taking power, the members of the ousted government into exile.[1] He never spoke out against the ugly and dangerous behaviors of some of his subordinates. During the 1930s, Ciro Freitas Vale, his ambassador to Hitler's Germany, openly hated Jews. Vargas gave wide berth to his brutal police chief, Felinto Müller, and he offered no comment when his justice minister, Francisco Campos, referred to refugees from Nazi Germany seeking haven in Brazil as *rebotalho branco* ("white trash"). He charmed his American suitors, lobbying hard to secure Brazil's support for the Allied effort, but he also negotiated, more discreetly, with the Reich's ambassador. Always the pragmatist, as a gesture to the Allies in 1943 Vargas abruptly removed both Müller and propaganda head Lourival Fontes as the authoritarian façade of his dictatorship started to crack.

Vargas always seemed to have a knack for being in the right place at the right time. His career started precisely at the point when his state's powerful machine needed new blood. He entered national politics when the old regime was disintegrating from within, and when dissident elites from outlying regions of the country were seeking allies among urban and military counterparts.[2] There were about 30 million Brazilians in 1930, a number that would jump to 41 million in 1940 and 52 million in 1950. Coming to power in a military coup, he mobilized urban Brazilians into a future base of personal political support, even though most of his reform measures were designed to maintain (and often increase) state control. He crafted a new role for government and a drive for industrialization, economic development, and national integration. In a very real sense, we can say that modern Brazil was born in 1930 and came to maturity on August 24, 1954. On this date, in the early morning hours, Vargas shot himself to death as he waited in the presidential palace for his generals to remove him from office.

It is uncertain to what extent Vargas was influenced by the fascist ideologies of the 1920s and 1930s. Brazilian corporatism, which borrowed from European fascism, also was influenced by the New Deal. On the whole, though, even though Vargas was a nationalist, he relied on pragmatism more than ideology, thus contributing to his characteristic unpredictability. Vargas frequently shifted directions, like his contemporary, Franklin D. Roosevelt. Vargas was, as was another Roosevelt, Theodore, an orthodox heretic and a conservative reformer.

---

1. Getúlio Vargas, *Diário*, vol. 1, 1930–1936 (Rio de Janeiro: Siciliano/Fundação Getúlio Vargas, 1995), entry for October 20, 1930.
2. Ruth Berins Collier and David Collier, *Shaping the Political Arena* (Princeton: Princeton University Press, 1991), 108–110.

Whereas the United States preserved its democratic framework throughout this period, Brazil had none to save. It had no modern tradition of national political parties, making it easy for Vargas to govern by patronage and negotiation. His tenure in power was propped up by two military coups, in 1930 and 1937. Another coup removed him, in 1945, and the imminent threat of still another led to his suicide. Coups and near coups continued after his death, resulting in the harsh military dictatorship imposed in 1964 and lifted some twenty-one years later.

The 1930s transformed Brazil and opened it to the outside world. Vargas oversaw significant growth in government at all levels. Most of his programs were social and economic; prior to 1930, only a handful of states – notably Rio Grande do Sul and São Paulo – had paid attention to these issues, and then only on a very limited scale. Vargas organized regional agencies to deal with drought, electric power, and commodity production. Decrees prepared the way for civil service reform and a national minimum wage. Professions and crafts were regulated; new government bureaus systematized the collection of statistics and set out to improve municipal administration. The government awarded pensions to selected workers, as well as job protection and workers' compensation. A federal university system was started. Radio, professional soccer, and the movies not only drew Brazilians into the national culture but linked the country to the outside world. Few Brazilians knew the names of Vargas's cabinet ministers but millions knew Tom Mix and Mickey Mouse. They also knew that the country's new roads led to jobs, leading to massive migrations of population, whereas decades earlier few ventured beyond their birthplace except when driven by famine.[3]

Since for Vargas governing was chiefly a question of administration, he invited a succession of foreign experts and commissions to visit Brazil and propose measures to further its modernization. He negotiated impressive economic aid from the United States, though at the same time he feared that alliance with the United States would force Brazil into long-term dependency. Brazil's economy diversified and expanded. Coffee exports, once half of Brazil's agricultural output, fell to a 16 percent share between 1939 and 1943. Vargas's government invested in hydro-

---

3. The administrative reforms are examined in detail by Beatriz M. de Souza Wahrlich, *Reforma Administrativa na Era de Vargas* (Rio de Janeiro: Fundação Getúlio Vargas, 1983).

electric power, improved ports, drilled for petroleum, and created a model industrial city, Volta Redonda, to produce steel. Influenced by positivism in his youth, he believed that "order" was a precondition for "progress."

WATERSHED YEARS

Vargas's regime ended the political culture of the oligarchic First (or Old) Republic (1889–1930), which was characterized by a federal system under which the wealthier states – all in the Center-South – ran the country, leaving crumbs for the poorer units of the federation. A tiny minority of Brazilians lived in comfort. The vast majority lived in poverty. Millions of Brazilians could not afford shoes. But although Vargas knew this, his era was about politics and economics, not the human condition.

Even though the 1930s were a time of hardship for most, for those with skills new opportunities presented themselves. Brazil needed statisticians, broadcasters, electricians, architects. Youths (mostly young men) went from small towns to larger cities seeking to make their fortunes. Impoverished rural families migrated south, lured by the promise of urban jobs. Overall, the apex and base of the social pyramid stayed largely the same: the wealthy "good families" at the top and millions of illiterate, destitute rural poor, roughly half of the population, at the bottom. In 1930, skilled industrial workers numbered fewer than 300,000; most worked long hours in dirty, unsafe factories for pitiful wages. There was an acute shortage of technical and administrative workers. Many firms preferred to hire immigrants for these positions, disparaging the work ethic of nonelite Brazilians. Society, after all, had always divided people into gente decente (decent people) and the povo (the masses), and there was little incentive to do things differently.

Some of Vargas's officials sought to change this, but after 1935 the repressive atmosphere drove out the progressive reformers who had been attracted to the promise of the 1930 Revolution. Still, Vargas's government, imbued with a mission to achieve national regeneration, included officials who shared his vision. Many of them who knew the countryside firsthand were shocked at its widespread poverty, at the de facto Argentine control of southern border areas, and at the lack of basic federal programs. They came away contemptuous of the way landowners and their clients ruled as local potentates – Góes Monteiro called them "greedy pigs" – and of how much of Brazil was ignored by the central government.[4]

Few rural Brazilians attended school for more than a year or two, and some never went at all. As sharecroppers, they fell into debt to the local stores and went through their lives undernourished. Families coped by seeking favors from their patrons, usually the landowners on whose properties they worked in exchange for loyalty and unquestioned obedience. Rural people were considered by their more cosmopolitan countrymen to be guileless and lazy. They were called by a variety of names – *caipiras* and *jecas* in São Paulo, *tabaréus* in Bahia, and *caboclos* in the Amazon and generally.[5] The terms conveyed different cultural meanings but, on the whole, disparaged their unschooled mannerisms and their mixed-race origins.

Vargas, himself born into the oligarchy, although from its geographic periphery, believed that Brazil could be modernized rapidly through industrialization and social engineering. A ruse or not, from the start of his political career he showed sympathy for ordinary people, and as a positivist he felt that they could be taught how to live in the modern world, much as one instructs school children. On occasion he was moved by their plight: he commented in his personal journal on the squalid housing conditions he found during visits to the North.

Vargas's supporters trumpeted the coup that brought him to power as the "Revolution of 1930." The victory was accompanied by what critic Antônio Cândido called, with some hyperbole, a "gust of intellectual radicalism and social analysis" that not even the banality of state propaganda was able to quench. Curiously, the Depression stimulated domestic intellectual production: the devaluation of Brazil's currency caused a sharp increase in the price of imported books. This made Brazilian books competitive in the local market for the first time since the early nineteenth century and spurred publishing of Brazilian authors as well as translations of foreign authors.[6] Sociologists like Gilberto Freyre

---

4. See Todd Diacon's excellent "Bringing the Countryside Back In: A Case Study of Military Intervention As State Building in the Brazilian Old Republic," *Journal of Latin American Studies*, 27 (1995), 569–592. See also Captain Pedro Aurélio de Góes Monteiro's reminiscences of the Paraná campaign, 1925, *The Brazilian Army in 1925*, ed. Peter Seaborn Smith (Miami: Florida International University Latin American and Caribbean Center, 1981).
5. Charles Wagley, *Introduction to Brazil* (New York: Columbia University Press, 1965), 109–110.
6. Randal Johnson, "The Dynamics of the Brazilian Literary Field, 1930–1945," *Luso-Brazilian Review*, 31:2 (Winter 1994), 12.

probed the roots of Brazil's racial heritage; historians like Sérgio Buarque de Holanda explored provocatively the roots of the nation's distinctiveness; others, influenced especially by French social scientists, founded the University of São Paulo and sustained a generation-long search for explanations of Brazil's singularity under the gathering storms of war in Europe.

LIMITED CITIZENSHIP

In 1889, Brazil's government changed from a constitutional monarchy to a secular federal republic based on orthodox principles of economic liberalism, ruled dictatorially for much of its first decade, and whose civilian presidents after 1896 lived under the threat of military intervention. Things stabilized after 1898 under the rule of the *paulistas*, and the national government grew under the Republic. From 1900 to 1930, central government expenditures grew annually at more than 5 percent, triple the 1930–1945 rate despite all of Vargas's new agencies.[7]

Still, Brazilians enjoyed neither democracy nor opportunities to improve their lives. The year 1930 saw upheavals throughout the region: incumbent governments fell not only in Brazil but in four other Latin American countries. The coup that brought Vargas to power implanted a military-backed provisional government, which consolidated its control further in 1935 by declaring a state of siege and which instituted an authoritarian dictatorship between 1937 and 1945, at which time Vargas overstayed his welcome and was ousted. Five years later, voters returned the old dictator to power, only to endure further instability after Vargas's death in 1954. The next decade saw another military coup, which suppressed individual rights until the mid-1980s. Only then were representative democratic institutions restored, buffeted by vast economic disparities, hyperinflation, corruption, impunity, and uncertainty about the country's political future, despite the tenacious survival of basic democratic institutions.

During most of these decades, citizenship in practice extended only to the elite. Human rights abuses were commonplace. Even during periods without formal censorship, newspaper editors instinctively downplayed or altogether excluded news about strikes, especially against large landowners (as in the case of the 1931 strike against the Albuquerque

7. Steven Topik, *The Political Economy of the Brazilian State, 1889–1930* (Austin: University of Texas Press, 1987), 20–21.

Lins coffee plantations), and against foreign-owned railroads.[8] Military authorities ran concentration camps for political prisoners, one of which, in Clevelândia do Norte in distant Amapá, revealed decades later graves filled with cadavers of prisoners who had been injected with morphine or had been forced to ingest quantities of broken glass.[9] Except for religious activity, society saw little associability. Village life, overshadowed by the power of the landowning class, lacked the tradition of autonomy enjoyed by villages in Mexico or Peru.

Vargas sought acknowledgment that his programs would influence future generations but he never coveted personal wealth. Abelardo Jurema, who visited the palace days before Vargas's death, commented later that when he saw the president's bedroom, he was struck by its bareness. Among the sparse furnishings was a plain bureau holding bottles of patent medicine, just like his grandfather's in the interior. On the other hand, Vargas permitted members of his family to take sinecures and sometimes positions of power, such as when he named his despised brother Benjamim ("Beijo") to be Rio's chief of police during his presidential term. And he shut his eyes to violence committed by agents of his government against citizens.

Populism and Corporatism

Care must be taken to separate general definitions of terms describing political thought and practice applied in Latin America from the ways these terms were understood elsewhere. The term "populism," for example, has been used to characterize a wide variety of political styles, including, in the United States, the racist People's Party (1892–1900), an antiurban movement in farming communities in the South and Midwest as well as in mining communities in the West that led, in the Deep South, to the Jim Crow laws of the early twentieth century. In Latin America, populism has encompassed many forms, but all have shared qualities of being urban-based, multiclass coalitional, hierarchical, cooptive, ad hoc, and nonrevolutionary, led by ebullient (if not charismatic) figures who promised to redress popular grievances and to build social solidarity. Argentina's Juan Perón (1943–1955) and Chile's Car-

---

8. Left-wing newspapers in and outside of Brazil did report at great length. See, for example, Bryan Green, *Brazil* (New York: International Publishers, 1937), published by an arm of the American Communist Party.
9. *O Globo* (Rio de Janeiro), February 1, 1996, 1, 8.

los Ibañez (1927–1931 and again in 1952–1953) represented variations on strong-man populist regimes. Colombia's Jorge Eliéser Gaitán, whose assassination in 1948 provoked violent civil insurgency, and Peru's Haya de la Torre were populist leaders whose political fortunes were less successful. Mexico's Lázaro Cárdenas (1934–1940) was another successful populist, although his was a variety of political leadership inherited from an older ideology, that of the Mexican Revolution. Overall, Latin American populists tended to sidestep democratic niceties. They disputed the vested interests of the region and, although they spawned bureaucracy, they often opposed the authoritarian-technocratic regimes that follow them.

Populist political movements are nationalistic in character but often have no consistent ideology or agenda; rather, they adopt a range of issues to fit the needs of the times, and often express themselves in a distinctive political style centered on leadership by a single figure. Latin American populist politicians tended to use labor organizations for their own ends, refusing to challenge the prevailing understanding among elites that strict control over workers would preserve social stability, provide industrialists with disciplined workers whose wages could be kept low by competition from a large reserve pool of workers, and preserve the rate of capital accumulation.

The Great Depression set in motion political events that brought populist governments to power – in Latin America, ones usually propped up by the armed forces. The vast changes in economic life after the end of World War I and the collapse of the postwar economic boom, after 1929 taking the ominous form of the Great Depression, touched the lives of everyone in the Western world. In Europe, the aftermath of war led to the rise of Mussolini in Italy, to the flaunting of Versailles, and ultimately to the rise of Nazism in Germany. In Portugal it led to the rise of António de Oliveira Salazar and his fascist Estado Novo, and in Spain to civil war. In the United States, Franklin D. Roosevelt's New Deal launched massive relief programs that Republicans called socialist and that intellectuals on the left derided as state capitalism. By any name, this was massive governmental recapitalization for purposes of economic development; it involved state cartelism (less aggressive than state capitalism because it does not seek growth). Roosevelt sponsored dozens of sweeping legislative packages, addressed major areas of social and economic need, waged war with Congress, and threatened to tinker with the Supreme Court. In comparison with Vargas's Brazil, for example, the New Deal was not enacted by decree; there were no military interventors in the states, and Roosevelt never suspended the rule of law under any state of war or state of siege. In common with the United States, Vargas and his fellow corporatist-populists endorsed the notion of sweeping government welfare programs addressing social needs, although nowhere except in the United States and Canada were there conscious efforts to create long-term domestic markets by building infrastructure in undeveloped regions of the country.

Brazil's experience with populism was complicated by the fact that there were two significant populist movements, both of which changed over time. The first was the _tenente_ movement, which erupted in 1922 when a handful of idealistic young officers revolted against the federal government over a question of military honor. This nationalist movement ultimately divided sharply into factions on the far right and far left. The right-wing _tenentes_ themselves branched off, their main body becoming Plínio Salgado's fascist Integralist Party, a populist movement of a sort. Left-wing _tenentes_ and their civilian allies split in 1930 into one camp made up of social democrats active in Rio de Janeiro and in the Northeast (Pedro Ernesto, Anísio Teixeira, João Café Filho) and another comprising the Communists, to which the _gaúcho_ hero of the Long March of the mid-1920s, Luís Carlos Prestes, was recruited.

Vargas's populism differed, and it changed as he adapted it to his political needs. It started out in the 1930 Liberal Alliance platform as a broad-based appeal to recognize workers' needs and to regenerate the nation. Under the provisional government it took on a more corporate coloration, culminating in the Estado Novo dictatorship in which Vargas's public appeals in favor of the work ethic and patriotism took the form of a propaganda campaign advanced by the Propaganda Ministry, or DIP. A more authentic populism emerged during the mid-1940s, when Vargas responded to rising calls for democracy, and culminated in his 1950 presidential campaign, which shared much in common with the campaigns of other Latin American populists, including Peru's Haya de la Torre.

Unlike the United States and Mexico during the 1930s, where populist goals were accompanied by massive state intervention, in Brazil, efforts at economic reorganization stopped far short of channeling public resources to create jobs or to make vast regions productive. Corporatist populism was a vehicle for holding political power, imparting autonomy and influence to the central state, and never relinquishing real control. As far as Brazil was concerned, Vargas's social legislative programs were essentially manipulative, carrot-and-stick techniques to channel the en-

ergy of emerging groups – mainly the salaried urban middle and working classes – into government-controlled entities. Brazilians welcomed
Vargas's initiatives because it promised them better working conditions,
job security, and opportunities for subsidized housing. We will discuss
how many actually benefited from these promises. Still, from the outset,
we should note that Vargas's goals differed from Roosevelt's and were
much closer to the goals of the European heads of state in Lisbon,
Madrid, and Rome, if not Berlin. At home, reactionaries advocated aggressively negative policies: combating communism, feminism, cosmopolitanism, labor militancy; resisting immorality; fighting liberalism
and individualism. To Vargas's credit, except for ferocious police repression of the left, he stressed the positive: building the nation, erasing regional inequities, promoting unity.

REVOLUTIONARY PROMISES

Vargas's legislative programs derived from two main sources, both dat-
ing from well before 1930. One was the Rio Grande do Sul experience
with social legislation carefully controlled by a disciplined political machine; the other was the idealistic (but no more democratic) *tenente*
movement of the 1920s. The tenentes, joined later by mainstream military officers, shared the conviction that republican politicians had self-
ishly neglected the needs of rural Brazil and the peripheral regions of the
vast country that many of them saw in their outpostings and during the
Prestes Column trek through the hinterland, which was aimed at mobi-
lizing popular support for the *tenente* cause. The Liberal Alliance coalition in 1930 focused on the need to reach out to new groups, to
recognize the needs of industrial workers, to extend the government's
presence to the hinterland, and to enlarge the electorate to enfranchise
women.

The reforms were paternalistic and rooted in a firm sense of moral
and patriotic responsibility. Vargas called on intellectuals to come
down from their ivory towers and to participate actively in the task of
nation building – but within his guidelines. One of Vargas's main goals
was to teach Brazilians to take pride in their nationality, to discipline
themselves, and to learn the proper values of self-reliance, the sanctity
of marriage and the family, and the value of work. The state took steps
to regulate the sale of liquor, to restrict smoking in the workplace, and
to provide bathrooms in factories. "The mouth is a cavern of microbes,"
one Estado Novo poster declared, and in the 1950s the national gov-

ernment launched a "Safe Kissing Campaign" to teach personal hygiene.

Elites went along because the reforms sidestepped the issues of control and power. They also combated laws and directives they thought too costly to obey. Laws against child labor, excessive hours, and poor working conditions were ignored whenever convenient for management; minimum-wage requirements were never extended to the countryside and even today remain ignored in parts of Brazil like Acre. Factory conditions remained precarious: workers suffered alarmingly high rates of injuries on the job, and most employers did nothing to provide safety equipment. Photographs commissioned to show industrial progress show workers in metal and chemical plants without shoes, gloves, or helmets. Men wielding acetylene torches wore no eye protection. Children as young as seven or eight and pregnant women worked long days in the fields or in sweatshops, in spite of laws making such work illegal.

In some ways, Vargas-era reforms widened the gap between the coast and interior, the modern Center-South and the vast rest of the country. Further, elites combated expressions of ideology directed at raising the consciousness of workers about their right to organize independently. Workers, after all, could not be trusted to think about their condition lest they challenge the system. For its part, as well, industrial and other salaried workers refused to accept the government's paternalistic approach to industrial relations, creating the basis for the standoff between workers on one side and employers and the government on the other, still unresolved sixty years after Vargas's coming to power.

Corporatism's attack on liberal ideas during the 1930s helped workers internalize authoritarian values. Brazilians more and more came to rely on the bureaucracy, not on legislative action or the private sector, as the source of change and benefits in exchange for political docility. Business leaders accepted this formula gratefully, because it assured that the state would play a mediating role between employers and their workers, and it promised to assure protection and a steady supply of capital. In the Vargas era, the elite restructured the relations between the state and its citizens. The power of the central government grew, especially after 1941, when Vargas endorsed state-sponsored industrialization, although it remained affected by the survival of a strong tradition of discretionality, whereby rules were or were not followed depending on who was involved.

To solve the enigma of Getúlio Vargas, we must look at the ways that Brazil changed after 1930 and at the ways it stayed the same. During the years Vargas was chief of state, Brazil's population not only grew but it shifted from a rural to an urban base. Its economy diversified, transforming the Center-South while leaving the rest of the country further behind in a time warp. Raft fishermen, rubber tappers, and landless peasants in the reachless interior lived harsh lives of poverty, while São Paulo's economic engine steamed ahead and Rio de Janeiro became a glittering international tourist destination. National institutions developed that eclipsed the formerly powerful states. The country saw vast changes in transportation, in the degree of foreign influence (especially from the United States), and in Brazil's emergence as a hemispheric diplomatic voice.

At the same time, even though the composition of the elite changed, its privileges did not, nor did traditional barriers to social mobility (except for the descendants of some immigrants). Patronage and the need for personal connections and favors (*jeitos*) continued to affect who received benefits and who did not. Public education and health care remained grossly insufficient for a country of Brazil's size; the rich were not taxed and land remained a source of power regardless of productivity. Reform always came from the top, and was inevitably accompanied by steps to maintain (or increase) social control. Mass mobilization was forbidden, and most Brazilian citizens lived on the margins of the market economy and outside the political arena. Constitutions came and went. The armed forces command took for granted that it could intervene as it wished, and civilian elites accepted the military's moderating role.

Who was Getúlio Vargas? What were the motives of the man Franklin D. Roosevelt, in a speech in Rio de Janeiro in 1936, credited with being "one of the two people who invented the New Deal"?[10] Why was Vargas despised by some as "Machiavellian"? What did President Fernando Henrique Cardoso – a distinguished and knowledgeable social scientist – mean when he declared at the outset of his term in 1994 that his administration would bring about "the end of the Vargas era"? The following chapters examine Vargas as a product of his origins in Rio Grande do Sul, as protector of powerful interests, as a proponent of government activism, and as a national leader who made millions revere him.

---

10. Franklin D. Roosevelt, November 27, 1936, text (430.22.42) in Itamarati Archive, Rio de Janeiro.

CHAPTER TWO

IN THE SADDLE, 1883–1937

Getúlio Dorneles Vargas was born on April 19, 1883, in São Borja, a small riverside frontier town near the Argentine border of Brazil's southernmost state of Rio Grande do Sul. His mother, Cândida Francisca Dornelles (1850–1936), and his father, Manuel do Nascimento Vargas (1844–1943), were from families that had arrived during the seventeenth century, when the region was first settled by Jesuit missions. His paternal grandfather was said to have been a direct descendant of Francisco de Paula Bueno, a *bandeirante* pioneer who trekked south from the captaincy of São Vicente, later São Paulo. His parents' marriage brought together the two warring clans in the region, one republican, the other federalist.

São Borja sat at the center of smuggling, political adventurism, and wars. Over the centuries, its history – and the history of Rio Grande do Sul – was unusually contentious and violent. The Vargas family defended its interests fiercely. One of Getúlio's brothers, Viriato, killed a fellow cadet while at military school and another was accused of two assassinations. Seventy-six citizens of São Borja complained to the governor in 1919 about the Vargases coercive activities.[1] In 1933, while he was Brazilian chief of state, two of Vargas's nephews were killed in a border clash.

Getúlio's[2] mother, who bore five sons, was described by her nephew

---

1. Joseph L. Love Jr., *Rio do Sul and Brazilian Regionalism, 1882–1930* (Stanford: Stanford University Press, 1971), 217.
2. In Brazil, first names and nicknames are used for public figures, even in circumstances where foreigners would expect surnames to be mandatory. Thus Getúlio Dornelles Vargas was known popularly as "Getúlio," or "Gegê," or "GV," just as Franklin D. Roosevelt was known as "FDR." Juscelino Kubitschek was known as Juscelino, or "JK"; Jânio Quadros was called Jânio; João Goulart, Jângo. Public figures less esteemed publicly tend to be called by their last names, as in the case of the military generals who seized power in coups.

Spártaco Vargas as "short and fat and pleasant," as many expected married women to be then. Her side of the family became *maragatos* (federalists) in Rio Grande do Sul's civil war, while the Vargases fought on the *chimango* (republican) side headed by Júlio de Castilhos. Getúlio's paternal grandfather, Evaristo José Vargas, had fought in the Farroupilha Revolt (1835–1845), a conflict with republican overtones that had attracted Garibaldi to Brazilian soil. Manoel do Nascimento Vargas, his father, was one of fourteen children, an influential rancher, and Paraguayan War hero. A proud and dominant man who lived to be ninety-nine, Getúlio's father allied himself with the chieftains of the principal republican family clans in the state, including the Guerra and Flôres da Cunha families who controlled everything from São Borja to Uruguaiana. Higher up the Uruguay River, in Itaqui and São Borja, the Vargases and Aranhas dominated. In São Luís, the Oliveira clan maintained control. Rio Grande do Sul lived under the shadow of rival Argentina, which at the turn of the century was one of the richest five or six countries in the world. Brazil, in comparison, was a sleepy agricultural nation, but it was awakening rapidly, and the *gaúchos* strived to bend that change to their own formula.

Getúlio studied at a private primary school on São Borja, although he did not finish. At the age of twelve, he and his older brothers were sent to military school in Ouro Preto, then the capital of Minas Gerais. Getúlio was not particularly popular; cadets taunted him by calling him *xuxu* (a pearlike vegetable), a reference to his five-foot, two-inch height and his rotund shape.[3] The violent *gaúcho* tradition also followed him. Following a row in a café over drunken singing, Carlos Prado, a cadet from a prominent *paulista* family, was shot to death by Getúlio's brother Viriato, who was accompanied by Protásio and other *gaúcho* cadets. Although Getúlio had not been involved, the academy sent the three packing.[4] On his return to Rio Grande, Getúlio enlisted in the infantry, seeking appointment to the military academy in Rio Pardo. When he was fifteen, however, he became involved in a student protest in the barracks over the lack of water, and again he had to leave, along with twenty other cadets. Some time later, an amnesty permitted him and the other insubordinate cadets to return.

After being transferred to a barracks in Porto Alegre, the state capital, he attempted to resign so that he could switch to law school, but his

---

3. The tale of Getúlio at military school is told by Affonso Henriques in his hostile *Vargas, o Maquiavélico* (São Paulo: Palácio do Livro, 1961), 3–22.
4. The incident is described at length by Henriques (ibid., 22–29).

BRAZIL IN 1940

discharge was delayed because he needed a medical examination before
the papers could be processed. Just at that moment, the old boundary
dispute between Brazil and Bolivia over Acre broke out, and his battalion was ordered to Matto Grosso. The experience marked him – he was
disillusioned, although in later years he said that living under difficult
conditions had taught him how to judge others -- and on his return he
again asked for a discharge. This time he managed to get a medical paper saying that he had epilepsy, which was untrue, and he was released
from his military commitment.

He audited ~~law school classes~~ in Porto Alegre while studying for the entrance examination and subsequently was admitted.[5] Adapting easily to the elite student culture, he became ~~active in the student republican faction~~ and served as an ~~editor of the law school newspaper~~, *Debate*. He and his republican friends endorsed the positivist goals of political boss Júlio de Castilhos and went out of their way to demonstrate their loyalty. A successful speaker, Getúlio was elected ~~orator of his class~~, and sought to display, in the words of one admirer, "vigor, a certain masculine coloration [to] ~~enlighten and persuade~~."[6] Since his family remained in São Borja, he lived in a series of *repúblicas*, fraternity-like boarding houses known for their atmosphere of pranks and bohemian life but also useful places for building personal networks. Among his acquaintances were two cadets attending the city's military academy, Pedro Aurélio de Góes Monteiro and Eurico Gaspar Dutra. He received his degree in 1907, although he ~~had no desire to practice law~~.[7] Instead, at the age of twenty-four, his father secured for him the coveted post of ~~assistant district attorney~~. It was so obvious that he had received the position because of his connections that the opposition newspaper, *Petit Journal*, printed a cartoon showing governor Borges de Medeiros surrounded by small children. "Do you want some candy?" Borges asked. "No," the child representing Getúlio said, "I want to be district attorney."[8] Such an appointment typically was the first step in a political career. Two years later, in 1909, he was elected to the state ~~Chamber of Deputies~~. Vargas was only twenty-six. ~~Congenial, he was well liked~~. He became known for his ability to temporize, and to hold his cards close to his vest.

In March 1911 Getúlio ~~married~~ Darcy Lima Sarmanho, in São Borja. For the next forty-seven years until his death, she stayed in the background, although when Vargas was head of state ~~she devoted herself to public charity causes~~. She supervised the family's households in the presidential palace in the federal capital and in São Borja. Darcy practiced

5. Alzira Vargas do Amaral Peixoto, *Getúlio Vargas, Meu Pai* (Porto Alegre: Editora Globo, 1960), 7.

6. *Revista Republicana*, October 5, 1885, 5, cited by Andrew J. Kirkendall, "To 'Order and Progress': Republican Discourse among São Paulo Law Students, 1878–1889," SECOLAS Annals, 27 (March 1996), 91–96, esp. 94.

7. For a good overview of Vargas's early career, see Sérgio da Costa Franco, *Getúlio Vargas e Outros Ensaios* (Porto Alegre: Universidade Federal do Rio Grande do Sul, 1994), 7–23.

8. Paulo Frischauer, *Presidente Vargas* (São Paulo: Companhia Editora Nacional, 1943), 115.

Roman Catholicism while Getúlio remained indifferent; he was agnostic, although for political reasons he maintained close relations with influential clergy. The couple had five children: Lutero, who became a physician; Jandira; Alzira, an astute and politically judicious young woman and law school graduate who became his favorite and confidant; Manuel (Maneco); and Getúlio (Getulinho), who died in 1943. Vargas participated in numerous sexual dalliances, and in 1937 took a mistress to whom he remained devoted – his diaries published a half century later confirm this – but if Darcy knew about it, she shrugged it off as something many Brazilian men did. He hid his inner life carefully, although he played golf every Sunday at the elite Itanhangá Golf Club, went by car to cowboy movies in theaters on the Largo de Machado, and could be seen on the grounds of the presidential residence at Catete smoking cigars or hand-rolled cigarettes.

Vargas's entry into political life coincided with the nation's first popularly contested presidential election. In the 1910 campaign, lawyer and diplomat Rui Barbosa attacked political corruption and warned of the dangers of military encroachment, a veiled allusion to the fact that his opponent was Hermes da Fonseca, the nephew of Brazil's first military head of state and the current minister of war. Hermes was declared the winner, setting off a wave of interventions in state governments to punish the factions that had backed Barbosa. The campaign was the first time the republican system had been called into question publicly and the first campaign in which one of the candidates appealed directly to the electorate.

The assassination in 1915 of the powerful *gaúcho* senator Pinheiro de Machado altered the delicate balance between Rio Grande do Sul and the dominating states of the Republic.[9] Changes were taking place within Rio Grande as well. Whereas the old-guard positivists of Castilhos's generation, convinced of the moral superiority of their positivist heritage, belittled national politics, those of Getúlio's "Generation of 1907" set out to remake the country, as they often said, to "RioGrandize Brazil." Following the French philosopher Auguste Comte's motto of "order and progress," the *gaúchos* endorsed positivism in theory, although in practice they disregarded its endorsement of freedom of conscience and of expression. Comte's emphasis on the family also likely appealed to them, as well as his lack of sympathy for the mass of the population.[10]

At the end of 1916 Vargas turned down an offer from governor Borges

9. Peter Flynn, *Brazil: A Political Analysis* (London: Ernest Benn, 1978), 42.
10. See Love, *Rio Grande*, 35; Costa Franco, *Getúlio*, 12–13.

de Medeiros to become Rio Grande do Sul's police chief. Instead, he ran for the state senate, won, and was named majority leader. Vargas was in Rio de Janeiro when eighteen reckless young officers, who came to be known as the *tenentes*, raised the banner of revolt against President Artur Bernardes in July 1922. Vargas became briefly caught up in the 1923 civil war in his state, caused by resistance to Borges's fifth reelection as governor, and was asked to assume the command of a military unit, but not wanting to become involved in the conflict, he ran for a seat that had fallen vacant in the federal Chamber of Deputies and departed for the national capital as soon as his credentials were validated. In 1924 he rose to leader of his state's delegation. His most noteworthy achievement as a congressman came in 1925, when as a member of a commission studying constitutional reform he advocated greater government authority.

CHANGING TIMES

The 1920s were turbulent years for Brazil. Prosperity for the elite was on the rise, but the 1922 *tenente* crisis revealed that nationalistic aspirations stood in conflict with the federal system of government dominated by the landed oligarchy. The outbreak of radical labor militancy among dock and transportation workers and strikes in factories led the ruling class to ponder the "social question," defined as the threat to the established order posed by subversive agents and their followers.[11] Fear of class conflict led the government to pass the Eloy Chaves Law in 1923 requiring railroad companies to provide pensions for their workers and a year later to establish a National Labor Council. The Chaves law was extended to other categories of workers in later years, but until 1930 this and some statutes regulating child labor and promising paid vacations were the only labor laws of any importance in Brazil, and they were often ignored.

Late in 1926 incoming president Washington Luís Pereira da Souza nominated Vargas to be finance minister, although Vargas had no fiscal experience. It was a purely political deal based on the practice of dividing important cabinet posts among the powerful states. A year later, in November 1927, when the resignation of Borges created a political vacuum in his home state Vargas resigned from the cabinet to run un-

---

11. See Stanley E. Hilton, *Brazil and the Soviet Challenge, 1917–1947* (Austin: University of Texas Press, 1991), 18.

opposed for the governorship. Vargas remained friendly to the Washington Luís administration and maintained his national ties, urging political reconciliation. His two-year tenure in Porto Alegre was energetic. At one point, Vargas vetoed dishonest election results that had produced a victory for his own political party.[12] He also brokered a cease-fire between the state's two warring factions, ending decades of conflict.

As governor, Vargas achieved bipartisan support for his government, for the first time in generations. His economic program, carried out by his friend (and fellow *gaúcho*) Oswaldo Aranha, extended credit to cattle raisers and organized interventionist cooperatives, or cartels, to pool resources and lower costs for agricultural exporters in the face of falling prices. Vargas accomplished this with great political dexterity. He showed himself to be an effective problem solver and a skilled mediator willing to tackle large-scale problems. His popularity in part came because he was not considered to be personally ambitious. As governor, he had displayed a gift for wearing his politics lightly. He was a proud man, but he preferred to win someone over rather than to bear a grudge.

He was a cultured man despite his rustic trappings. Typical of many in his generation, foreign books were the source of his education, rather than his university studies, which were perfunctory. Vargas spoke French and read daily (one of his favorite books was a biography of Mussolini; he also liked Nietzsche, Spencer, and Darwin). He could be an erudite conversationalist, and his interests ranged widely. Shortly after he took power in 1930 he started to read a treatise on revolution by the German political sociologist Karl Bücher. He hid his intellectual side from view, preferring to cultivate his image as a rancher pursuing a government career reluctantly.

In 1929, the collapse of international commodity prices combined with a sudden split within the national government transformed Brazil's political calculus. Conflict over coffee price supports, banking policy, and the insistence of President Washington Luís to name Júlio Prestes, another *paulista*, as his successor led to a secret agreement between Minas, Brazil's most populous state, and Rio Grande do Sul to have Vargas run for president under the newly formed opposition Liberal Alliance banner. His selection puzzled many because he was seen as a machine politician, "as representative a politician of the old regime as any," and

12. John W. F. Dulles, "The Contribution of Getúlio Vargas to the Modernization of Brazil," in Eric N. Baklanoff, ed., *The Shaping of Modern Brazil* (Baton Rouge: Louisiana State University Press, 1969), 40.

his desertion to the opposition is said to have come as a surprise to many of his friends.[13] But as a low-key cabinet minister he had behaved himself; he did not threaten the more flamboyant members of the opposition, notably the *tenentes*, whose leaders remained in exile but who provoked the political arena through well-placed newspaper articles calling for radical change. When he accepted the Liberal Alliance draft, he sent a letter to Washington Luís explaining that if he did not accept the *mineiro* offer, he feared that his state would suffer dire consequences.

He did not, then, burn his bridges. A few months later he negotiated privately an agreement with Washington Luís that as a candidate he would not appear publicly outside of his home state. Further, Vargas pledged that if the official candidate won, he would give his support. In exchange, he won the promise of reciprocal acceptance of his presidency if he won. Meanwhile, the more radical members of the Liberal Alliance coalition discussed with the expatriate *tenentes* the possibility for an armed revolt. The *tenentes* included Siquieira Campos, Juárez Távora, and Luís Carlos Prestes, the most left-leaning of the group and who during the next few years would go to Moscow and become the titular head of the illegal Brazilian Communist Party. Prestes, we now know, met secretly with Vargas in Rio Grande do Sul at least twice, in late 1929 and early 1930, but Prestes considered Vargas insufficiently revolutionary, and they struck no deals.

Vargas's campaign from the outset invoked a bold nationalistic and reformist agenda. He proposed a comprehensive labor code, although union leaders – many of whom were Communists and anarchosyndicalists – did not support him, considering him just another incumbent politician. His platform advocated the secret ballot and voting rights for women. Vargas proposed a drive to improve the nutritional intake of the poor and to address social problems. He made it clear, however, that change would come from above, drawing on the precedents set by the *gaúchos* under Borges (1890–1927) and during his own two-year term. He reminded voters that Rio Grande do Sul had shown unprecedented sympathy to workers' demands during strikes in 1917.[14]

With tensions heightened by the reeling economy and the emotion-

13. Mauricio A. Font, *Coffee, Contention, and Change in the Making of Modern Brazil* (Cambridge, Mass.: Basil Blackwell, 1990), 231.
14. See Joan L. Bak, "Cartels, Cooperatives, and Corporatism: Getúlio Vargas in Rio Grande do Sul on the Eve of Brazil's 1930 Revolution," *Hispanic American Historical Review*, 63:2 (May 1983), 255–275.

al energy released by the electoral battle, Vargas decided to disregard the scenario that had been worked out in advance. He abandoned his pact, traveling to Rio de Janeiro on New Year's Day 1930 for a public rally in which he and João Pessoa, his vice-presidential candidate, introduced the Liberal Alliance platform. The election campaign became spirited and Vargas was startled by the fervor of the cheering crowds that came to greet him. This reception contributed to an incipient sense in his mind that he had been chosen to lead the Brazilian people out of their wilderness. Liberal Alliance "caravans" were dispatched to northern cities, headed by Pessoa, who was from Paraíba. After incidents of violence in several states against Alliance rallies, however, Vargas drew back abruptly, withdrawing to his ranch, naming Aranha acting governor of Rio Grande, and claiming that he would no longer campaign due to "moral scruples." In late February, a political civil war exploded in Pessoa's state. Washington Luis's government backed the anti-Vargas forces in Paraíba and in Minas Gerais.

Vargas's strongest backer in the press was Assis Chateaubriand, his friend since Vargas's arrival in Rio as a deputy, and the head of the largest chain of newspapers in the country. Chateaubriand had become so close to Getúlio that he began to affect gaúcho colloquialisms. Getúlio did not like the man's drive to amass a personal fortune, but he understood the importance of having a news baron behind him.[15] On March 1, 1930, however, the Liberal Alliance coalition ticket was declared the loser. The official vote count claimed that he received 700,000 votes against a million for São Paulo's Júlio Prestes. That there were 30 million Brazilians with such a small percentage voting shows that Brazil's democracy was a very limited one, and it is commonly believed that there was extensive electoral fraud on both sides. Still, more votes were cast in the 1930 presidential election than ever before, and Vargas's initial acceptance of defeat signaled that the system was holding firm, even if riddled with irregularities.

The Liberal Alliance refused to accept the results of the presidential election. Assis Chateaubriand led ferocious attacks on the government and on its complicity in political fraud. Aranha, considered the brains behind the eventual coup, deposited in a Buenos Aires bank account a large sum of money for the purchase of armaments. In late July, news arrived of the murder in Recife of João Pessoa over a question of personal

15. Fernando Morais, Chatô, o Rei do Brasil (São Paulo: Companhia das Letras, 1994), 202.

honor. The opposition blamed the federal government for Pessoa's death and for the deteriorating economic climate. Behind the scenes, Vargas's Liberal Alliance negotiated with Washington Luís, offering him a compromise that would have preserved the Republic. The president's fatal mistake was to assume the support of the armed forces, and he rejected compromise. The Republic, whose stability rested on consensus within the oligarchy, quickly fell apart when that consensus was broken.[16]

In the early hours of October 3, 1930, the Liberal Alliance launched its revolution. In three states and in the federal capital, its troops attacked government buildings and sealed off barracks holding loyalist soldiers. Two days later forces led by Prestes Column–veteran Juárez Távora took Recife and secured control of the Northeast, at which point he prepared to head south through Minas Gerais. On November 20, President Washington Luís took refuge in the Copacabana Fort and ceded control of the government. The key to victory was the attitude of the military command, which ended the Republic just as it had started it a half century earlier. The regime took political prisoners, holding them for more than a year in Recife and transferring them after that to the harsh federal penitentiary in Fernando de Noronha when they rioted.[17] Behind the scenes, the armed forces continued to maintain pressure on Vargas, whom they had put into power. Many of them mistrusted his political program but considered him malleable. They presumably approved of the fact that Vargas wore his old army uniform in the first photographs to appear in the press.

LIBERAL ALLIANCE VICTORY

Reaction to the triumph of the opposition forces was immediate and enthusiastic. A "New Brazil" seemed to be dawning. Cheering crowds milled in city streets; speakers at rallies attacked the plutocrats, "the rotten ones, the worm-eaten ones" of the departing government.[18] Talk of revolution, however, proved premature. Many of Vargas's civilian supporters wanted little more than to switch places with the politicians they had ousted. Vargas's assumption of dictatorial powers blocked the aim of

---

16. See Flynn, *Brazil,* 42–50.
17. Getúlio Vargas, *Diário,* vol. 1, *1930–1936* (Rio de Janeiro: Siciliano/Fundação Getúlio Vargas, 1995), entry for January 18–22, 1932 (p. 88).
18. Leôncio Basbaum, *História Sincera da República: de 1930 a 1930* (São Paulo: Ed. Edaglit, 1962), 13.

some *tenentes* for popular mobilization, even though dozens of new political parties and nationalist organizations formed in the weeks following the coup, promoting plans for government action that in some cases were far-reaching, even visionary. Vargas had promised no less than national reconstruction, but once in office, he kept a low profile, busying himself with mundane matters. The fever stirred up by events receded, especially as the economic impact of the Depression worsened. But Vargas had awakened hope, even among the poorest Brazilians. He sensed that he had touched a nerve, and it drove him to stick to his goals, albeit slowly and deliberately. For the time being, Brazilians accepted a regime without parties that would govern the country by decree.[19]

Brazil in late 1930 occupied a vast, mostly underpopulated territorial expanse from the Amazon rain forest to the flat lands of the far South. Most major cities, with the exception of Belo Horizonte, built by *mineiro* urban planners earlier in the century, rested on the coast. Politicians and businessmen espoused free-market policies, although they demanded government intervention in the economy when they stood to benefit from it.[20] The Republic's highly federalist structure had allowed the more solvent states to retain most of their resources while the rest of the country languished in grinding poverty. Prosperity was tied to world market prices for sugar, cacao, rubber, and coffee, and therefore was affected severely by the 1929 Crash. In the fast-growing Center-South, the Depression facilitated entry into the elite by immigrants and their descendants, many of whom married into the economically declining families of the old aristocracy. In other parts of Brazil status depended less on capital liquidity than on family lineage, limiting opportunities for mobility.

Most Brazilians could not read or write and only a minority held regular jobs. Diet was limited to staple foods – manioc, rice, black beans, a little dried beef – and life expectancy was low. Rural families often had ten, fifteen, or more children, although many died in infancy. Transportation between states was limited to coastal shipping routes and poorly maintained roads. Railroad tracks connected plantations and mines to the ports. Only during Vargas's tenure did road building get underway in earnest, and after World War II Brazil would gain a modern network

19. See Ronald M. Schneider, *Brazil: Culture and Politics in a New Industrial Power-house* (Boulder, Colo.: Westview Press, 1996), 58–59.
20. See Eugene Ridings, *Business Interest Groups in Nineteenth-Century Brazil* (Cambridge: Cambridge University Press, 1994).

of airports, courtesy of the Americans who built them for military use. Elite Brazilians preferred to travel abroad than to other Brazilian cities. Tourism was undeveloped (although Rio had several world-famous casinos), and wealthy Brazilians had little interest in other Latin American countries, even neighboring Uruguay and Argentina.

The forty-seven-year-old Vargas's parlor car arrived at Rio de Janeiro's central station on October 31 and he was installed as provisional president four days later. His train had traveled slowly from Rio Grande during a nearly continuous driving rain. Vargas stopped frequently to make speeches and participate in local rallies in the mud. He ran the government from his parlor car. "All of the steps have been taken," he wrote in the diary that he had begun on October 3, "all of the connections carried out. [Our] 'adventurous thrust' should take place today, at 5 P.M." While his generals readied their troops to overthrow the government, Getúlio dined with his family, played his usual game of ping-pong with his wife, and took a nap. He faced possible defeat stoically: "If we lose," he wrote, "they'll say I did it out of ambition, who knows? I'm afraid that only the sacrifice of one's life can repay for the error of failure."[21]

On the day Vargas arrived in the federal capital, mounted *gaúcho* soldiers were photographed at the Senate building, an image calculated to show that the old order had ended. But Vargas personally cast off his *gaúcho* ties. As his son Manuel Antônio remarked years later, "He left [Rio Grande do Sul] here a *gaúcho* and arrived [in Rio de Janeiro] a Brazilian." Nevertheless, *gaúchos* formed much of his inner circle. Oswaldo Aranha, Lindolfo Collor, Baptista Luzardo, Maurício Cardoso, João Neves da Fontoura, and others played prominent roles in his administration, while an old friend from law student days, Firmino Paim Filho, became his honcho, dealing secretly with the opposition behind closed doors. Vargas reiterated his campaign pledges to open up government and end corruption, but privately he doled out patronage almost every day. Even former president Epitácio Pessoa visited the presidential palace at Catete to ask for a favor for his son-in-law. Vargas's hand was strengthened by rumors that there would be a military coup to remove him – they were without foundation – and that a Communist insurrection was imminent. On January 19, 1931, Vargas ordered Communists arrested and their property seized. This would not be the first time in the decade that Vargas would use a Communist threat to tighten his own hold on power.

21. Vargas, *Diário*, entry for October 3, 1930.

Few breaks opened in the heavy rains that poured down on the Atlantic coast during the first weeks of Vargas's revolutionary government. The political atmosphere remained as unsettled as the weather. Not only did Vargas have to appoint the entire upper level of the federal government but also the interventors in the states, some of whom, especially in the Northeast, had to be replaced almost as soon as they took office for becoming involved in local political squabbles. Vargas was hampered by the fact that his backers represented a mostly incompatible coalition of civilians and *tenentes*, some seeking major changes, others working to preserve the old system with themselves in control; worse, the *tenentes* themselves could not agree. In November, Luís Carlos Prestes issued a revolutionary manifesto from Buenos Aires, calling for the dissolution of the new regime. In January, Communists in Rio held a hunger march which was broken up by police, who then arrested its organizers. Rumors flew almost daily in the closing months of 1930 of attempted right-wing coup activity, worrying Vargas greatly. He ignored Prestes but dutifully visited the Realengo Military Academy and the Naval War College to show his loyalty to the armed forces. Although prohibited by the constitution, he arranged for a public patriotic mass to be celebrated by Cardinal D. Sebastião Leme, the prelate of Rio de Janeiro.

The provisional government closed the republican congress and assumed absolute powers. He appointed military interventors – most of them young and inexperienced *tenentes* – to administer the states. Legislatures across Brazil were dissolved. Things moved so quickly that Vargas's initial measures did not follow any comprehensive plan. It was one thing to make electoral promises, quite another to translate them into concrete action. Aranha, named justice minister, admitted the regime's uncertainty in a newspaper interview: "I have no program except that of the Revolution. I am here as the people's delegate. I will do nothing against the people and will follow their wishes. To now, the people have followed the government; now the government will follow the people. The people want us to carry out our revolution. . . . I will work relentlessly against all that is superfluous, and we will eliminate all waste."[22]

The economic crisis posed an especially difficult problem for the new government, so Vargas, ever the pragmatist, invited a British financier, Sir Otto Niemeyer, to advise him in early 1931 on how to reform the monetary system and handle the debt. Niemeyer told Brazilians what was rarely admitted in public – that the principal weakness of the coun-

22. *Correio da Manhã*, November 5, 1930, 1.

try was its excessive dependence on a few export crops. Vargas used Niemeyer's prestige to support his own calls for diversification and economic development. Throughout his tenure in office, Vargas solicited advice from foreign commissions to gain expertise and to furnish legitimacy to his far-reaching goals.

Vargas acknowledged that his administration was provisional and would be replaced by a new popularly elected government as soon as a new constitution could be written. At the same time, he clearly wanted to cultivate popular backing and to stay in power as long as possible. His daughter Alzira claimed that the provisional government was a "democracy led by a dictator kept in power with the people's support."[23] Although a laughable assertion, the statement illustrates Vargas's tactic in picturing himself as a people's leader, not as a political broker. Ignoring the affluent classes, he turned to industrial and white-collar workers, roughly 20 percent of the work force, to provide the core of his regime's backing. He extended to workers the protection of law and set down the guidelines for labor's participation in national politics. One month after he took power he established two new cabinet ministries, for health and education, and for labor, industry, and commerce, also known as the "Ministry of the Revolution." Previous Brazilian governments had been uniformly hostile to labor, considering it, in words attributed to Washington Luís, the last president of the Old Republic, "a matter for the police." Washington Luís's opinions were long held: as São Paulo's mayor in the previous decade, he set out to cleanse working-class neighborhoods of their "vicious mixture of scum of all nationalities, all ages, all of them dangerous."[24]

Vargas faced major difficulties throughout his first few years as head of state. In late October 1931, soldiers calling for a soviet-style revolution seized control of their barracks in Recife for two days before being subdued. Strikes, especially against railway companies and on the docks, were frequent, and often led to bloodshed. In Rio Grande do Norte in March 1931, manual laborers hired with government relief funds to build a road from Natal to Macaíba demanded more food relief for their

---

23. Vargas do Amaral Peixoto, Getúlio Vargas, 290.
24. Cited by Joel W. Wolfe, Working Women, Working Men: São Paulo and the Rise of Brazil's Industrial Working Class, 1900–1955 (Durham, N.C.: Duke University Press, 1993), 49. The mayor's speech was quoted in Maria Célia Paoli, "Working-Class São Paulo and Its Representations," Latin American Perspectives, 14:2 (Spring 1987), 204–225, but no date was given.

families. Among the arrested strike leaders was shoemaker and Communist organizer João Praxedes de Andrade, who four years later would participate in an ill-fated and quixotic insurrection that gave Vargas the excuse to impose martial law.[25]

Things would have not have been so difficult had not Vargas continued to receive implacable opposition from the old landholding oligarchy throughout the states as well as business and industrial leaders in the Center-South. As a result, Vargas's decree legislation more often than not proved empty and was inadequately enforced. Although Brazil's republican government before 1930 had been active, indeed, more than many other Latin American countries, Vargas's assumption of decree powers did remove all remaining obstacles to centralized administration, but the country remained too vast and uncoordinated to give teeth to most programs administered in Rio de Janeiro. Vargas's predecessors had never seen the need to have federal ministries representing the interests of labor, education, or public welfare; Vargas added them all. *Paulista* industrialists in 1928 had created an institute (CIESP) whose projects included some social and economic welfare measures; but there were no other such bodies anywhere else.[26] Vargas also paid unprecedented attention to the problems of the vast, backward Northeast, crippled by drought and depressed agricultural output. He set into motion the steps to create strong centralized agencies, but they remained mired in factional infighting and in the end simply became repositories for political patronage.

Where Vargas succeeded was due to his political skills. Yet he was never comfortable with the influential members of elite high society, nor with the authoritative members of the *mineiro* and *paulista* oligarchy that his 1930 Revolution sought to topple but with whom Vargas eventually had to do business. He chomped on Havana cigars, cursed frequently, and never abandoned his superstitious beliefs in witches and demons, something that his suave, ambitious (and pro-Nazi) police chief, Felinto Müller, never let him forget. Still, that Vargas rose to Brazil's presidency even given his family's comfortable and powerfully connected status in the São Borja region was evidence of the tremendous changes

25. Maocyr de Oliveira Filho, *Praxedes, um operário no poder* (São Paulo: Ed. Alfa-Omega, 1985), 38.
26. See Barbara Weinstein, "The Industrialists, the State, and the Issues of Worker Training and Social Services in Brazil, 1930–50," *Hispanic American Historical Review*, 70:3 (August 1990), 379–404.

occurring in Brazilian society in the early twentieth century. Few members of a family as influential as Vargas's would ever have taken an army assignment that required serving with men so socially unacceptable. Once in the political arena, Vargas displayed a talent for bringing opposing sides together in conciliation. There was a practical reason for this: Rio Grande do Sul had been bitterly divided between warring factions for decades, and Vargas understood that in order for the state to carry weight nationally in proportion to its growing economic importance, it would have to present a united front.

His personal conviction that class conflict and the interests of capital and labor needed to be harmonized drew from notions of corporatism not only tested in Italy and Portugal during the 1920s but present in the writings of some *tenentes*. Vargas founded symmetrical hierarchies of associations for employers and workers, assuring institutionalized contact between the two at all levels, and establishing the state as arbiter between them. Corporatism, unlike liberal democracy, rejected the notion of the paramount freedom of the individual; in the atmosphere of gathering worldwide depression, and Brazil's seeming inability to respond to its social needs, Vargas welcomed a benevolent, interventionist model of an organic state, viewing society as a collection of groups differentiated and ranked according to their productive or economic role. As such, Brazil continued to be governed by the same old elites, men dressed in their white linen suits directly related to planter oligarchy or to the rising industries, but with a different style, more bureaucratic and more immediately manipulative. By September 1931 Vargas had decreed censorship of the press and relied on a small group he called his "revolutionary soviet" to run the country: the army, navy, and justice ministers; the minister of public works, General Góes Monteiro, and Rio de Janeiro interventor Pedro Ernesto, the sole social progressive in the group. Vargas agreed to lift press censorship three months later but he had made his point very clearly that it could be restored at any time.

The *tenentes* found themselves edged out as an independent political force. For a while it had seemed that the nationalistic Third of October Club would prevail. The club, named for the day on which the revolution had started, was a mix of civilians (including Oswaldo Aranha and its first president, the "civilian *tenente*," Pedro Ernesto) and military men (including Góes Monteiro and Juárez Távora). Soon, however, Vargas managed to ease most of them to the periphery. The *tenentes'* weakness was their political clumsiness, and they never understood the resilience of the old state oligarchies (and Vargas's willingness to make alliances at the state level that suited his needs). The *tenentes* were also authoritarian: when the Rio de Janeiro newspaper *Diário Carioca* attacked Vargas's failure to convoke elections, the Third of October Club sent thugs to smash the newspaper's offices and to beat its employees. Vargas understood this, and he used strong-arm tactics as well when he had to. The *tenentes* desired fast-paced change, centralized government, and an end to the pretenses of liberal democracy and the old elite-dominated system of oligarchic control, but they were less cynical than Vargas, who refused to burn his bridges of support from these interests.

The Liberal Alliance victory represented a profound shift in political power as well as philosophy. The federalist republic had been controlled by the old rural landed elite of the wealthiest states. Representatives of the oligarchies of the powerful states continued to exert considerable power, but Vargas widened opportunities for individuals from lesser states as well. Free-market economic liberalism had helped the rich to get richer and more powerful while the rest of the population languished unprotected. The idea of nationalism attained new meaning in Brazilian politics: it now referred to the national good. Still, it was a pragmatic nationalism. Faced with a decision about what to do about a controversial one-million-hectare Amazonian concession given in 1927 to Henry Ford, Vargas, who needed revenue badly, ruled in favor of the Ford plantation even though its fifty-year exemption from taxation was legally dubious.[27]

The regime's most tempestuous crisis came in mid-1932 when São Paulo launched an attack on Vargas's government. São Paulo dominated the rest of the country, producing more than 40 percent of total manufacturing output. One industry, the Antarctica brewery, paid more taxes than each one of fifteen states paid to the federation.[28] *Paulista* leaders smarted over their political defeat in 1930 and were further angered by *tenente* João Alberto Lins de Barros being imposed as interventor. Vargas had passed over *paulista* candidates to name an outsider, who governed "the proud and powerful State of São Paulo" (in the words of the American chargé) as if it were under military occupation.[29] Vargas also named *tenente* Miguel Costa police chief, another affront to the *paulis-*

27. Warren Dean, *Brazil and the Struggle for Rubber* (Cambridge: Cambridge University Press, 1987), 72–73.
28. Karl Loewenstein, *Brazil under Vargas* (New York: Macmillan, 1942), 335.
29. Walter C. Thurston, Rio de Janeiro, to Secretary of State, Washington, July 15, 1932, National Archives, Washington, D.C.

tas. At issue was the old state elite's anger at having been shoved from power. The *paulistas* responded to the campaign for "autonomy for São Paulo," moving Vargas, in July 1931, to accept João Alberto's resignation. The reluctance of state leaders to accept Vargas's nominee to be the new interventor further inflamed the volatile atmosphere. In late August 1931, Vargas had reinforced the federal government's control over the states, including in economic matters. Demands for a constituent assembly to set the stage for an elected government increased. This angered Vargas, because he saw the "proconstitutionalization" movement as simply a cloak for the efforts of the old regime to return to power.

São Paulo's militia's revolt was joined by the local federal garrison and civilian volunteers and some old-guard *mineiros* hostile to Vargas who crossed the border to join the fight. Within days, most of São Paulo rose in revolt against the federal government. The state had more than 40,000 troops, but half were untrained volunteers; government forces numbered more than 70,000 on three fronts. After two months of fighting, however, concentrated in the economically desolate Paraíba Valley, the insurgents surrendered. Ironically, the rebels added to their side's cache of arms by collecting armaments from local factories, rifles and other weapons stockpiled to put down worker insurrection. Workers, needed to increase production, were also bribed with new comprehensive fringe benefits, including free health and dental care. During the civil war, factories operated twenty-four hours a day. Impressed by the willingness of their workers to respond to incentives, after the conflict ended *paulista* industrialists embraced some of Vargas's ways of dealing with labor, namely government-initiated welfare capitalism under a corporative framework.

Although several formerly close compatriots defected to the opposition, including Borges de Medeiros, Lindolfo Collor (who left the Labor Ministry in March 1932), and Baptista Luzardo, Rio de Janeiro's chief of police, hoped-for aid for the rebellion from other states and from abroad never materialized. Hundreds of *paulistas* died, mostly untrained university-age students. The national government never revealed its number of dead and wounded. To dissuade other states from entering on São Paulo's side, Vargas coldly ordered dozens of politicians imprisoned, including ex-president Artur Bernardes and Borges de Medeiros. Yet he did not punish São Paulo after the fighting ceased. Behind the scenes he took steps to pacify the situation and assure the state's industrialists and landowners that his calls for sweeping change would not threaten their hegemony. He named as interventor Armando de Sales Oliveira, the son-in-law of Júlio de Mesquita, one of the leading members of the *paulista* oligarchy, to replace *tenente* João Alberto. Eugénio Gudin was appointed to head a new commission to investigate irregularities in loans contracted by states and to "expose to the nation the nasty secrets of earlier governments."[30] The commission met continually for more than two years, uncovered nothing, and expired. In the end, the constitutionalist crisis made Vargas less beholden to old allies and more of his own man. When he had to replace Minas's interventor in 1933, he chose neither of the obvious candidates but Benedito Valladares, "a man Vargas invented" (as one of his enemies said) and a distant relative to boot. Oswaldo Aranha and some of his other cronies told him that Valladares was "mentally incompetent" and an "imbecile," but he liked Valladares's modesty and held his ground.

Vargas had helped precipitate the crisis by delaying too long his promise to end his provisional government by calling a constituent assembly, which he had promised the governments of Rio Grande do Sul and Minas Gerais in return for their support in 1930. By now, he had taken things into his own hands. He was fortunate that opposing groups remained split ideologically. Liberal Alliance civilians in Rio Grande do Sul and Minas Gerais had lost their revolutionary fervor. To stand up to the military, Vargas named as many civilians as he could to be interventors in the states. When Rio Grande do Sul chieftain Borges de Medeiros broke publicly with Vargas in 1932 (and was punished by exile to Pernambuco), the former protégé remarked: "This is something. I backed old man Borges's dictatorship for twenty-five years and have nothing to complain about. Now he's protesting because I've been dictator for two years."[31] After the bloodshed was quelled, Vargas bought time by declaring a blanket amnesty and by absorbing the state's war debt. He also agreed finally to implement the selection process for a constituent assembly. Some months later he admitted to himself that he was fed up with it all. "[Is it] fatigue . . . disillusionment?" he wrote in his diary. "Wouldn't it be better for me to leave office at this point?"[32]

The absence of national political parties created an atmosphere in which many groups – some urban, some rural, some class-based, some

30. Eugénio Gudin, deposition, CPDOC archive, Rio de Janeiro.
31. Juracy Magalhães, cited in Valentina da Rocha Lima, *Getúlio: Uma História Oral* (Rio de Janeiro: Ed. Record, 1986), 66.
32. Vargas, *Diário*, entry for June 19, 1933 (p. 219).

traditional, some newly emergent – continually jockeyed for influence. Vargas did not object because it made things fluid, giving him more opportunities to enlist support for his government. Given the dependent nature of Brazil's economy, none of these groups was strong enough to impose its own model of political order on the others. Vargas, seeking to hold together the diverse coalition that had placed him in power, shrugged off the infighting among his supporters. Instead, his provisional government vacillated from one stance to another, while never relinquishing power. As provisional chief of state, he reserved the right to initiate all policy, and therefore the central government became the main generator of resources for national development. Power was redistributed after 1930 to a new elite, but Vargas remained the leader and moderator in all of the conflicts generated by the process.

Vargas governed atop an authoritarian system in which he and his hand-picked representatives at the national as well as state and local level held all power. The provisional government was Brazil's first formally established dictatorship that strove for legitimacy, ushering in a centralized authoritarian system that survived well beyond the end of the provisional government in 1934. Now, Vargas, as he noted in his diary, had the luxury of being able to surround himself with generals, not *tenentes* (lieutenants), a reference to the fact that he had been able to assert his independence of the idealistic young nationalist officers who had so deeply influenced the Liberal Alliance program and who, in the first days of his government, had been his most trusted aides.

Vargas implemented his policies through decrees and sometimes through the use of coercion. To give his interventors practical control of their states, the power of rural *coronéis* had to be crushed. Rural boss control was one of the reasons that Júlio Prestes had handily defeated Vargas in 1930. In Juazeiro, for example, along the São Francisco River in Pernambuco, Vargas lost by a margin of 2,285 to 352. After Vargas's coup, his interventors set out to settle scores in such districts. The power of *coronéis* to act with impunity in their private domains was attacked. Vargas disarmed the *coronéis*, curbed the ability of the bosses to use hired thugs and personal armies, and, once this was on the way to being accomplished, arrested or killed thousands of bandits, including, in 1938, the most notorious of all, Lampião (Virgolino Ferreira da Silva), who with his band had terrorized the rural interior for twenty years, attacking towns, giving interviews to the press, and otherwise playing Robin Hood. With the pacification of the hinterland, the kinds of local autonomy permitted under the old system – whereby the political machines of rural states bought fraudulent ballots from rural chieftains in exchange for patronage – yielded to decision making in Rio de Janeiro by federal bureaucrats. On the other hand, rural dominant family clans continued to prevail, perhaps in less brazen a manner than before, but still wielding considerable might.

A survey conducted in mid-1934 by visiting officials from the United States Department of Commerce revealed how daunting the task faced by Vargas was. It was found that skilled laborers in São Paulo earned eight milreis per day, worth fifty-six cents in the United States. Most workers did not earn this, and even those who did were frequently laid off when supplies were late or when orders lagged. There was no accident or health insurance, no pensions. The families of these workers averaged more than five dependents, often having to live on the equivalent of fourteen dollars a month. Men and women often worked without shoes and socks because they did not own them. Housing conditions and diet were found to be terrible.[33] And this was in São Paulo, with the most skilled work force in Brazil and the highest level of wages.

The selection of Lindolfo Collor to head the Labor Ministry showed Vargas's willingness to bring into his administration men from more diverse backgrounds than would have been possible under the Old Republic. Collor was the son of a shoemaker. His father, João Boekel, and his mother, Leopoldina Shreiner Boekel, were descendants of the first German settlers to arrive in Brazil in 1824. After his father died, in 1893, and his mother remarried João Antonio Collor, a man who ran a small shipping fleet, he took the name Collor. A Protestant, he studied for three years in a Presbyterian seminary in the city of Rio Grande, and later entered pharmacy school. In 1909 he moved to Bajé, where he worked as a journalist. He then moved in 1911 to Rio and became close to Senator Pinheiro Machado. There he worked as a journalist, studied law, and became friendly with members of the gaúcho "Generation of 1907" in the capital, one of whose members was Getúlio Vargas. In 1914 Collor married Hermínia de Sousa e Silva, the daughter of a deputy from Paraná, and thus secured social and political respectability. He learned well: seeking a political career, he patterned himself after Borges de Medeiros, making public statements about the need for order, party discipline, and "absolute submission to the head of the party." For his loy-

---

33. Horace D. Davis and Marian Rubins Davis, "Scale of Living of the Working Class in São Paulo, Brazil," *Monthly Labor Review* (Washington, D.C.), 33 (January 1937), 245–253.

alty he was elected state deputy in 1921. He then served as federal deputy and held posts in Washington Luís's administration before defecting to the Liberal Alliance.

Collor worked hard as labor minister to increase industrial production while keeping workers pacified. Strikes by anarcho-sindicalist and other independent labor unions continued to hinder transportation and production. Collor's reforms set the stage for the Vargas era's approach to labor: extend benefits to workers in exchange for their cooperation. Job protection was extended nationwide to all those with more than ten years' service. A comprehensive reorganization of the entire industrial relations system was unveiled in March 1931 based on the corporatist model and borrowing as well from the pattern of conflict avoidance pioneered in Rio Grande do Sul by the ruling Republican Party. Businessmen endorsed the new system, which included notions of planned factory management (Taylorism) and which effectively banned strikes; the government also promised that the system would respect private property. Industrialists barely tolerated the initiatives, but they accepted the concept of authorized *sindicatos* replacing independent unions, which were far less pliable, and which Collor harassed and ultimately shut down. Bureaucratic inefficiency and worker suspicion, however, slowed the process of conversion to Vargas's system. Although by 1940, two thousand unions existed on paper, in reality the labor ministry's ability to apply its new programs remained limited to the federal district of Rio de Janeiro, right under its nose. One legal scholar called the ministry a "monster with an enormous head, and with almost no body."[34]

Vargas intended his "Ministry of the Revolution" to serve as the means by which the government acknowledged the right of labor to organize, even if only under tightly controlled circumstances. He named archconservative Oliveira Vianna to be the new ministry's legal advisor, therefore signaling his true intentions, although in his public statements Vargas projected a progressive, even radical, defense of the interests of workers. Wages were standardized industry-wide, thus stabilizing a labor market that had been unstable since World War I. Workers' benefits were given at the price of giving up their rights to strike. The new labor courts barely functioned. Ministry programs yielded more foot dragging on both sides than compliance. Labor decrees remained uncodified for more than a decade. Ministry bureaucrats were so out of touch with the

34. Joel W. Wolfe, "The Faustian Bargain Not Made: Getúlio Vargas and Brazil's Industrial Workers, 1930–1945," *Luso-Brazilian Review*, 31:2 (Winter 1994), 82.

states that during the entire 1930–1945 period they referred in their memos to the entire country outside of Rio de Janeiro as "the interior."[35] Workers' complaints sent to Rio were returned to Labor Ministry offices in the respective states, where they were ignored. Violence against dissenting labor voices remained commonplace. The Labor Ministry established hundreds of unions, run by "yellow dogs," later termed *pelegos*, loyal to their bosses in the bureaucracy, not to the combined total of more than a half million rank-and-file Brazilians on union rolls by 1944. Vargas-era *pelegos* later were eased out of power during the late 1950s and early 1960s, but under Vargas they reigned supreme.

The ministry's attempts to regulate working conditions were timid at best. São Paulo's 1926 code restricting minors to six hours a day of work and prohibiting employment of minors under the age of fourteen was more stringent than Vargas's child labor law, although employers frequently ignored such regulations. Political realities also frustrated Vargas's goals. One of the problems was that he found it difficult to delegate authority, and although he spent countless hours poring over paperwork, he did not manage to impart his personal dedication to others. Government officials continued to come to their offices late in the morning, take three-hour lunches, and sometimes not return in the afternoon. Shortages of paper forms often meant that a bureau would be unable to attend to the public for weeks or longer. Vargas centralized the government but did little to change attitudes or to make government machinery move more expeditiously. It was one thing to issue decree after decree, still another to have bureaucrats carry them out. Insofar as they worked at all, his programs were successful in the Federal District but rarely elsewhere in the country. Another problem was that the young and inexperienced *tenentes* he had named to replace the state governors faced irresolute resistance from the entrenched ousted oligarchies.

IDEOLOGY AND NATIONALISM

The Brazilian Roman Catholic Church played a key role in stabilizing support for the provisional government. The church hierarchy had decided at the turn of the century to take a conservative social stance, and therefore watched Vargas's election campaign very closely. Working through the conservative Cardinal Sebastião Leme, who cultivated Vargas's support from the outset of the provisional government in 1930,

35. Wolfe, "The Faustian Bargain Not Made," 81.

Catholic nationalists worked to mobilize public opinion and to "rechris-
tianize" Brazil, which at the outset of the Republic had formally sepa-
rated church and state. They attacked the offending 1891 Constitution
as "atheistic" and urged Vargas to enact measures supporting the family
(against divorce), and supporting religious education in the schools and
chaplains in the armed forces. The Brazilian church accepted corporatism as consistent with its emphasis on social unity over class conflict,
and its labor policies were consistent with this model.[36]

Vargas's policies favoring centralization complemented the emphasis
of Rome's Ultramontane movement on papal authority and orthodoxy,
although Vatican doctrine's opposition to modernity in its forms of liberalism, scientism, and secular expression did not agree with Vargas's positivist vision of reform. Understaffed, with a high percentage of priests
foreign-born, the church opted to reach the Catholic population through
legislation and the state, with the single exception being the choice of
the dark-complexioned Our Lady of Aparecida as Brazil's patron saint in
1904.[37] Vargas saw eye to eye with many Church opinions. He despised
spiritism, which the church had called "a factory of madness."[38] He welcomed the effort to increase the Catholic school network, because this
would reduce costs. For its part, the church wanted to insert religious instruction into the public school curriculum, because this would reach the
majority of the population too poor to send its children to private school.

Ironically, Vargas's decision to ally with the Catholic Church dismayed leaders from his home state more than from anywhere else.
Protestantism and Freemasonry were especially strong in Rio Grande do
Sul, and positivism's anticlerical feeling remained strong. Politicians –
including former governor Borges de Medeiros – still smarted from the
efforts of the Church in 1926 to form a rival Catholic Party in his state.
Vargas did not care; he welcomed the legitimacy that church support
could provide. He authorized religious instruction in public schools for

36. See Jeffrey D. Needell, "History, Race, and the State in the Thought of Oliveira
    Vianna," *Hispanic American Historical Review*, 75:1 (February 1995), 1–30; and
    Dain Borges, "Brazilian Social Thought in the 1930s," *Luso-Brazilian Review*,
    31:2 (Winter 1994), 137–150.
37. See Juliana Beatriz Almeida de Souza, "Mãe Negra de um Povo Mestiço," *Estu-
    dos Afro-Asiáticos*, 29 (March 1996), 85–102.
38. Ubiritan Machado, *Os Intelectuais e o Espiritismo* (Rio de Janeiro: Edições
    Antares, 1983), 129–141, cited by C. F. G. de Groot, *Brazilian Catholicism and
    the Ultramontane Reform, 1850–1930* (Amsterdam: CEDLA Incidentele Publi-
    cations, 1996), 59; see also 118–119.

the first time in forty years, permitted crucifixes to be placed in classrooms and government offices, and backed constitutional prohibition of
civil divorce. Streets, beaches, and even *favelas* were named for Catholic
figures. In October 1931 Vargas and his entire cabinet attended the con-
secration of the striking Christ the Redeemer statue atop Corcovado hill
overlooking the federal capital of Rio de Janeiro, accompanied by a procession from the central train station to the metropolitan cathedral celebrating Our Lady of Aparecida, with air force planes flying overhead
and an estimated half million people in attendance.[39]

Because of his family's tradition, Vargas was perhaps more sensitive to
Catholic issues than many of his contemporaries, although he personally was believed to be an agnostic. The church hierarchy, dominated by
the lay intellectual Jackson de Figueiredo in the 1920s, a decade later was
led by Alceu Amoroso Lima, a nationalist intellectual and journalist
whose personal Catholicism deepened later. Under his influence, church
policy took on the conservative social reformist coloration expressed in
Pius XI's encyclical, *Quadresegimo Anno* (1931). It was a nationalist alternative to liberalism and socialism, a synthesis of Jacques Maritain's political philosophy with Alberto Tôrres's conservative reformism.
Amoroso Lima called for a neo-Thomist union of church and state, a
"morally restrained, socially just capitalist economy," an ordered, plural-
istic society, and a corporatist and mildly authoritarian government.[40]
When the Brazilian branch of Catholic Action was established in 1935,
Amoroso Lima became its president, consolidating by incorporation
most of the formerly independent Catholic social action groups that had
operated before that date. Catholic Action was instructed by the church
hierarchy to refrain from open political activity, choosing to exert political influence behind the scenes. The bishops approved the organization
of the Catholic Electoral League, a pressure group charged with getting
out the vote and persuading individual candidates to back church positions. The church and its allies – mostly conservative businessmen – were
antirevolutionary, conservative, and committed to law and order.

Much more aggressive were *tenente*-connected right-wing intellectuals led by *paulista* Plínio Salgado and Gustavo (Dodt) Barroso, a Ceará-

---

39. de Groot, *Brazilian Catholicism and the Ultramontane Reform*, 146–147; Almei-
    da de Souza, "Mãe Negra," 91–93.
40. Ludwig Lauerhass Jr., "Getúlio Vargas and the Triumph of Brazilian National-
    ism: A Study on the Rise of the Nationalist Generation of 1930" (Ph.D. diss.,
    University of California, Los Angeles, 1972, 161.

born novelist. Barroso was a member of the Brazilian Academy of Letters and an enfant terrible who wore a pistol in a holster. He wrote scurrilous anti-Semitic tracts and praised the Nazi Reich. Not all Brazilian conservative nationalists were fascists but they repeatedly pressured Vargas to govern by decree, to restore the link between church and state, and to root out socialist ideas and what Barroso called "liberal cosmopolitanism," which he used as a code word for Jewish and liberal ideas. The nationalists were backed by some of the most powerful members of the military high command.

In 1932 Salgado founded Ação Integralista Brasileira (AIB), a paramilitary political party whose members marched in green uniforms, jack boots, and with the sign of the Greek letter Σ on their sleeves – the Σ not only appearing roughly like a swastika at a distance, but the mathematical sign of the integer, the sum of all parts, a perfect corporatist symbol. Salgado's movement borrowed its paraphernalia from the European fascists, its clerical strain from Portugal's Salazar, and its charitable programs from Catholic Action groups in Europe. Integralists sought a kind of anachronistic dystopia, seeking return to moral and family values that had never been practiced. Their argument that ordinary Brazilians needed discipline and instruction was shared by many members of the elite, some of whom put on dark green shirts and claimed that for them integralism was the solution to Brazil's Depression-era ills. The Integralists cheerfully coexisted with local Nazis among German, Italian, and Polish communities in southern Brazil and also drew support in major cities from the lower middle class (including some blacks) and culturati nurtured on the modernist movement of the 1920s, in which Salgado had played a role. Modernism, in some ways, fit neatly into Brazil's intellectual transformation from the experimentation and soul-searching of the 1920s and early 1930s to the Estado Novo, which adopted Salgado's *modernista* notion of celebrating the nation as fusion, a basis for authoritarian government.[41]

CONSTITUTIONAL INTERLUDE

The turning point for Vargas's provisional government came on May 3, 1933, when he decreed elections for members of a new Constituent Assembly. This gave São Paulo what it had waged war to achieve, and it

41. Dain Borges, "The Recognition of Afro-Brazilian Symbols and Ideas, 1890–1940," *Luso-Brazilian Review*, 32:2 (Winter 1995), 70.

provided a way to legitimize his control and, if successful, to implement his goals for national regeneration. He no longer seemed to need to surround himself with aides, and his "inner" cabinet began to be phased out. Many Liberal Alliance veterans by now had left politics, and the dapper Oswaldo Aranha had been packed off to Washington as ambassador.[42] Vargas confirmed that once the Constituent Assembly finished its task, it would convene to elect a president, thereby avoiding direct elections but giving the appearance of democratic choice.

The 1933–1934 Constituent Assembly consisted of delegates from every Brazilian state as well as forty deputies representing "class" interests according to the corporatist formula. Pro-Vargas deputies, a coalition of representatives from most of the outlying states, the "class" delegates, and minority representatives from the major states, opposed the efforts of São Paulo, Minas Gerais, and Rio Grande do Sul to limit the power of the central government. If Vargas was dismayed at losing the support of his home state, he did not show it. His former ally and close friend Flôres da Cunha attacked Vargas angrily: "Rio Grande will do everything to normalize the country's political life and to remove from certain heads the thought of implanting another dictatorship, whatever its coloration. If such should happen, I believe that Rio Grande would arise as one man to protest with arms against the terrible adventure. Let the nation know that I would struggle until the last drop of blood."[43] Vargas ignored such threats, and despite his rhetoric, Flôres da Cunha ultimately was exiled to Montevideo, where he spent most of his time at gambling casinos.

The new constitution was ratified on July 16, 1934, without any national referendum. A day later, the Constituent Assembly voted Vargas president of Brazil for a four-year term by a 175–59 margin over the symbolic candidacy of the veteran *gaúcho* politician Borges de Medeiros. Sworn in on July 20, Vargas named only one *gaúcho* to his new cabinet,

---

42. On Aranha, see Stanley Hilton, *Oswaldo Aranha: uma Biografia* (Rio de Janeiro: Objectiva, 1994).

43. Cited by Carlos E. Cortés, *Gaúcho Politics in Brazil: The Politics of Rio Grande do Sul, 1930–1964* (Albuquerque: University of New Mexico Press, 1974), 67. See also Joan L. Bak, "Political Centralization and the Building of the Interventionist State in Brazil: Corporatism, Regionalism and Interest Group Politics in Rio Grande do Sul, 1930–1937," *Luso-Brazilian Review*, 22:1 (Summer 1985), 9–25; Dulles, "The Contribution of Getúlio Vargas," 41; Nize Pellanda, *Flores da Cunha* (Porto Alegre: Tchê! Editora, 1986); Regina Portella Schneider, *Flores da Cunha: o Ultimo Gaúcho Legendário* (Porto Alegre: Martins, 1981).

Bank of Brazil president (and crony) Arthur da Souza Costa as finance minister. In reaction to Vargas's taking office in 1934, Flôres da Cunha remarked that Brazil now had its "Third Emperor." He was not far from the mark. Between 1934 and 1937 he ruled by decree. Congress was virtually powerless, and there was no independent judiciary. The old state political machines had been dismantled by Vargas's interventorships, and Vargas – perhaps because his hold on power was still shaky and subject to military approval – did not move to establish a national political party.

Conservatives considered the 1934 charter a victory over secularism and a defeat for the enemies of *brasilidade*. Borrowing from the 1919 Weimar Constitution and the Spanish Constitution of 1931, it added to the 214 delegates elected by voters a layer of 40 "class" deputies representing employers, employees, public servants, and members of the professions. The Constitution guaranteed the right to join unions although it did not make union membership compulsory. The hybrid nature of the new Constitution satisfied no one; Vargas himself, in his first address as constitutional head of state, did not attempt to hide his disappointment, and privately he said that he would be "the first one to revise it."[44] Vargas's earlier electoral reforms were codified into the new constitution. He curbed the power of the Senate, long dominated by the smaller (and antireform) states of the federation. He instituted a secret ballot to prevent the intimidation of voters, long a common practice. His 1932 code had made the vote secret, led the way to extending it to women, and lowered the age requirement from twenty-one to eighteen, with literacy the sole remaining requirement. The creation of national political parties a decade and a half later was facilitated by Vargas's 1945 electoral code, one of Vargas's last decrees before his ouster.

Much of the Constitution, and most of Vargas's subsequent decree laws, were prescriptive. They set aside, for example, a percentage of federal tax revenues to alleviate regional problems; provided incentives for the development of commercial radio, coupled to the requirement that all stations carry the government's daily *Hora do Brasil* program; shifted emphasis from religious to patriotic holidays; and required in 1935 that Carnival *samba* associations register with the government and therefore submit themselves to control. Yet although the Constitution seemed to

---

44. Getúlio Vargas papers, 34.07.15/2, cited by Aspásia Camargo, et al., *O Golpe Silencioso: As Origens da República Corporativa* (Rio de Janeiro: Rio Fundo, 1989), 30.

give Vargas everything that he had wanted, it proved unwieldy when put into practice. The new Congress was divisive, just as the republican Congress had been. Within weeks of its enactment, Vargas showed signs that he would bypass it.

At the same time, its provisions creating regional agencies and permitting intervention in the national economy aided Vargas's other measures to strengthen the central government. One of the most critical aspects of this was Vargas's reorganization of the national armed forces and the assertion of federal coordination and ultimately control over the formerly quasi-independent state militias. Vargas then quietly disarmed a military coup being plotted against him by supporters of army general Góes Monteiro and consolidated his power.

President Vargas stood by as Integralists clashed in the streets with their left-wing counterparts, members of the Aliança Nacional Libertadora, a popular front organization headed nominally by Luís Carlos Prestes. The ANL brought together Communists, trade unionists, and sympathetic antifascists to combat integralism, which by 1935 had attracted approximately 180,000 members nationwide, and to demand social justice. Behind the scenes, the Comintern (Third International), operated out of Montevideo, manipulated the ANL and used it as cover for clandestine operations. Instructed by Moscow that Latin America was ripe for revolution, the Comintern planned insurrections in Chile, Argentina, Uruguay, and Peru, as well as Brazil. None of them amounted to anything, but they gave officials justification for cracking down on the left and crushing suspected pockets of communism. Vargas used Prestes's radical demands to impose a draconian National Security Law in June 1935 and to close the ANL. Further, the confrontational atmosphere brought the Catholic Church into alliance with the military and with propertied interests "to combat all progressive forces that could be viewed as allies of the communists."[45]

Despite the fact that Rio de Janeiro was tipped off in advance by the British Intelligence Service about the Comintern's plans, in November barracks revolts broke out in Recife, distant Natal, and Rio de Janeiro's Praia Vermelho, a few kilometers from the presidential palace, in Urca. In Recife, the interventor was absent, en route to Lisbon aboard the dirigible *Hindenburg*, thereby making coordination of the resistance difficult. The revolutionaries toppled the government of Rio Grande do Norte and held power in the name of a soviet Brazil for three days, un-

45. Schneider, *Brazil*, 63.

der the ANL banner of "Bread, Land, and Liberty." The army and police quelled all three of the revolts. Civil rights were never restored. The
insurrections provided the pretext for governing under a state of siege,
which remained in place until the proclamation of the Estado Novo dictatorship on November 10, 1937. They illustrate the sorry unworldliness
of the Latin American left during these years, a condition that resulted
in the imprisonment or deaths of many thousands of well-meaning sympathizers following orders or caught up in events.

Vargas used the insurrections to drive the final nail into the coffin of
the 1934 Constitution and to end any chance for the exercise of representative democracy. The Constitution had served some of Vargas's purposes; it was not a complete failure. It had facilitated the creation of regional agencies, and its endorsement of intervention in the economy
complemented Vargas's goal of strengthening the central government.
The Constitution had enabled Vargas to reorganize the armed forces and
assert federal coordination and ultimately control over the formerly
quasi-independent state militias, one of which, São Paulo's, had risen
against the national government in 1932. Foreign observers had scoffed
at the hysteria being stirred up in Brazil against the Communist threat,
but the November events quieted them. A diplomat in the American
embassy had written: "A measure of Communism is perhaps inevitable
in a country in which ignorant and poverty-stricken masses live in jux-
taposition with an indolent and parasitical moneyed class. But in spite
of the undisciplined character of the people it is difficult to believe that
with their happy-go-lucky temperament they would be much inclined
to accept communistic dogma."[46]

The failed uprisings gave the upper hand to the hard-liners. Savage
repression followed. Felinto Müller, the army officer named by Vargas as
federal police chief, scolded foreigners who were appealing for leniency
in the cases of "Prestes and his henchmen" for depicting Brazil as a
"semibarbaric country."[47] In a driving rain on March 5, 1936, fifty soldiers surrounded the "safe house" of the head of the Brazilian Communist Party and entered, firing wildly. The Brazilian legation in Portugal
and the Consulate in Buenos Aires both had informed Foreign Minister
Macedo Soares that Prestes had obtained a false passport as "Antonio
Villar," and had even forwarded a copy of the passport application com-

---

46. George A. Gordon, U.S. Embassy, Rio de Janeiro, to Secretary of State, Report
    730, July 11, 1935, 958, National Archives, Washington, D.C.
47. Quoted by Hilton, *Brazil and the Soviet Challenge*, 111.

plete with photographs of Prestes and his wife, the German-born Communist, Olga Benário, who it was said later, had been ordered by the KBG to marry him.[48] They were arrested along with several foreign Comintern agents (including an American, Victor Allan Barron, and German-born Arthur Ewert and his wife Elise). The police even arrested Prestes's former maid, administering beatings and electric shocks. Barron died under torture; Ewert was abused with great intensity, then kept caged behind a stairway in the police headquarters building for over a year, sleeping on the floor and living in his own filth, until he nearly went mad. Elise and Olga – who was seven months pregnant – were deported to Nazi Germany, where they died in death camps, although Olga's daughter Anita, who was born in Berlin, survived. Anita believes that the women were deported as a gesture by Vargas to show Hitler his willingness to pursue good relations between their countries. Aranha wrote to Vargas that the anti-Communist hysteria was being overdone but Getúlio replied that the threat was as serious as the government had been maintaining. Responding to pleas sent from abroad to stop the mistreatment of political prisoners, Vargas declared on May 10 that the police had been "magnanimous" toward prisoners and treated them "benignly." Müller also denied "stooping to violent methods."[49]

The Balance Sheet

Vargas had attempted to hold together the diverse Liberal Alliance movement by casting his 1930 presidential platform in "the widely acceptable mold of liberal democratic nationalism" but he quickly moved away from the liberal *tenente* position and stood ready to rely much more heavily on those who advocated antidemocratic solutions. The consolidation of power by the central government at the expense of local and state interests became the cornerstone of his administration. Yet in some ways, however, little changed during Vargas's first seven years as head of state. His decrees bringing benefits to salaried workers went far beyond the limited and rarely enforced laws of the Old Republic, but they were

48. Letter, M. Nobre de Mello to the Brazilian Foreign Ministry, March 21, 1936; letter, M. Paranhos, Vice-Consul in Buenos Aires, to J. C. de Macedo Soares, March 9, 1936, DOPS archive, Arquivo Público do Estado do, Rio de Janeiro, Setor Geral, Lata 1860, M. 36110.
49. Hilton, *Brazil and the Soviet Challenge*, 84; Anita Leoncadia Prestes, "Olga Benário Prestes, Minha Mãe," in *Não Olhe nos Olhos do Inimigo* (Rio de Janeiro: Ed. Paz e Terra, 1995), 13.

only incompletely carried out, especially outside of Rio de Janeiro. So-cial welfare legislation had come at the price of individual freedom. Workers now had to carry work booklets (*carteiras*) that gave employers and the police the ability to blacklist anyone who had gotten into trou-ble for participating in strikes or political activism. Unionization briefly flourished after Vargas took power – there were nearly five hundred unions in 1935, mostly in Rio and São Paulo – but the number of non-recognized unions declined steeply after the November insurrections and the resulting police crackdowns. After 1935, strikes were for all practical purposes outlawed. The centralization of government had dealt a near fatal blow to the state political machines, although the clans that dominated individual states remained powerful because Vargas did nothing to neutralize the resilient political culture rooted in patronage and government-by-favoritism.

The expansion of government into wholly new areas transformed everyday life in many ways, especially as a result of the drive to regulate and control. Soccer, which became a craze throughout South America in the early years of the century, had started out as an elite, amateur sport played in private clubs originally established for rowing and socializa-tion. The sport spread to the lower classes when English factory owners started to field employee teams, but it did not become a national insti-tution until 1933 when the sport became professionalized under the Brazilian Sport Confederation (CBD). Overnight, elite teams rushed to acquire working-class athletes, creating an institution that combined the passions of rich and poor alike. The government seized on this, ap-propriating the nationalistic symbol of the all-Brazilian team's victory in the 1932 South American Cup and approving the use of black players (initially resisted by CBD officials) on Brazil's World Cup teams of the 1930s.[50] Vargas's government also appropriated the popularity of Car-nival samba – another expression of popular culture newly appreciated by the elite – in the same way, requiring samba associations, tradition-ally located in Rio's *favelas*, to register and submit to censorship in ex-change for tourist subventions and other stipends. In so doing, Vargas's government elevated samba to a national institution and extracted from it a host of symbolic values that enhanced its own image.

Where it counted, however, little was done to provide needed hous-ing or to improve public health. A few of Vargas's regime's reforms had

---

50. See Robert M. Levine, "Sport and Society: The Case of Brazilian *Futebol*," *Luso-Brazilian Review*, 17:2 (Winter 1980), 233–252.

effects, mostly in the Federal District, although the removal and arrest of interventor Pedro Ernesto Baptista (who had established several major social and educational programs in Rio de Janeiro) and the subsequent persecution of progressives affected adversely some of the brightest reforms, especially in education. Consider Vargas's record in this area. The right of all Brazilians to a free primary education had been included in all Brazilian constitutions since 1824, but only after 1930 did the federal government play a role. Calls for educational reform had surfaced as early as the 1920s, when reformers, aware of movements for progressive education in Europe and the United States, organized the Brazilian Education Association. In 1932, they issued a manifesto calling for massive aid to public education, demanding such innovations as coeducation, education in hygiene, and free secular, pluralist education. Some of the reformers were hired by Vargas's new Ministry of Education, but it received only limited resources. As a result, gains were modest at best, especially in the hinterland. Catholics and other conservatives attacked the education reformers as "materialists" and Communists, and after 1935, efforts to reform teaching methods were derailed, although the regime continued to allocate resources to build new schools.

Only thirty of every one thousand children completed the primary grades when Vargas took power. Educational policies at all levels were uncoordinated, and the number of schools very small, since Brazil was a rural country. Although Vargas made promises about education in most of his speeches, and in spite of the fact that he seemed to be genuinely personally concerned about the need for reform, the 1940 census revealed that fewer than one-quarter of school-age children under the age of fourteen attended class.[51] Public secondary schools were especially rare, and vocational education mostly limited to "training institutes" and state institutions that were more reform schools than anything else. The Catholic Church did maintain a network of schools, but mostly for children of the elite. Very occasionally, schools were funded by individuals or by community organizations, although most of these were for children of immigrants – and these schools would be closed in 1938 when Vargas outlawed the use of foreign languages in schools or in the press. Teachers across Brazil remained ill-trained, often having less than a high school education themselves, and teacher salaries remained at or below subsistence levels in most parts of Brazil. Many teachers were un-

51. See David N. Plank, *The Means of Our Salvation: Public Education in Brazil, 1930–1995* (Boulder, Colo.: Westview Press, 1996), 63.

married women forced to live in poverty, although in many cases they paid for books and supplies because their students' families had even less. Although Education Minister Gustavo Capanema was an effective administrator, calls for reform slowed appreciably after the repressive aftermath of 1935. Conservatives attacked efforts to put boys and girls together in the same classrooms, to teach hygiene, and to depart in any way from the traditional curriculum, which emphasized rote learning.

Any dissatisfaction with this was muted by the eclipse of civil liberties after 1935, especially after the implementation of the draconian National Security Law and successive declarations of states of national emergency to combat the Communist threat. Public attention shifted to other issues. By 1937, the economy had begun to rebound, nearing pre-Depression levels. Vargas complied with the requirement that there be a presidential election in 1938, and in the preceding year he set the machinery into motion. The electoral campaign, however, soon took on a mood strikingly similar to the contentious Vargas-Júlio Prestes campaign eight years earlier. José Américo de Almeida, a Paraíban from the progressive *tenente* wing, was the choice of press baron Assis Chateaubriand and others who wanted a veteran of the Liberal Alliance to symbolize the drive to renew the failed promise of that movement. A national convention on May 25, 1937, formally endorsed José Américo, who immediately initiated a campaign attacking dictatorships of the right as well as of the left. His adversary, São Paulo's Armando de Sales Oliveira, made Brazil's lack of democracy under Vargas his main issue and attacked José Américo as a potential demagogue. Vargas probably accepted José Américo's candidacy because he thought it weak and likely divisive.

As early as January 1936, Vargas had written to Oswaldo Aranha in Washington that the "Communist virus contaminated us earlier and with greater intensity than one could imagine." Suppressing the Communist threat would not be enough, he added. The Brazilian people need "healthy stimuli of a moral and ideological nature," he added, telling Aranha that he intended to coordinate the efforts of the Education Ministry, the Army General Staff, and the League for National Defense to launch a national campaign. Within weeks, Gustavo Capanema created a special Education Ministry committee to censor children's literature and announced a lecture series whose opening talk would be by Catholic Action's Alceu Amoroso Lima on the threat posed to education by communism.[52] What Vargas was doing was, in Ronald M.

52. Hilton, *Brazil and the Soviet Challenge*, 88.

Schneider's words, engineering a "controlled escalation of the crisis," fostering polarization by encouraging integralism and fanning fears of communism by permitting disclosure of the "Cohen Plan," an Integralist forgery alleging a left-wing conspiracy aimed at bringing down the state and burning churches.[53] He named General Dutra as war minister and Góes Monteiro to be the army chief of staff.

This was nothing new: Vargas always had been quick to use the threat of Communist subversion to justify repressive measures against leftists and their sympathizers. In March 1931 he contracted with the New York City Police Department to send two specialists in anti-Communist tactics. In 1935 he decreed the National Security Law, suspending habeas corpus and instituting a civil-military tribunal, the Supreme Security Tribunal or TSN, to hear cases brought against persons suspected of threatening Brazil's "national integrity." He met regularly with military leaders and worked with them to transfer trusted officers to positions where they could handle any trouble. Brazil remained under successive states of national emergency during the entire period from November 1935 to November 1937, when with military backing he overthrew his own government and imposed the Estado Novo, openly based on the fascist regimes in Portugal, Poland, and Italy. Explaining his reasons, Vargas claimed that "moral and political deceptions" had been eliminated and that the country could go forward to "construct its history and destiny."[54]

Integralists within the military, led by General Newton Cavalcanti, the regional commander in the Northeast (and the president of the Brazilian Boy Scouts), took up the anti-Communist crusade with relish. Vargas's speeches took on, in Stanley E. Hilton's words, "an increasingly Integralist tone," appealing for reinforcement of the "ties of family, religion, and state," and warning that Communists wanted to "annihilate the fatherland, family, and religion."[55] On November 1, 1937, Vargas stood on his balcony and reviewed a parade of twenty thousand Integralist militia, with two generals identified with the Integralists at his side. He clearly was signaling his readiness to move to the right, although other business of government went on as usual. Rumors flew that a coup was imminent. It seemed apparent that the country was moving to the far right and to fascism.

53. See Schneider, *Brazil*, 62–63.
54. Getúlio Vargas, *A Nova Política do Brasil* (Rio de Janeiro: J. Olympia, Editora, 1938), 5:19–32; Dulles, "The Contribution of Getúlio Vargas," 46–47.
55. Hilton, *Brazil and the Soviet Challenge*, 92.

Months before, one of the songs written for 1937 Carnival had commented on the political scene:

> Will it be Sales?
> Or will it be José Américo?
> Between the two,
> My heart is wavering.
> Because at H hour
> The one who will stay
> Is Gegê [Vargas].[56]

Vargas seemed unconcerned by these signs. He spent weekends with
his family, playing dominoes to kill time, and if he enjoyed power he
never admitted it to himself. Rainy days depressed him, and his day-to-
day presidential activities were borne with tedium. "Darcy's reception,"
he wrote on one occasion, "got in the way of getting away from the capital this weekend, as I had hoped. Nothing interesting is happening
these days: conversations, intrigues, little boring things, a speech by candidate Armando Sales filled with promises."[57] Following a meeting with
General Goés Monteiro and J. S. Maciel Filho – the journalist who
would become almost his alter ego fifteen years later – Getúlio wrote
cryptically in his secret diary that the old sense of adventure was back,
that it posed "risks to life itself," but that risk was worth taking. Within
days, he cheered up. "I went to the Jockey Club," he wrote on August 1,
using flowery language unusual for him: "It was a clear and bright Sunday, with the sun illuminating the magnificent scene watched by a mul-
titude." His diary entries reverted to the old style, although now he began to hint that the presidential campaign was bothering him. "There
have been negative repercussions in the political arena of the extremist
speeches in favor of José Américo [de Almeida's] candidacy, especially the
candidate's own speeches."[58] The political atmosphere, he wrote in late
September, "is deteriorating." In less than two months, the entire structure of Brazil's government would be pulled down, not by popular action,
but by Vargas himself with the military standing firmly behind him.

One week before the Estado Novo coup, Vargas celebrated the sev-

---

56. Vargas do Amaral Peixoto, *Getúlio Vargas, Meu Pai*, 308.
57. Getúlio Vargas, *Diário*, vol. 2 (Rio de Janeiro: Siciliano/Fundação Getúlio Var-
    gas, 1995), entry for July 16–18, 1937 (p. 60).
58. Ibid., entries for July 25–27, 1937; August 1, and August 28–30 (2:61–67).

enth anniversary of his ascension to power. "There were commemorative as well as spontaneous celebrations," he noted blandly in his diary, "but I did not attend them." He spent the day conferring with aides about the price of coffee but devoted the evening to a "long" conversation with General Goés Monteiro. The next day Vargas and Francisco Campos, who had been identified with the right-wing *tenente* movement earlier in the decade and who admired European fascism, talked about Vargas's request for Campos to draft a new national constitution. On November 5 Vargas railed at a *Correio da Manhã* story about "intrigues within the armed forces." Vargas's diary entry showed rare anger: "How did the censors let that be published?" The next day the censorship apparatus was transferred from the civilian justice ministry to Felinto Müller's Federal District police. Justice Minister Macedo Soares was fired, replaced by Campos. On November 7 Vargas confided that the planned *golpe* could not be turned back, that Congress would be closed and a new constitution put into place. He spent November 8 working through a "mountain of paperwork" from the Education Ministry. He began to inform his cabinet ministers of what was coming, and quietly named new interventors in two states, Bahia and Pernambuco, where soundings about the intended coup had suggested that the interventors would not comply. One of them, Juracy Magalhães in Bahia, had been a *tenente* and former close ally. At ten in the morning of November 10, the cabinet was asked to sign the new constitution; only the agriculture minister, Odilón Braga, refused, resigning on the spot. At eight in the evening Vargas informed the nation of the *golpe*. Brazilians accepted the news compliantly. "The movement of November 10th," he said in an interview some months later, "was, without doubt, brought about by the national will." "We had need of order and security in order to carry on; conspiring against that was the critical state of political decomposition to which we had arrived."[59]

59. Getúlio Vargas, Interview, March 1938, cited in E. Bradford Burns, A *Documentary History of Brazil* (New York: Knopf, 1966), 348.

CHAPTER THREE

THE ESTADO NOVO,
1937–1945

On the morning of November 10, 1937, writer Joel Silveira, then a young law student in Rio de Janeiro, found the iron gates of the law faculty building locked. "Getúlio pulled off a coup," another student told him. "He closed the Chamber, the Senate. There'll be no classes today." Traveling downtown by streetcar, Silveira saw soldiers guarding the legislative palace, standing around smoking cigarettes. That evening, Vargas addressed the nation over the radio. He spoke gravely, in his usual monotone. "[His words] tumbled out," Silveira recollects, "heavy, measured utterances, unctuous, dull, dripping like oil. We were told that with the help of the military we have been saved. Vargas explained, like a teacher, that a Communist plot was imminent. . . . He, Vargas, and his praetorian guard would stand watch over us. From that moment, we, citizens of Brazil, workers of Brazil, could rest assured. . . . In the wings stood, without a doubt, the SS of Major Felinto Müller, the gauleiter of the capital."[1] This version, of course, benefits from hindsight and literary license, since Silveira wrote his memoirs four and a half decades later. If others felt similarly, they kept their reaction to themselves. Across Brazil, life went on as usual.

Waldo Frank, touring Latin America, described the Brazilian leader some time later: "Vargas has the small, square hands, hairy and hard, of a worker. His head sits on his shoulders like a precocious student's: there is the discrepancy between it and his oldish body, which reveals excess development of mind over emotion. The head is harmoniously shaped; the eyes have cunning and humor; both head and eyes give him the air

---

1. Paraphrased from Joel Silveira, *O Presidente no Jardim* (Rio de Janeiro: Editora Record, 1991), 43–45.

of youth. Vargas has lived hard, but saved emotion." As psychoanalysis, Frank's characterization was amateurish, but he was an astute observer, and in the span of a short visit he sized up what many others took years to express. Vargas, he wrote, "is a marginal man in Brazil," referring to his birthplace on the Argentine border and his excellent knowledge of Spanish. Vargas "is as cool as a glacier, and nearly as slow. He is known to be fearless . . . [partially] due to his deliberate and controlling strength of reason."[2]

Cool as ice or not, Vargas masterfully orchestrated the events through which the Estado Novo was imposed. He secured the support of the military command and assured journalists, especially foreign correspondents reporting from Brazil, that things were under control. The presidential elections were unceremoniously canceled and the 1934 Constitution abrogated in favor of a new document written by the archconservative jurist Francisco Campos. This constitution ceded virtually all power to the head of state. It was based on the Italian Carta del Lavoro and fascist Poland's 1935 charter, which proclaimed that the "sole and individual authority of the State is concentrated in the person of the President of the Republic." Opponents nicknamed the Estado Novo constitution "the *polaca*" ("the Polish one"), alluding to the term's meaning as slang for European prostitutes.

Vargas opted for the coup because it was the only way he could remain in office beyond his legal term, which would have ended in a few months. He had become adamant that only he could move Brazil forward to national integration, and the election campaign between Armando de Sales Oliveira and José América de Almeida dismayed him as a choice between a *paulista* restoration and uncontrolled radical populism. "To combat the poverty and disorganization of [Brazil's] public life," he told his radio audience, the presidential campaign, "transformed into an unruly exchange of charges and demagogic promises," had to be canceled. His concluding promise was that "I will continue to serve the nation."[3] He then permitted a story to circulate in the press affirming the existence and threat of the scurrilous "Cohen Plan," although this was a blatant lie, and blamed Communists for bringing

2. Waldo David Frank, *South American Journey* (London: Victor Gollancz, 1943), 342.
3. Affonso Henriques, *Ascensão e queda de Getúlio Vargas* (Rio de Janeiro: Distruibuidora Record, 1966), 428–429. See also Thomas E. Skidmore, *Politics in Brazil, 1930–1964* (New York: Oxford University Press, 1967), 29.

Brazil to the edge of calamity. This was preposterous, and even some of Getúlio's closest supporters, including Oswaldo Aranha and Assis Chateaubriand, reacted with anger after the Estado Novo was imposed. Aranha resigned from the government. But if Vargas was upset, he did not show it. He welcomed the opportunity to crack down on the opposition and on dissent. He had Müller tap the telephones and open the mail of everyone in the government, even General Góes Monteiro, to whom Müller gave his "word of honor" that his phone conversations would remain private.[4]

Vargas surrounded himself with officials who shared his outlook. Francisco Campos, the author of the 1937 Constitution, justice minister, and the major intellectual defender of authoritarian corporatism, flatly rejected liberal democracy on the grounds that the entry of the masses into political life required repressive measures to resist degeneration into class conflict, "Muscovite inundation," and anarchy. Instead, Campos advocated a strong centralized state to serve the entire nation, not class interests.[5] The role of the state was to guide, not to control. Labor was to be organized vertically, from local *sindicatos* (unions) up through national confederations, representing in organic fashion not only the workers but management, producers, and the state. Azevedo Amaral, explaining the Estado Novo's position, argued:

> Docile submission to the authority of the State is not repugnant and cannot be repugnant to normal individuals, for they intuitively understand that in order for a people to transform itself into a nation, it must organize itself into a hierarchical structure. The solidity and efficient functioning of this structure requires the action of an authority capable of coordinating and orienting the elements which are juxtaposed in society.[6]

Powerful interests, like the São Paulo industrialists, were incorporated into the decision-making process, but organized labor was treated

---

4. Transcript of telephone conversation between Góes Monteiro and Dep. Jayme Correa, November 5, 1935, recorded by secret police, reproduced in *Bras-Notícias*, October 19, 1995, Sinopse, 6.
5. Francisco Campos, *O Estado Nacional; sua Estrutura, seu Conteudo Ideológico* (Rio de Janeiro: José Olympio Editora, 1940), 23, 39–40, 61.
6. Antônio José do Azevedo Amaral, *O Estado Authoritário e a Realidade Nacional* (Rio de Janeiro: José Olympio Editora, 1938), 171, cited by K. P. Erickson, *The Brazilian Corporative State* (Berkeley: University of California Press, 1977), 18.

paternalistically and manipulated. Vargas-era syndicalism was imposed from the top down. Vargas, Erickson shows, held his coalition together through concessions, force, and the promise to mobilize a national effort to bring Brazil out of the Depression.[7] Pluralism in Brazilian society was permitted only if it did not challenge the government. Furthermore, Vargas remained in power only with the backing of the military. Before 1937 there had been a pretense of popular support; after 1937 this was no longer claimed as a justification for dictatorship.

Free from the restraints of liberal constitutionalism, Vargas was able to restructure the government as he wished. The ban on political activity also extended to self-help voluntary associations, including groups organized by blacks in São Paulo earlier in the decade. Citizens' groups like the *paulista* Society of Friends of the City (SAC) remained in operation but without effect; all initiatives now came from the state. Mayors were no longer elected but appointed by Vargas's state interventors. Vargas imposed a policy he called *desacumulação*, a decree forbidding anyone from holding more than one public job. This dealt a blow to thousands who had accumulated several public jobs as patronage, but also had harmful effects, hurting poorly paid university professors who needed to hold more than one post to make a living.

To circumvent the old bureaucracies, Vargas created the Administrative Department for Public Service (DASP), a federal super ministry accountable only to him, along with similar agencies at the state level. This afforded the government freedom to innovate, to create regional agencies able to avoid power struggles among jealous state interests, to expand welfare policies, and to invest directly in steel, iron ore, and river valley development, among other activities.[8] The Estado Novo built its programs of social justice and "economic democracy" on Vargas's earlier initiatives. Unlike Mussolini, he never attempted to organize a mass political party to support the regime. His cynical (and former Integralist) labor minister, Alexandre Marcondes Filho, affirmed Vargas's premise that only within a framework of social order and tranquility, based on Christian principles, could the government discharge its duties

---

7. Erickson, *The Brazilian Corporative State*, 22.
8. Barry Ames, *Political Survival: Politicians and Public Policy in Latin America* (Berkeley: University of California Press, 1987), 106. See also Morris L. Cooke, *Brazil on the March: A Study in International Cooperation* (New York: McGraw-Hill, 1944), 56.

by providing for the needs of the working class and preventing class struggle.[9]

Vargas had never shied away from heavy-handedness, and he welcomed his new dictatorial powers because he had always felt impatient with political delay. Authoritarian government suited him, and his actions gave the strong impression that he had accepted the ideological position of the conservative far right. Soon after the coup, he let it be known that the Integralists were welcome to join his government by offering the education post to the green-shirt chieftain Plínio Salgado. The Integralist leader initially accepted but then changed his mind, holding out for a more powerful portfolio, possibly justice. When Vargas refused, he sulked. Given that Vargas's antidemocratic proclivities were shared by many in the armed forces, had Salgado accepted, fascism would have probably taken a firmer hold. But Salgado's rejection of the post set into motion events that abruptly undermined his pretensions to amass power and permitted Vargas to consolidate his hold more firmly than ever.

On May 8, 1938, dozens of armed Integralists in the early hours of the morning attacked the Catete palace. Vargas, his daughter Alzira, and his personal staff were forced to barricade themselves and shoot back from their windows. For several hours the military did nothing to intervene, although relief was nearby and the armed forces command had been informed of the assault by telephone. Clearly the military command waited to see what would happen. When loyal troops finally arrived, they quickly quelled the assault. Vargas followed up by banning the AIB and dispatching Plínio Salgado into exile in Portugal. This was a soft punishment – in contrast to Prestes's harsh imprisonment – but Vargas presumably did not want to alienate the European fascist powers. The attempted *putsch* would have been comic had there not been live ammunition on both sides. It short-circuited a more elaborate plot by members of the ex-Democratic Party in São Paulo, led by João Mangabeira, for a second constitutionalist uprising against Vargas, this time in alliance with the Integralists. The assault on the palace was triggered by two green-shirted militia men presumably acting on their own, Lieutenant Severo Fournier and a physician, Belmiro Valverde. Vargas, catching his breath, seized upon the attack to liquidate all pockets of remaining opposition in the country. This stopped the jockeying for pow-

---

9. Ludwig Lauerhass Jr., *Getúlio Vargas e o Triunfo do Nacionalismo Brasileiro* (Belo Horizonte: Itatiaia, 1986), 247–248.

er that had started with the Liberal Alliance campaign in 1930. Vargas was now firmly in control, although the generals watched him carefully; they were the ones who held ultimate power.

The justification for abandoning representative government was bluntly stated by Agamenón Magalhães, the dour new labor minister who had earned a reputation for nastiness in suppressing dissidents in his home state of Pernambuco. Brazil, Magalhães declared, was "the land of electoral clientelism, of incompetence, of favors, of bureaucratic waste." We need radical solutions, he added: "simpler ones, more rational, more intelligent, more efficient."[10] Vargas shared Magalhães's view wholly. Yet for most Brazilians, the Estado Novo did not seem a sinister police state. Persons picked up by police – unless they were wealthy or from the "better" families – expected to be beaten, sometimes savagely; but this always had been the case and was not the result of Vargas's suspending habeas corpus or imposing the Estado Novo. A visiting political scientist in 1941 characterized the regime as a "mild-tempered, semi-totalitarian dictatorship."[11]

To be sure, Vargas never embraced military fascism. The Estado Novo was administered by bureaucrats, not soldiers. Vargas's paternalism was not new to Brazil but continued the legacy of generations.[12] The Estado Novo was centralized and nationalistic, but in a slack, fragmentary way. Once it was installed, Vargas ceremoniously lowered state flags and replaced them with Brazil's striking green, blue, and yellow national emblem. But this was only theater; Vargas's policies under the Estado Novo simply continued his earlier measures. He championed economic independence and the progress that would come from abandoning partisan and state-based interests. He banned the use of foreign languages in schools and pressed communities of Germans, Italians, Poles, and Japanese to acculturate. In the name of Brazilian unity, foreign-language newspapers and magazines were prohibited. This *Brasilidade* campaign was so effective that individuals who spoke no Portuguese were publicly ostracized in their communities, even in places heavily populated by immigrants. But Brazilians responded positively to the nationalistic measures, and no protests were raised against government actions that inconvenienced individuals and small groups. When Vargas sent troops in 1944 to join the United States Fifth Army in Italy, he boasted that sol-

10. Agamenón Magalhães, in *Folha da Manhã* (Recife), September 18, 1940, 1.
11. Walter R. Sharp, "Methods of Opinion Control in Present-Day Brazil," 3.
12. Erickson, *The Brazilian Corporative State*, 15.

diers would serve from every single Brazilian state, to affirm Brazil's drive for national unification. That the soldiers were sent virtually untrained went unsaid.

Police and armed forces intelligence agents targeted for arrest or close surveillance tens of thousands of suspected opponents of the regime, most of them leftists. Antigovernment publications were taken from newsstands and incinerated, as were the National Library's back issues of many Communist newspapers. Many persons unsympathetic to the regime fled into exile. Among those who were imprisoned were the distinguished writers Graciliano Ramos and Monteiro Lobato. For having written a letter criticizing Vargas's petroleum policy as "malevolent,"[13] Lobato was arrested in his house at four in the morning and sentenced to five months in prison. Ordinary Brazilians also suffered indignities. Government clerks steamed open mail, made verbatim copies of letters for their files, sealed the envelopes, and sent them on their way. Many Brazilians learned only decades later that their privacy had been violated during the entire Estado Novo and that they had been considered potential subversives.

Political prisoners fared very badly. Thousands languished in the regime's penitentiaries. Some of the worst were the Maria Zélia and Paraíso prisons as well as the public jail in São Paulo, the Ilha das Cobras stockade in Rio de Janeiro, Recife's fetid House of Detention on the banks of the Capibaribe River, with more than four thousand prisoners crammed into tiny cells, and the penal colony on Fernando de Noronha island off the northeastern coast. Prison space was so much in demand after the November 1935 uprising that naval ships were converted into floating jails anchored in the sweltering heat of Rio's harbor. Arrested persons who were not citizens were deported. The Supreme Security Tribunal (TSN) handed down long prison sentences. Security officials let their own prejudices influence their work. Because Müller and others considered Jews potential Communists, the secret police kept a wide variety of Jewish social and cultural societies under surveillance.[14] When arrested, Jews, blacks, and union militants frequently received harsher treatment than others. Afro-Brazilian religious cults were considered deviant and therefore suppressed by the police. Nazi Party mem-

13. Letter, Monteiro Lobato to Getúlio Vargas, May 14, 1940, CPDOC archive, Rio de Janeiro.
14. DOPS Archive, Arquivo Público do Estado do Rio de Janeiro, Setor Geral, Pasta 7, Dossier 11.

bers, German nationalists, and fascist Integralists were watched, although they were rarely arrested or mistreated. Generals Góes Monteiro and Eurico Gaspar Dutra, the two most powerful members of the military high command, were friendly to the Integralist movement, and Police Chief Müller maintained almost weekly contact with Integralist officials.[15]

The accelerated expansion of the centralized government after 1937 and the maintenance of a ponderous censorship system were accompanied by propaganda extolling the "new mentality in our country" and the regime's promises to improve the quality of Brazilians' lives. "A country is not just a conglomeration of individuals within a stretch of land," Getúlio told a May Day gathering in 1938, "but above all a unity of race, a unity of language, a unity of national spirit." Vargas's words were the products of Brazil's patriarchal tradition. He was benevolent and judgmental, "perpetually smiling rather than stern, accessible rather than distant, relaxed rather than formal."[16]

The regime celebrated the Estado Novo's first anniversary in November 1938 with an elaborate "Exposition of Anti-Communism and Estado Novo Propaganda" in Rio's elegant Municipal Theater.[17] Visitors viewed displays showing weapons seized during the 1935 Communist insurrection, dioramas and maps pinpointing Communist ventures throughout the world, and graphics depicting the Estado Novo's programs and goals. A display taunting the Spanish Republic was considered so offensive that it led to a formal complaint by the Spanish embassy and, in turn, recognition of Franco by the Brazilian foreign ministry. Police chief Müller regularly received "educational" materials from the Gestapo, and some of it was likely used on this occasion.

The DASP notwithstanding, Brazil remained too vast and inefficient a country to be administered wholly from Rio de Janeiro. As a result, each state fared differently under the Estado Novo depending on the style and motivation of Vargas's appointed interventor. In some states, hardly anything changed. This was not the case in Pernambuco under Agamenón Magalhães. Taking an aggressively populist stance, he an-

---

15. Augusto do Amaral Peixoto and Jeová Mota, cited in Valentina da Rocha Lima, *Getúlio: Uma História Oral* (Rio de Janeiro: Ed. Record, 1986), 107–108.

16. Susan K. Besse, *Restructuring Patriarchy: The Modernization of Gender Inequality in Brazil, 1914–1940* (Chapel Hill: University of North Carolina Press, 1996), 202; Getúlio Vargas, *A Nova Política do Brasil*, 5:205, cited by Besse, 206.

17. Dossier, "Exposição Anti-Communista e de Propaganda do Estado Novo," Itamaratí Archive, Lata 685. M. 10.044, Rio de Janeiro.

nounced a program to pressure firms to limit extravagant profits and to lower prices. Citizens were invited to report cases of price gouging and other improper behavior. Magalhães paid subsidies to the Catholic Worker Educational Centers, established privately during the mid-1930s. In 1939 he launched a program to tear down some of the more unsightly *mocambo* shantytowns on the outskirts of Recife. The state administration installed an anti-Communist pavilion at the annual trade fair, and he went after not only Communists and fellow travelers but, in quieter ways, some of the members of the local oligarchy linked to pre-Estado Novo factions. In December 1937, state police arrested 269 alleged subversives, all without habeas corpus. The federal Justice Ministry assisted by providing Pernambuco with 40 percent of the entire national budgetary resources earmarked for the "repression of communism."[18] Purges removed intellectuals from their jobs; many were arrested, deported, or savagely harassed. When Ulisses Pernambucano, a psychiatrist and pioneering health administrator in Recife, lay ill with heart trouble, unmarked police cars parked outside his home and honked their horns all day. He died shortly afterward.

Pernambuco under Magalhães was more the exception than the rule. São Paulo mostly ignored the Estado Novo and its decrees. Minas Gerais went along with Vargas, yet it received relatively little in funding or new programs. The poorer states received even less. This reality, Vargas's paternalism, and the fact that for most Brazilians life went on much the same as before the coup, muted the hard edge of the new order. Vargas continued to guard his privacy, and he refused to speak on or off the record about the specifics of his administration. He remained symbolically accessible to all citizens but there was little follow-up. He mastered the art of the political visit, dressing comfortably so as not to appear a stuffed shirt, always smiling and waving his hand, cultivating accessibility even if he said little of substance. It was not what he said in public but how he said it. He became a calming, familiar presence in the lives of nearly all Brazilians, unheard of before in Brazil. He traveled great distances for official visits – ninety thousand miles in 1942 – dedicating public projects, cutting ribbons, and speaking from makeshift wooden platforms never built so high that they would separate him from his audience.

His way of speaking evolved. Before 1938, he spoke of "my govern-

18. Dulce Chaves Pandolfi, *Pernambuco de Agamenón Magalhães* (Recife: Ed. Massangana, 1984), 55–57.

ment," "our organization," "your will"; but starting in 1938, under the guiding eye of his Propaganda Ministry, he began to use the term "I." He had made the transition to self-identification with the masses, whom he addressed as "workers of Brazil," and his spoken expressions eliminated any intermediaries between people and government. He now made it clear that he stood at their side; that he and the people were one. He implored Brazilians to celebrate the dignity of work and traditional values. He enlisted the working class to his side: "order and work," "union and work," and, by the mid-1940s, working with the people to achieve the economic emancipation of Brazil. By following him, Vargas guaranteed, they would be assured employment with dignity and just wages and benefits, even though for most Brazilians these were empty promises.[19]

Vargas put his government behind efforts to instill a common and affirmative sense of national identity. He asked members of the Brazilian Academy of Letters to reformulate rules for written Brazilian Portuguese, simplifying spelling and affirming the language's distinctiveness from the Portuguese of the mother country. This was a matter of national pride, a way of institutionalizing the undisguised disdain many Brazilians felt toward the "valiant little Portuguese people" in their tiny country.[20] The Education Ministry, headed by Gustavo Capanema from 1934 to 1945, worked to improve the public school network in a variety of ways but also to inculcate the regime's values. It commissioned textbooks to stress national unity and to remind students of the "indifference of past regimes to social questions."[21] Capanema created new agencies, such as the National Book Institute (Instituto Nacional do Livro) to disseminate patriotic culture. School curricula were altered to encourage national pride, discipline, good work habits, family values, thrift, and morality. Brazilian history, geography, and literature received new emphasis. Schools were asked to produce citizens with the kinds of attitudes conducive to national improvement. Officials experimented with newer approaches to the nationalization of culture and the "emotional diffusion of national values."

19. For a valuable analysis of Vargas's techniques in speaking, see Michael L. Conniff, "Getúlio Vargas: 'Workers of Brazil! Here I Am at Your Side!,'" in John Charles Chasteen and Joseph S. Tulchin, eds., *Problems in Modern Latin American History: A Reader* (Wilmington, Del.: S R Books, 1994), 116–117.

20. For a Portuguese view, see Agostinho de Campos, "Poesia e Idioma," *Comércio de Porto* (July 14, 1935), n.p., sent by the Brazilian Consulate to Itamaratí in Rio de Janeiro.

21. *Cultura Política*, 1:1 (March 1941), 51–60.

The most important civilian agency of the Estado Novo regime and the one most involved with these newer approaches was the Propaganda Ministry, the DIP. By late 1938, 60 percent of all newspaper and magazine articles were DIP handouts. Its mandate included censorship of all public media as well as responsibility for promoting nationalist sentiment through public events and through the school system.[22] Four years later, the DIP prohibited the broadcast of 108 scripted radio programs and 373 songs, many of them written for performance at Carnival. At the same time, the regime enlisted popular culture to teach popular values. "It Is Good to Marry," went the title of one Carnival samba. *Malandros*, knife-wielding street thugs whose dark exploits had fascinated urban residents, were transformed into conforming, guitar-strumming zoot-suiters, as lovable as actors in the American musical *Guys and Dolls*.[23] Estado Novo publicists sanitized the image of such characters, even, in the case of one propaganda piece, calling Getúlio Vargas the "greatest rogue of all" because he "used his guile" to entice industrialists to behave nicer to workers, as well as protecting workers in other ways with his cleverness.[24] The regime welcomed this "sonorous climate," Alcir Lenharo argues, and used it as a counterpoint to the more caustic (and uncontrollable) compositions that censors were trying hard to domesticate.[25]

Not only did it censor the press but the DIP "suggested" that editors publish its handouts. Those refusing ran the risk of having press runs apprehended or burned. The *Estado de São Paulo* for several years was placed under direct government control, and the editors of Rio de Janeiro's *Diário de Notícias* were pressured by Lourival Fontes personally. Nationwide, many formerly independent newspapers increasingly fell under the domination of networks like the Diários Associados, which by 1937 had also branched out into radio. Assis Chateaubriand's Radio Tupi ("O Cacique do Ar"), launched in São Paulo, soon acquired the most powerful signal in Latin America.

22. Antônio Pedro Tota, "A Glória Artística nos Tempos de Getúlio," *Istoé*, January 2, 1980, 46–47.
23. See Ruben George Oliven, "Malandragem na Música Popular Brasileira," in Ruben George Oliven, ed., *Violência e Cultura no Brasil* (Petrópolis: Editora Vozes, 1983), 52–53; Henrique Dias da Luz, *Os Morros Cariocas no Novo Regime* (Rio de Janeiro: Gráfica Olimpica, 1941), 15–16.
24. Mário Lago, *Na Rolança do Tempo*, 3rd. ed. (Rio de Janeiro: Civilização Brasileiro, 1977), 9.
25. Rui Ribeiro, *Orlando Silva, o Cantor das Multidões* (Rio de Janeiro: FUNARTE, 1985), 11–16.

Vargas's crony, Lourival Fontes, a second-rate journalist from back-water Sergipe, headed the ministry. It was Fontes's idea to portray the bland head of state as the "father of the poor" (*pai dos pobres*) by blanketing the nation with propaganda, popularizing a new vocabulary of hero worship (*voz*, or "voice," as in "voice of the people," was one of the anointed words; another was *povo*). Vargas worked long and hard at perfecting the mannerisms and turns of phrase that contributed to his image of paternalistic competency. His talks were always short and simple, averting the rhetorical flourishes of traditional politicians and avoiding stilted words.[26] Vargas used speech writers – not only Fontes but, during the 1950s, newspaper editor and confidant J. S. Maciel Filho – but he always protected his control of what would be said and how it would be expressed. When Vargas was sent a batch of draft speeches during the 1950 presidential campaign, he rejected them because he found them "very academic, very correct," "not addressed to the masses." "They are more for highbrows," he commented; "they don't deal with the heart of the social and economic crisis that we are undergoing."[27]

Vargas reached his largest audience by radio, speaking frequently on the evening *Hora do Brasil*, a compendium of music, general news, uplifting speeches, tips on farming, nutrition, child rearing, agriculture, and anything else deemed appropriate by the DIP. His major speeches were reserved for holidays – Christmas and New Year's Day, as well as Independence Day and May Day. Whenever Vargas made a public appearance, it was filmed, so that the scene could be repeated across the country via newsreels, short clips accentuating the regime's accomplishments shown in movie theaters before the featured film. Newsreels powerfully shaped the perceptions of every Brazilian with incomes above the subsistence level because cinemas blanketed the country and brought the outside world to their audiences.

Knowledgeable Brazilians understood full well that most of this was a facade. Official broadcasts had the ring of Orwellian truthspeak: in an Independence Day broadcast, Vargas assured the nation that he had brought freedom to Brazil through the Estado Novo, which he termed a "functional democracy." For ten minutes each day the Estado Novo la-

26. Michael Conniff, preface to translation of Lourival Fontes and Glaucio Carneiro, *A Face Final de Vargas* (*os bilhetes de Getúlio*) (Rio de Janeiro: Edições O Cruzeiro, 1966), in Chasteen and Tulchin, *Problems in Modern Latin American History*, 117.
27. From Fontes and Carneiro, *Face Final*, 119.

bor minister, Marcondes Filho, addressed the nation on the *Hora do Brasil*, starting his talk with the phrase *Boa noite trabalhador* ("Good evening, worker"), reaching the hearts of the listeners in ways never heard before in the country's history.[28] Workers, he said, were "the producers of Brazil's wealth"; they "were manufacturing a new Brazil with fuller rights, social justice, and human dignity."

CHANGING TIMES

Many of the Estado Novo's propaganda claims proved hollow. The enlarged bureaucracy and continued use of patronage to fill government sinecures created the need for thousands of *despachantes*, personal expediters who for a fee could cut through red tape and receive favored treatment for their clients. The DIP churned out propaganda asserting and reasserting Vargas's compassionate championing of the poor. By telling the working classes that they were the bedrock of his political movement, he expanded his popularity while police raided nongovernmental unions.

Yet there was substantial progress in other areas. The Education Ministry created vocational schools and funded agronomy institutes, in part at the prompting of visiting United States technical missions. Production of electric power increased, and cement production and mineral extraction improved. In turn, the unprecedented demographic and technological changes that were transforming Brazil from a rural to an urban nation facilitated the dissemination of Estado Novo propaganda. Nearly a million radio sets by 1940 were able to tune into programs emanating from Rio de Janeiro. Migratory streams of unskilled northeasterners poured into southern cities, arriving crammed into open trucks that bounced along on the new roads built by the government. The DIP used posters and billboards to carry its messages, and distributed millions of photographs of Getúlio Vargas that were placed in homes, businesses, and government offices. Newcomers to Brazil, more than any other group, benefited from the regime's encouragement of industrial development. Nearly half of the founders or chief developers of firms with

28. See Frank, *South American Journey*, 12, 58; Pandolfi, *Pernambuco de Agamenón Magalhães*, 54; Michael A. Ogorzaly, *Waldo Frank: Prophet of Hispanic Regeneration* (Lewisburg, Pa.: Bucknell University Press, 1994), 135. In comparison with Vargas, Franklin D. Roosevelt, who also used the radio to great advantage, spoke much less frequently. During the dozen years of his presidency, Roosevelt averaged less than three "fireside chats" each year. Vargas spoke with much greater frequency.

more than one hundred employees in São Paulo were immigrants, another one-quarter had foreign-born parents, and another 11 percent were grandchildren of immigrants.[29]

Foreign observers tried to see in Vargas a Latin American version of Mussolini or Franco, but the descriptions never seemed apt. He is "cold, plump, and spider-like," Waldo Frank wrote in *Foreign Affairs* after a visit, not bothering to explain what he meant by "spider-like."[30] Frank and others were dismayed at Vargas's anticommunism as the justification for the imposition of authoritarian rule. "Communism," Vargas reported in his 1936 New Year's address, was "the most dangerous enemy of Christian civilization" because it brought disorder and, for workers, a regime of slave labor under the guise of proletarian freedom. Brazilian workers, he exhorted, would resist Bolshevism, exported from those countries whose vitality had been sapped by World War I. "National security," he stated in a speech in July 1936, necessitated the sacrifice of lesser goals and requires a climate of labor peace. A new Brazilian nationality would soon emerge, he promised, stretching from North to South and rooted in respect for order and resistant to the agents of subversion working clandestinely. Workers would be protected by the National Security Law, which would rid the country of subversives.

Vargas succeeded in using the political stability brought by the Estado Novo to transform Brazil's productive structure and to mold its economic evolution. Creating new economic policy instruments not only accelerated the growth of needed infrastructure but it reduced the traditional power base of the landed oligarchy.[31] During the entire period, developments abroad continually influenced Brazilian politics. Leftists sympathized with the Spanish Republic; at least sixty-five men volunteered to fight in the International Brigades. Comintern-backed newspapers ran story after story about Italy's invasion of Ethiopia, about the growing abuses of Hitler's Reich, and about lynchings of blacks and capitalist exploitation in the United States. Integralist newspapers praised the European fascists. Groups within the police and armed forces stirred up cam-

29. Joseph L. Love, *São Paulo in the Brazilian Federation, 1889–1937* (Stanford: Stanford University Press, 1980), 19.

30. Could he have been playing with the meaning of the name of Oswaldo Aranha, which means spider? See Frank, *South American Journey*, 32.

31. Antônio Barros de Castro, "Renegade Development: Rise and Demise of State-Led Development in Brazil," in William C. Smith et al., eds., *Democracy, Markets, and Structural Reform in Latin America* (Coral Gables, Fla.: North-South Center, 1994), 186–187.

paigns against Jews in Brazil, motivated by the fact that many Communists and socialists were immigrant Jews. Foreign embassies stepped up their cultural programs to curry favor with educated Brazilians. The Alliance Française offered language classes and sponsored French theater. After the fall of France in 1940, both Gaullist and Vichyist organizations vied for the attention of Brazilian elites. The Nazis targeted a narrower group, sending films, books, and other materials designed to stir pride about Teutonic culture to every teacher in German-speaking communities in southern Brazil. Pi sudski's Polish regime sent Brazilian-born Polish youths to Warsaw to train as pilots. The Spanish government worked hard to win support for its cause although in January 1939 Vargas recognized Franco and added Spanish Republicans to the list of enemies of the Estado Novo. In 1942 the United States's Office of Inter-American Affairs (OIAA) sent movie producers, filmmakers, dance troupes, and scholars to Brazil as part of the Good Neighbor Policy.

The major powers jockeyed for position in Brazil, a source of critical resources (especially rubber) and potentially a vast market for trade and technology as Vargas's drive to diversify the economy proceeded.[32] Foreign governments were upset at Brazil's high protective tariffs but were not willing to risk antagonizing Vargas. In foreign policy, Vargas maneuvered between the world powers, negotiating extensively with Wilhelmstrasse's ambassador Curt Prüfer about trade and armaments. On June 11, 1940, Vargas made a speech aboard the carrier *Minas Gerais* that seemed to favor the Axis. Observers suspected that the speech was a lever to extract economic aid and military armaments from the United States, but it was also known that he deeply feared the repercussions on his policies of economic independence that would come from an American alliance.[33] Germany offered to give Brazil all the weapons it want-

---

32. In the case of the United States, private philanthropy was active even before 1930. The Rockefeller Foundation gave millions for medical education, public health, and programs to combat epidemic diseases, and oversaw the reorganization of the University of São Paulo's medical school. Nelson A. Rockefeller, who headed the Office of Inter-American Affairs during the war, channeled extensive amounts of funding into programs to eradicate malaria and to improve hygiene among Amazon rubber workers. In the decade after 1945, Rockefeller channeled foundation aid to programs in Brazil ranging from public administration to medicine to food distribution.

33. See John D. Wirth, *The Politics of Brazilian Development, 1930–1954* (Stanford: Stanford University Press, 1970); Ricardo Antônio Silva Seitenfus, *O Brasil de Getúlio Vargas*, 324–325.

ed, whereas the United States demanded that Brazil pay for them over a ten-year period, and even that was held up by agency infighting in Washington. From Rio de Janeiro, United States Ambassador Jefferson Caffery warned Sumner Welles at the State Department in June 1940 what would happen should the Reich prevail in Europe:

> Here in Brazil the Army can make and unmake Governments, can remove President Vargas any day it sees fit to do so: if it is literally impossible for us for well-known reasons to help them to acquire arms, et cetera, in the United States, the Army will turn to Germany, accept the arms, et cetera, from them and almost inevitably receive German military and air missions as well. In other words, it will be very, very, very difficult to keep them from aligning themselves openly with a victorious Germany.[34]

Vargas relished the opportunity to use Brazil's neutrality to play both sides against one another. In May 1941, Vargas dispatched a telegram to Hitler with "best wishes for your personal happiness and the prosperity of the German nation."[35] He kept up pressure on the United States through the aftermath of Pearl Harbor, extracting, in March 1942, funding from the Export-Import Bank in Washington for the creation of the Companhia Vale de Rio Doce to mine iron ore and ultimately to generate hydroelectric power. Twenty million dollars was also granted for a Brazilian steel mill at Volta Redonda, a wholly planned industrial city, the symbol of Vargas's goal of economic independence. More than anything else, however, it was Vargas's fear that falling into the American orbit would doom any chance of postwar economic independence for Brazil. He was too much the realist to believe otherwise. It was the inevitability of the eclipse of Brazilian sovereignty, not any real admiration for the Nazis or their collaborators, that led Vargas to delay his decision until the last minute, leaving him with a sardonic tinge at the bargain that he had made.

By 1942, the United States had pledged financing for Brazilian railroad improvement, the manufacture of aircraft engines, allocation of

---

34. Confidential letter, Jefferson Caffery to Sumner Welles, Personal No. 150, Rio de Janeiro, June 24, 1940, 810.24/112-1/3, National Archives II, Washington, D.C.
35. *New York Times*, May 10, 1941, cited by Dulles, "The Contribution of Getúlio Vargas," 48.

needed chemicals and steel products, price supports for unsold coffee and cacao, and arms. Nelson A. Rockefeller's Office of Inter-American Affairs, funded by his family's foundation, ran medical and sanitation programs in the Amazon as part of a frantic Allied effort to increase rubber production by improving the health of workers. On the whole, though, the war set back Vargas's plans. Railroads and ports stagnated and suffered equipment breakdowns and fuel shortages; plans for petroleum drilling were stalled, and other promised aid from the United States only materialized after the war ended.

On the home front, Vargas's aides initiated a speaking campaign in which they thanked the chief of state for the social benefits decreed by the government, including the eight-hour day, paid vacations, and the creation of pension institutes for members of *sindicatos*.[36] Vargas was credited for expanding the vision of Brazilian government: he was bringing government services to rural areas, spokesmen said, consistent with the government's "March to the West" policy, encouraging colonization of the frontier and an expansion of national goals, a latter-day resurrection of the colonial-era *bandeirante* saga.[37] Vargas was the first head of state to travel to the far reaches of his country. In 1940, he spoke in Manaus, in the heart of the Amazon Basin, reminding his listeners of the centuries-old claim that Brazil's interior was the gateway to El Dorado. If access to the country's riches had been blocked in the past, he suggested, it was because of lack of political foresight, personal courage, capital, and technology.[38]

On the whole, the balance sheet for the 1940s was mixed. Vargas declared that ordinary Brazilians were "weakened by poverty, poorly fed, indolent, and lacking in initiative," but through education and example they would be lifted to higher levels.[39] But he took few concrete steps to aid them, and his *sindicatos* ignored the millions of lower-class Brazilians who lacked skills to find work. The government unions were for the

36. See, for example, Magalhães's speech as interventor of Pernambuco to Rio de Janeiro's Commercial Employees Syndicate, December 30, 1937, cited by Eulalia Maria Lahmeyer Lobo, ed., *Rio de Janeiro Operário* (Rio de Janeiro: Access Editora, 1992), 127.
37. See Cassiano Ricardo, *Marcha para Oeste* (Rio de Janeiro: José Olympio Editora, 1940).
38. Leo A. Despres, *Manaus: Social Life and Work in Brazil's Free Trade Zone* (Albany: State University of New York Press, 1991), 1.
39. Célio da Cunha, *Educação e Authoritarismo no Estado Novo* (São Paulo: Cortez Editora, 1981), 118.

cream of the working class, but despite the generous benefits offered to them, even most trained workers stayed away as well. During the whole of the Vargas period, the large majority of industrial workers refused to affiliate. São Paulo's Textile Workers' Union enrolled fewer than 3 percent of the city's millworkers; only 5 percent of metalworkers joined the official union for that sector. Few factories anywhere had more than 20 percent union members. In Minas Gerais, some *sindicatos* remained practically empty until Vargas initiated a membership campaign in 1943. There were more beggars on the streets of Recife than dues-paying members in unions. In some parts of Brazil, individual large employers dominated – for example, the St. John d'el Rey Mining Company in Morro Velho – offering benefits attractive to workers in the paternalistic tradition of urban industrial factories like Maria Zélia in São Paulo and Bangú in Rio de Janeiro.[40]

The Estado Novo generally ignored women, although they provided more than half the work force in the formal economy (mostly in textiles and as clerks and teachers) and an even larger percentage of the alternative, or underground, economy, producing lace, hats, hammocks, embroidery, and working as farm laborers, domestic servants, and nursemaids. Women, nonetheless, were discouraged from joining *sindicatos*, just as they traditionally had been excluded from independent unions, shunted instead into charity work. Catholic welfare agencies were often run largely by women, and the fascist Integralist movement segregated women members into women's auxiliaries that marched in Integralist parades, usually at the rear. The DIP praised women as homemakers, emphasizing that work was a masculine domain. Only 7 percent of the members of employees' syndicates in Rio de Janeiro in 1940 were women. In São Paulo, even though more women than men worked as factory operatives in textile factories and some other trades, women made up well under 10 percent of the members of the official unions in that state. A confidential summary of a fact-finding tour to the State Department by Mary Cannon, of the U.S. Labor Department's wartime

40. Joel W. Wolfe, "The Faustian Bargain Not Made: Getúlio Vargas and Brazil's Industrial Workers, 1930–1945," *Luso-Brazilian Review*, 31:2 (Winter 1994), 77–96. For Minas Gerais, see Maria Andréa Loyola, *Os Sindiactos e o PTB: Estudo de um Caso em Minas Gerais* (Petrópolis: Vozes, 1980), 51–57; Yvonne de Souza Grossi, *Mina de Morro Velho: A Extração do Homem; Uma História de Experiência Operária* (Rio de Janeiro: Paz e Terra, 1981); and Marshall C. Eakin, *British Enterprise in Brazil: The St. John d'el Rey Mining Company and the Morro Velho Gold Mine, 1830–1960* (Durham, N.C.: Duke University Press, 1989).

Women's Bureau, disclosed that Brazil's female work force suffered from absenteeism, "lack of ambition," an absence of incentives, lack of education and vocational training, lack of cleanliness and other comforts, lack of safety devices, and a disinterest in enforcing laws protecting women and children. Management and labor department officials believed that women should do the "easy" and therefore lowest-paid jobs, thereby making it more difficult for women to rise to better positions.[41]

After 1943, the regime's labor courts and conciliation commissions for the first time began to rule in favor of petitioners, likely part of Vargas's efforts to win political support from workers and leftist intellectuals. In addition, Vargas reduced the Estado Novo's authoritarian controls over industrial relations. In 1944 he permitted rural workers to join *sindicatos*. Some of his initiatives failed, however. Workers pushed for higher wages, bypassing the labor courts and refusing to listen to syndicalist officials urging caution.[42] Freeing labor from some of the Estado Novo labor codes backfired in other ways as well. Vargas released Luis Carlos Prestes from prison after nine years, a few weeks after the end of the war, as part of a calculated reach for Communist support, but Prestes refused to cooperate. Members of the Brazilian Communist Party, now legal, rushed to organize strikes, marches, and rallies, and established a Communist-dominated labor confederation, the Workers' Unity Movement (MUT).[43]

Despite Vargas's conviction that the authoritarian apparatus of the Estado Novo was necessary to achieve his nationalistic goals, however, many Brazilians were disgusted at the arbitrary stripping away of personal liberty. An outcry was raised when Louis Carlos Prestes, languishing in prison, was not permitted to attend his mother's funeral. Opposition to the regime on civil libertarian grounds began to emerge during the early 1940s, among law students, for example, in São Paulo and some other cities. Most Brazilians, however, acquiesced, especially as the European war spurred the economy because of import substitution and raised living standards. Some of Vargas's former allies who had left the

41. See Wolfe, "The Faustian Bargain Not Made," 13–14; Mary M. Cannon, Inter-American Representative of the Women's Bureau, U.S. Department of Labor, Confidential Report, August 1943, 832.4055/18.
42. Wolfe, "The Faustian Bargain Not Made," 11.
43. Eduardo Dias, *Um Imigrante e a Revolução: Memórias de um Militante Operário* (São Paulo: Brasiliense, 1983), 50–52; Gerald Michael Greenfield and Sheldon L. Maram, eds., *Latin American Labor Organizations* (Westport, Conn.: Greenwood Press, 1987), 78.

government when the dictatorship was imposed (including Oswaldo Aranha and Assis Chateaubriand) quietly returned to the fold.

WORLD WAR II

The year 1942 proved to be an important watershed for Vargas personally as well as for the dictatorship. En route to Rio's soccer stadium on May Day, the automobile carrying Getúlio and his wife was involved in an accident on the Praia do Flamengo in Rio de Janeiro; he fractured a number of bones and took several months to convalesce. His daughter Alzira and Foreign Minister Aranha more or less ran the government, clashing with Góes Monteiro, Dutra, and especially Felinto Müller, but managing to keep things on an even keel until Vargas returned. After his accident Vargas put on weight, taking up golf for exercise although he never seemed to enjoy it. He stopped writing in his diary after dutifully attending to it for twelve years.

Vargas delayed any decision about Brazil's role in the war for three years. During the second half of 1942, however, Nazi submarines had sunk 525 Allied ships in the Atlantic, making commercial shipping impossible and increasing American pressure for Brazil to join the Allies. When six Brazilian merchant ships were torpedoed in the Atlantic Ocean by the German navy between August 15 and 19, 1942, crowds in cities across Brazil attacked German and Italian-owned businesses and clamored for a declaration of war. In Rio de Janeiro and São Paulo, crowds carrying American flags attacked suspected Axis sympathizers.[44] The war minister and General Góes Monteiro told Vargas that Brazil was not prepared to commit troops to any conflict, but he overruled them – he wanted the boost in international prestige that a combat role would bring. Brazil declared war on August 22. Right-wing advisors Francisco Campos and Francisco José de Oliveira Vianna were edged aside; now Vargas's speeches embraced democracy and exhorted Brazilians to support the war effort and to look to a future nation that would defend "fuller [citizen] rights, social justice, and human dignity."[45] He ignored the embarrassing fact that Brazil had entered the war against the

44. Late in 1995 a rumor spread widely in Brazil that "documents" had been discovered that showed that the Americans had sunk the ships, to force Brazil into the war, but none was ever cited or reproduced.
45. *Hora do Brasil* broadcasts, 1944–1945, cited by Joel W. Wolfe, *Working Men, Working Women: São Paulo and the Rise of Brazil's Industrial Working Class, 1900–1955* (Durham, N.C.: Duke University Press, 1993), 96.

Axis with a fascist constitution. The military command, which had un-enthusiastically backed Vargas's declaration of war against the Axis, ul-timately sent more than 25,000 Brazilian soldiers to Italy, where many of them fought in the bloody 1944 campaign at Monte Cassino. Vargas's son Lutero, a fighter pilot, also served in Italy. The Brazilian Expedi-tionary Forces lost 450 soldiers in combat.[46]

Brazil contributed to the war effort at home as well as in Europe. Var-gas permitted American engineers to build airstrips throughout the coun-try and especially in the Northeast, shoring up defenses against a possible Nazi invasion from Africa. Vargas agreed to let the heads of several rub-ber companies participate in experimental programs sponsored by the United States Department of Agriculture in several Latin American countries to find ways of improving yields and combating plant diseases. In early 1942 Vargas authorized the recruitment of an army of some thir-ty thousand "rubber soldiers" with the goal of producing sixty thousand tons of rubber per year.[47] Rubber workers were first recruited voluntarily from among refugees from the northeastern drought and then drafted out-right, given the option of being sent to the Italian front or the Amazon. An undetermined number of rubber workers died from disease, and many deserted as soon as they could, escaping from the torrid rubber fields where they were worked to exhaustion. At least one government report, written by Dom Helder Câmara, an Integralist during the 1930s and a progressive cleric later, castigated the program for harming the rubber workers.[48] On the other hand, some soldiers in the "rubber army" considered their as-signment positive. In May 1943 a sergeant wrote to his fiancée in Ceará of his loneliness, but also of the fact that food was plentiful in the rubber fields, and that he was helping to ship boxes of oranges and bananas to feed the starving peasants in his home state. "If you come here," he wrote, "you will get fat just from eating fruits, your favorite food."[49]

46. See Getúlio Vargas, A Nova Política do Brasil, vol. 10 (Rio de Janeiro: José Olym-pio Editora, 1938–1947), 244; Frank D. McCann, "Brazil and World War II: The Forgotten Ally," E.I.A.L. 6:2 (1995), 61.

47. See Paulo de Assis Ribeiro, "A organização de um serviço de guerra," speech giv-en at DASP headquarters, Rio de Janeiro, August 3, 1943, in Revista do Serviço Público, 3:3 (September 1943), 13–20.

48. See Panflêto, which operated underground during the war and circulated legal-ly after 1945, especially issues (undated) carrying a series of articles in 1946 by Odálio Amorim entitled "30,000 Cóvas [Tombs] na Amazonia!"

49. Letter, First Sergeant José Paiva de Araujo, Altamira, to Maria José, May 31, 1943, in Brazilian National Archives, Rio de Janeiro.

The rubber campaign generated an intense debate in Brazil and, unlike most government programs, was opposed publicly by some influential members of the government. Valentim Bouças, the powerful editor of the Estado Novo's *Observador Econômico e Financeiro*, disparaged the way the program was being run; the defense was led by Felisberto Camargo, Vargas's head rubber administrator, who as a scientist had a much more accurate understanding of conditions and in the end was proved correct. Clandestine left-wing newspapers decried the program, which became a rallying cry for incipient nationalist feelings during the early 1940s that would come to maturity during Vargas's elected presidency.

Others opposed Brazil's entry into the war against the Axis. In 1941, a small group of armed forces officers conspired, unsuccessfully, to overthrow Vargas. His decision to back the Allies came after a secret meeting with Roosevelt aboard a United States Navy ship in the North Atlantic. As a result, Brazil became the only sovereign Latin American nation to send troops to fight. Nazi Germany had vainly attempted to win the alliance of both Mexico and Brazil, and, failing this, had developed plans for the military invasion of the Western Hemisphere in which troops would invade northeastern Brazil from Africa, then head north through the Caribbean to the Gulf Coast of the United States. In return for its alliance, Brazil received 70 percent of all United States aid given to Latin America during the war years. Washington used its new alliance with Rio de Janeiro to encourage Portugal's Salazar to join the United Nations against Germany.[50] Brazil hoped to boost its diplomatic influence in the hemisphere, long dominated by Argentina, and to win a permanent seat on the new United Nations Security Council. Argentina, in fact, had only declared war on the Axis in late March 1945, when Germany lay in ruins. But when the war ended, neither the British nor the Soviets paid heed to Brazil's wishes; Roosevelt had died, and Washington backed away as it lurched ahead toward the cold war and its more traditional concerns in Europe.

Sending Brazilian troops to fight in Europe sealed the fate of the authoritarian Estado Novo and moved the government to a new phase characterized by talk about democracy and activity to build a base of support for Vargas among industrial workers and the urban middle class. Affected by the cultural influence of the United States and wary of being identified with the Estado Novo, intellectuals began to distance them-

---

50. See Gerhard L. Weinberg, *The Greatest War: A Global History of World War II* (Cambridge: Cambridge University Press, 1994), 397.

selves from the regime, often resigning from posts they earlier had accepted eagerly. Law students in São Paulo organized against the regime. Many Brazilians had opposed the Estado Novo's cancellation of elections, and Vargas himself gave an interview on November 10, 1943, on the anniversary of the Estado Novo *golpe*, promising to call general elections when the war ended. In February 1945 Rio's *Correio da Manhã* defied the Estado Novo censors and published an interview with José Américo de Almeida (whose candidacy for the presidency had been sidelined by the Estado Novo coup) in which he called for elections. Within a month, most leading newspapers had stopped submitting articles to the DIP for approval, and in March Vargas closed the agency, although censorship continued on the state level well beyond the end of the war.

Early in 1945, Vargas, whom Frank had chided for "not trust[ing] the people," scheduled elections for December 2. Two national parties were created under government sponsorship: the Workers' Party (Partido Trabalhista Brasileiro, or PTB) and the Social Democratic Party (Partido Social Democrático, or PSD). Both named War Minister Dutra as their candidate, affirming, in so doing, that Vargas would step down as head of state. The PSD was based in the state political machines Vargas had nurtured, and was especially strong in rural and poor states. The PTB was organized by the Labor Ministry and dominated by *pelegos* (government honchos) loyal to Vargas if not to the Estado Novo. It sought to attract all workers, employed or not, and reach out to ordinary Brazilians not previously included in the political process.[51] The PTB became strong in some large cities (although curiously not in São Paulo) and in Vargas's home state of Rio Grande do Sul. São Paulo's reduced influence was accepted by its conservative representatives as a way to curb the potential power of its working-class voting bloc. The opposition União Democrática Nacional (UDN) formed around an anti-Vargas coalition of prodemocracy constitutionalists no longer in control of the state political machines, and affluent urban residents. The Allies, hostile to the Estado Novo, backed Vargas's enemies. Yet in some ways there was little promise of change. None of the new parties presented any clear-cut

51. Barbosa Lima Sobrinho and Ivete Vargas, cited in da Rocha Lima, *Getúlio: Uma História Oral*, 154, Alexandre Marcondes Filho, statement to the press, September 1945, Marcondes Filho archive, CPDOC, Rio de Janeiro. See also Maria Celina D'Araujo, *Sindicatos, Carisma & Poder: o PTB de 1945–65* (Rio de Janeiro: Fundação Getúlio Vargas, 1996).

ideological posture. Organizers within each of the three new parties came from within the state apparatus, a signal that the old clientelistic system was hanging on regardless of the trappings of representative democracy built into the new political system. The Communists, exhilarated by their newly granted legality, railed at the role of such men as Dutra and Góes Monteiro as "remnants of a putrid past," but few paid them any heed; nor did the poor, "the starving of the land, the victims of hunger" in PCB banners, rally any support.[52]

Vargas's endorsement of an open, populist political system estranged him from the military command and ended his fifteen-year-long alliance with it. Even if he knew that his days as chief of state were numbered, of course, he continued to go through the motions; when the first troops from the Brazilian Expeditionary Force returned home on July 18, 1945, he was wildly applauded as his automobile brought up the rear of the official welcoming parade. Six months earlier, at a New Year's Eve banquet of generals and admirals, Vargas had announced plans for a return to electoral democracy. Ironically, this was unsettling for some, including the United States State Department, which feared that Vargas would become a demagogue, like Juan Perón in neighboring Argentina, whom the Americans had wanted to oust.[53]

On October 28, 1945, Vargas named his brother Benjamim (Beijo), a lackluster, caustic man with a somewhat unsavory reputation, as the Federal District's chief of police and security, replacing João Alberto Lins de Barros, the old *tenente* whose incumbency had again become a liability, just as in 1932 in São Paulo. Rumors flew through the military command that this was Vargas's first step toward keeping himself in power. Fortified by the return of officers who had served in Italy, the armed forces command, with the blessing of Dutra and Góes Monteiro, decided to depose Vargas.[54] The motorized troops of the Rio garrison were instructed by the high army command to take over the city. The next day, with army tanks surrounding the most important buildings in the capital, including the presidential palace, General Cordeiro de Farias, former interventor in Rio Grande do Sul and Getúlio's personal friend, de-

---

52. Everardo Dias, *História das lutas sociais no Brasil*, 2nd ed. (São Paulo: Ed. Alfa-Omega, 1977), 51; Ames, *Political Survival*, 107; Joseph A. Page, *The Brazilians* (Reading, Pa.: Addison-Wesley, 1995), 52–53.
53. See Thomas E. Skidmore, *O Brasil Visto de Fora* (Rio de Janeiro: Paz e Terra, 1994), 207.
54. Stanley E. Hilton, *Brazil and the Soviet Challenge, 1917–1947* (Austin: University of Texas Press, 1991), 206.

livered the generals' ultimatum; he signed his resignation letter shortly after midnight. He was replaced by José Linhares, the colorless president of the Supreme Federal Tribunal, because the generals did not want to bother with establishing a temporary junta as had been done in 1930. Linhares took the oath of office at the War Ministry at two in the morning on October 30, appointing a caretaker cabinet. On the next day, Vargas traveled to São Borja under official guard, after publicly endorsing Dutra's presidential candidacy in a personal gesture to save face and to forestall being forced into exile outside of Brazil. Vargas and his family fumed, feeling that he had been treated ungratefully, but there was nothing Getúlio could do but ride his horses, hunt, and, after a while, discreetly begin to receive visitors with plans for the future. We do not know how Vargas felt privately, because he stopped keeping a diary after his automobile accident in 1942, and because he remained as circumspect as ever.

CHAPTER FOUR

POPULISM, VARGAS STYLE,

1945–1954

Vargas's humiliating ouster was set into motion earlier in 1945, when the nationalist General Góes Monteiro, who had opposed Brazil's entry into the war and who was angered by Vargas's attempts to redefine himself in populist prolabor terms, publicly called for Vargas to step down.[1] What the conservative anti-Vargas forces sought was to replace the Estado Novo without undermining its structure, thereby resisting an uncontrolled opening of the political process. The defeat of the Axis had eclipsed fascism's appeal and, as a result, confidence in representative democracy gathered momentum, and the elites no longer trusted Vargas to rein in his progressive impulses.

Once Vargas was safely back in Rio Grande do Sul, the 1945 electoral contest to restore democracy was played out between former Axis sympathizer Dutra, backed by Vargas's PSD and PTB, and former *tenente* hero Brigadier Eduardo Gomes, a stalwart partisan of the opposition UDN party, which had been created in April. Gomes openly courted the rural oligarchy, praising it for sustaining Brazil's economy for centuries. The two Varguista parties were run by the state interventors, who had been named by Vargas, and by labor bosses. In some ways, the atmosphere was remarkably different from the country's last such election; there were seven and a half million voters (half of them women) now, compared with barely more than a million in 1930. And, as a Vargas crony later pointed out, this was a contest between an air force brigadier and an army general, not between two weak state politicians as had been

---

1. See John D. French, "The Populist Gamble of Getúlio Vargas," in David Rock, ed., *Latin America in the 1940s* (Berkeley: University of California Press, 1994), 141–142.

the case for the 1938 campaign, which had been canceled by the Estado Novo coup.[2] Now, both candidates declared themselves "conservative-liberals" and spoke in platitudes, avoiding mention of Vargas and the Estado Novo. Although Gomes ("a handsome eligible bachelor," the press noted) cut a dashing figure compared with the "short, dull" war minister who had favored the Nazis before Vargas took Brazil into the war, Dutra won by a three-to-two margin.

His inauguration came on January 31, 1946, amid fears that Góes Monteiro, commander in chief of the army, might stage a coup to place himself in power.[3] Dutra took office cautiously, relying on support from Vargas's giant bureaucracy as well as from industrialists and landowners who favored the uncharismatic president.

Even so, a new era had begun. Brazilians who came of age between 1931 and 1946 had never voted in an election, and Vargas had banned all political parties. With his departure, dozens of new parties and political alliances rushed in to the vacuum. Some were holdovers; others represented new alliances seeking to capture the enlarged electorate. The Labor Party had been created for workers loyal to Vargas, whom they now called "The Old Man." Vargas's opponents signed with the UDN, led among others by José Américo de Almeida, who had been the frontrunner for president before the Estado Novo *golpe* canceled the 1938 election.[4]

More than anything else, Vargas's decision in April 1945 to release Luís Carlos Prestes, the *tenente* hero of the 1920s and the leader of the attempted 1935 popular-front insurrection, had displayed his pragmatism and, many said, his cynicism. Prestes had been the most well known political prisoner in Latin America and the object of years of international protests arguing for his release. As the war had drawn to its close, and with prospects of ties with the Soviet Union, Vargas had offered Prestes amnesty and granted legal status to the Communist Party. Tens of thousands of Prestes supporters jumped into the political arena, although Vargas set the terms by which the Communists could operate.[5] Shortly before, Marcondes Filho had launched the *queremista* ("We

2. Paulo Pinheiro Chagas, quoted in Valentina da Rocha Lima, *Getúlio: Uma História Oral* (Rio de Janeiro: Ed. Record, 1986), 158.
3. Amaral Peixoto, cited in Rocha Lima, *Getúlio: Uma História Oral*, 158. See also *Veja*, 27:14 (no. 1,334), April 6, 1994, 25.
4. See Interview, José América de Almeida, CPDOC Archive, Fundação Getúlio Vargas, Rio de Janeiro, 1978.
5. French, "The Populist Gamble," 153–155.

want Vargas") campaign, declaring "We want Getúlio" and "a Constituent Assembly with Getúlio." Vargas thought Prestes's release might offer him a chance to stay in power. Instead, the heated political atmosphere accelerated the demise of the Estado Novo and brought Vargas's fifteen years as chief of state to an abrupt end.

Soon after he departed, Vargas alertly took advantage of quirks in the new political system to reenter the fray. He was elected senator from two states and federal deputy from no fewer than seven more, although he prudently spent most of his time on his São Borja ranch. The postwar period was characterized by uncertainty about how accessible the political process would become. By 1947, after some stops and starts, the climate had settled, with the old conservative basis of Brazilian politics reasserting itself under Dutra. Doors that had been opened were closed, signaled by restrictions on labor independence. Political factions and interest groups battled for preeminence in a political arena characterized by divisiveness and lack of meaningful national unity. The 1946 Constitution, ratified by a Constituent Assembly on September 16, created a presidential system with a bicameral legislature, with the larger states, especially São Paulo, underrepresented. Dutra's PSD, the strongest party in Brazil from 1947 to 1964, continued to draw its strength from Vargas-appointed state and municipal administrators with control of patronage and resources. Despite competition from sixteen other parties in the 1947 congressional elections, the PSD remained the strongest party nationwide. The PTB, Vargas's workers' party, lagged well behind.

Dutra, who was sixty years old when he took office in late January 1946, committed his government to fiscal austerity. He experimented with free-market policies but drew back when industrial production fell, and his government suppressed demands for higher wages. By now agriculturalists no longer dominated the elite but shared influence with bankers and commercial interests, especially manufacturers. Industrial production output more than doubled between 1946 and 1955. Factory owners saw their own interests diverge as such new sectors as automobile manufacturing and durable goods became prominent. Major industrial associations, especially São Paulo's Industrial Federation (FIESP), lobbied successfully for continued protection against competition from foreign firms and for curbs on labor.[6]

6. Eli Diniz, "The Post-1930 Industrial Elite," in Michael L. Conniff, ed., *Modern Brazil: Elites and Masses in Historical Perspective* (Lincoln: University of Nebraska Press, 1991), 108–109.

Dutra's cabinet was dominated by PSD members, who now controlled the political machines in the states, and was supported by rank-and-file members in urban areas whose livelihoods were dependent on Vargas's bureaucracies for employment. Dutra recognized their demands and parceled out benefits in return for support. The UDN combined reactionary landed interests in the states, tied to the old rural oligarchy, and in the cities to bankers, manufacturers, and members of Brazil's high society. It favored free-market economic policies but opposed social reform, a legacy of its conservative rural base. The labor party, the PTB, was influential mainly among urban industrial workers but lacked electoral support elsewhere. Large agriculturalists preserved the system of subsidized exports, and manufacturers put tariff protection ahead of higher wages and investment in modern industrial capacity. Wages continued to fall, however, as government spending fell and as the brief postwar boom flattened out, although the economy picked up at the end of the decade, restoring confidence.[7]

Dutra cracked down on labor by dispatching troops to quell strikes and replacing militant unionists with more pliant ones. The total number of strikes dropped drastically, alienating skilled laborers but pleasing manufacturers. Salaries fell, but the government resisted adjusting the minimum wage that had been implemented in 1942. The general's somber presidential style subdued the heated political atmosphere that had been generated at the end of Vargas's tenure. Censorship no longer operated but newspaper editors, reflecting the conservative, probusiness climate, behaved cautiously. Few objections were raised in 1947 when Dutra banned the Brazilian Communist Party after it gained some electoral victories. Overnight, the government restored the anti-Communist climate of the mid- and late-1930s. Vargas's pursuit of Communists, real and imagined, would rival the Red Scare of the United States during the period of Senator Joseph R. McCarthy in the early 1950s.[8]

VARGAS'S FINAL CHAPTER

Brazil's population had grown to fifty-three million in 1950. From a rural country when Vargas first took power, Brazil now had become urban

7. Salvador A. M. Sandoval, *Social Change and Labor Unrest in Brazil since 1945* (Boulder, Colo.: Westview Press, 1993), 62.
8. There is massive documentation about this renewed anti-Communist campaign in the newly opened DOPS archive in Rio de Janeiro.

and industrial. For the first time, Brazilian-made products were more numerous than imported ones, although consumers avoided locally made items when they could. The low-wage structure still excluded most Brazilians from the national market and therefore limited opportunities for further industrial expansion, even though Brazil now produced its own hydroelectric power and steel, and government-owned Petrobrás controlled oil refining. Foreign corporations received handsome incentives to build factories in the Rio-São Paulo corridor, which within a decade would turn out Brazilian-made Alfa-Romeos, Renaults, and startling numbers of Volkswagen Beetles. Mercedes-Benz and Volvo built heavy trucks. Refrigerators, television sets, and washing machines for the first time were manufactured in the country. Telephone capacity was choked by great demand, and only in another two decades could Brazilians call from one city to another without having to be routed through New York or Lisbon.

Getúlio Vargas was sixty-seven years old when he received the PTB's draft nominating him for the presidency. Behind the scenes his backers maneuvered for the PSD to choose a weak candidate, one whose support would come from the same sectors that would likely vote for the UDN.[9] Lawyer João Café Filho, a fierce opponent of the Estado Novo, was selected as Vargas's running mate. He was an outsider from the barren state of Rio Grande do Norte, and had been persecuted after 1935 for his role in the popular front ANL and as a supporter of the progressive *tenentes*. Café Filho had spent several years in exile and on his return had helped organize a brief-lived opposition Social Progressive Party (PSP). Vargas chose Café Filho, it was believed, to prevent São Paulo's populist governor Adhemar de Barros from running, although it was further rumored that Vargas had agreed to support Adhemar four years down the road. Throwing caution to the winds, Vargas declared in July 1950 that "I know the people and have confidence in them. I know that I will be elected, but I also know that, as happened before, I will not be allowed to reach the end of my term. I will have to fight. How far will I go? If they don't kill me, how much will I be able to take? I'll tell you one thing: I will not tolerate being humiliated."[10] With the opposition divided and with the support of both political parties he had created in

9. Ronald M. Schneider, *Brazil: Culture and Politics in a New Industrial Powerhouse* (Boulder, Colo.: Westview Press, 1996), 70–71.
10. Quoted by Ivar Hartmann, *Getúlio Vargas* (Porto Alegre: Editora Tchê!, 1984), 97.

1945, Vargas won the October 1950 elections. Although working-class voters had received fewer benefits (except for skilled industrial workers) than the middle class, they would give Vargas his greatest margins in the election. Vargas received 48.7% of the total vote cast for three candidates, and, in the largest industrial cities, São Paulo and Rio de Janeiro, he received overwhelming support. Voters in São Paulo gave him almost three times as many votes (925,493) as Eduardo Gomes, the runner-up (357,413), and six times the total of the third candidate with 153,039. Vargas's margin in Rio de Janeiro was nearly as great.[11]

The presidential campaign permitted Getúlio to rearticulate his political goals. Speaking out in favor of electoral free choice, he stopped short of endorsing classical democracy, warning that "formal democracy" ignored "social equality." Rather, he campaigned against privilege, angering elites and creating the basis for the post-1950 three-way division in the country's political system between the PSD, Vargas's middle-class party, the laborites in the PTB, and the opposition UDN, heir to the pre-1932 legacy of the paulistas and their political and economic allies. At least twice during the 1947 campaign Vargas alluded to "socialist democracy" and "tomorrow's socialist Brazil" but this was likely a trial balloon, and he dropped socialism from his rhetoric.[12]

National progress in industrialization had made it possible for Vargas to create the Labor Party, which in turn rewarded him by nominating him as its candidate for president. The PTB mobilized workers, distributed patronage, punished its enemies, and created government jobs to reward loyalists. Vargas announced his candidacy at a press conference at the residence of João Goulart, the head of the PTB. "The people will climb the steps of the presidential palace with me," Vargas declared in a speech in Minas Gerais, "and with me they will remain at the head of the government."[13] As the campaign progressed, Getúlio stepped beyond his cautious, self-effacing image, making deals and raising the level of rhetoric. His closest advisor and confidant was now newspaperman J. S. Maciel Filho, a devout Catholic who had been a crony of Lourival Fontes during the Estado Novo period and who, starting in 1950, wrote most of Vargas's speeches and conferred with him almost daily.

11. Evaldo Vieira, Estado e Miséria Social no Brasil de Getúlio a Geisel, 1951–1978 (São Paulo: Cortez Editora, 1983), 21.
12. See Sérgio da Costa Franco, Getúlio Vargas e Outros Ensaios (Porto Alegre: Editora da Universidade Federal do Rio Grande do Sul, 1993), 20–21.
13. Quoted by Hartmann, Getúlio Vargas, 97.

Vargas's return to power had been accomplished by playing the two tactical cards of "Getulismo" and "Trabalhismo." The ploy ultimately backfired, dividing his supporters irrevocably, but it got him elected. Getulismo reflected his personal political style, seeking its identity in his government's social legislation and its economic nationalism. Getulismo also generated anti-Getulismo, knee-jerk opposition to everything the legacy stood for. This was seen most clearly in the banners of the UDN, a political party known more for what it resisted than for any alternative program of its own. "Trabalhismo" (or "Varguismo") centered on the political activities of the labor movement and on Vargas's PTB, which had been modeled in some ways on the British Labour Party although in the Brazilian case it relied more heavily on state favors to organized labor than to labor autonomy. "Trabalhismo" ceded to the state the responsibility for legislative initiatives, always seeking to preserve political harmony between capital and labor. Characteristic of Vargas's style was the way that Brazil's three political parties emerged as democratization unfolded: two parties completely loyal to Vargas, and a third intricately tied to it in opposition. The pragmatic basis of the arrangement typified Vargas's approach to politics: the PTB would reward workers for not succumbing to the propaganda of the Communists, and the PSD would reach out to government employees and others in the middle class who had benefited from government programs (pensions, public health, education, job protection) and who did not want to see a return to the old system. Labor Ministry officials initiated a *trabalhismo* (prolabor) doctrine as early as 1942, at the height of the authoritarian Estado Novo, anticipating a postwar political climate that would likely demand democratization. Without the ideological groundwork paved by *trabalhismo*, moreover, drafting Vargas to run under the *queremista* banner would have been impossible.

One of the curiosities about the 1950 electoral campaign was that decades later an allegation surfaced that the Argentine demagogue Juan Perón had provided secret financial support for Vargas. The money was transferred from the frontier town of Paso do Los Libres over the border to Uruguaiana in Rio Grande do Sul. While the allegation remains unproved, we do know that one of the first things Vargas did on assuming the presidency on January 31, 1951, was to sign an economic accord with Perón as well as a promise for future military cooperation. Dutra fulfilled his constitutional mandate and returned to private life after Vargas took office in 1951 although many members of the military high command urged that Vargas's return to power be impeded. Journalist Carlos Lacerda editorialized in his *Tribuna da Imprensa* that revolutionary means should be used if necessary to block Vargas from taking office. Such threats were nothing new. The president-elect took the high road, telling a nationwide radio audience on Christmas Day that Brazilians constituted a family, "unified and linked by common conditions, sentiments, and aspirations." Reaching for a theme that would be exploited frequently in the coming years, he warned of "dark clouds" and "sinister threats" on the international horizon. He concluded his address with his typical flourish: "Brazilian Workers! Your welfare is my constant concern. . . . We know one another well. You can count on me in the same way I always have counted on you!"[14]

What Vargas likely did not anticipate was that his victory, rather than uniting the electorate, would deepen old divisions. Voters were more numerous, younger, and stirred by an increasingly aggressive press. Buoyed by the open presidential campaign, newspaper editors now turned to tabloid tactics to sell newspapers and attack their opponents. Vargas met the challenge by joining the fray. "Those who think that the Brazilian people elected me to fish for sardines were roundly wrong," he boasted. "We are going after sharks."[15] Assailed by rumors of conspiracies on all sides, Vargas became for the first time in his political career an alarmist. His prewar fears about increasing Brazil's dependency had come true. The United States' share of Brazil's exports had risen from a quarter in 1938 to nearly a half after 1941. Brazil's armed forces, moreover, had been trained and supplied by the Americans, and by the 1950s Brazil had become the major power in its region.[16] Vargas knew that he had little control over the military, and that intervention could come at any moment.

For these reasons, Vargas adjusted the nature of his political style. He defended his goals aggressively, no longer waiting to hear from all sides and then moderating compromises, as he had done earlier. He was exasperated by congressional bickering and affronted by the personal attacks that democratic systems permitted. Like Roosevelt had done in the 1930s, Vargas used the presidential pulpit to counterattack, castigating

---

14. Getúlio Vargas, "Mensagem do Natal de 1950," in *O Governo Trabalhista do Brasil*, vol. 1 (Rio de Janeiro: José Olympio, 1952), 17–18.

15. New Year's Address, December 31, 1951, in *O Governo Trabalhista do Brasil*, vol. 2 (Rio de Janeiro: José Olympio, 1952), 67.

16. Stanley E. Hilton, *Brazil and the Great Powers, 1930–1939* (Austin: University of Texas Press, 1975), 220–221.

his enemies and polarizing the debate. In private he became conspiratorial and manipulative, leaning on labor officials for support and punishing them when they did not deliver. Strikes broke out intermittently, although police coercion remained moderate by pre-1950 standards. Battling to maintain his control, Vargas proclaimed that only through stability and decisions made for the common good could the interests of the downtrodden be protected. Government needed to be strong and benevolent, not weak and indecisive, as liberal democratic governments were labeled.[17]

Vargas's new presidential style blended clientelistic and populist strategies, a pragmatic response to the fact that as elected president under a democratic constitution he could no longer rule by decree. He attempted to broaden his appeal, promising more and more and casting blame on his enemies, real and imagined. Every time Vargas announced a presidential initiative in this manner, his opponents would accuse him of seeking dictatorial powers. In the first months of his administration the economy fared well, and he was able to brush aside this disapproval. As conditions deteriorated and inflation ate into wages, he increased the intensity of his rhetoric but he was able to do little to alleviate the hardships that the lower and middle classes increasingly faced.

The confrontational mood was exacerbated by the widening gap between what Vargas promised and what he was able to accomplish. His nationalist program made it easy for him to shrug off attacks from the left – in 1950 Luís Carlos Prestes issued a manifesto calling for struggle against "feudal-bourgeois dictatorship in the service of imperialism,"[18] but few Brazilians understood this vocabulary and fewer still identified with Marxism. Vargas's nationalism was moderately progressive: Vargas supported, for example, the United Nations' Economic Commission for Latin America, an agency whose planners helped articulate solutions to Latin American economic dependency. His government invested heavily in transportation and energy development, financed by its new National Economic Development Bank (BNDE), but the bureaucracy remained bloated and unproductive. Inflation became a recurrent obstacle, and Vargas's nationalistic policies kept import duties high. Vargas had been forced to increase the minimum wage four times between

17. Sandoval, *Social Change and Labor Unrest*, 62, 78–79.
18. From Prestes's 1950 Manifesto, cited by Joseph L. Love, *Crafting the Third World: Theorizing Underdevelopment in Rumania and Brazil* (Stanford: Stanford University Press, 1996), 175.

1940 and 1954. The goal was to reestablish a 1943 level of purchasing power, but by 1955, real wages for industrial workers were worth only 53 percent of workers' salaries in 1943. Real wages by 1954 fell to their lowest levels in the entire nineteen-year period between 1945 and 1963.

Vargas continued to counterattack. Not only did he constantly identify himself with the poor, but he assailed trusts, monopolies, and, increasingly, foreign meddling in the Brazilian economy, although his own government a decade earlier had avidly courted foreign investment. He kept rapid industrialization as his major goal, to bring about national independence and to strengthen the labor sector. He proposed numerous schemes to reform government and to curb needless bureaucracies, and he indirectly acknowledged that the Estado Novo's labor system had not worked. As in the past, however, a gap remained between what he said and what he did. He proved unable to negotiate with the legislative branch, a legacy of his personal prejudice that it was wasteful and contentious. Formerly, he had governed by decree and by political maneuvering; now he had to deal with a recalcitrant and factionalized Congress. He considered workers his principal constituency, yet as his term progressed Vargas's Labor Ministry succeeded in keeping wages below their 1950 level while at the same time holding labor unions under control.

In 1952 Vargas delegated responsibility for the labor movement to João (Jângo) Belchior Marques Goulart, his vice-president, close friend, and fellow *gaúcho*. Vargas had been a friend of Goulart's father, and when the elder Goulart died, he left his ranch, which was adjacent to Vargas's, to his son. They saw a good deal of one another during Vargas's exile after the 1945 coup, and many commented that Goulart had become as close as if he were Vargas's son. Trained as an attorney, he was elected to the state legislature in 1945 on the PTB ticket and later served as state secretary of justice. In 1950 he rode the Vargas bandwagon to election to the federal Chamber of Deputies. Goulart, who did not hide his ambition to be Vargas's successor, purged officials not loyal to him and substituted others deemed more pliable. He was ousted from his post on February 22, 1954.

In São Paulo, within the labor movement, the initiative passed from the *sindicatos* to factory labor commissions, formed by unionists in allegiance with some dissident *pelegos* who agreed to bring grass-roots leaders to the bargaining table. In his May Day 1952 speech, Vargas himself had turned against the official union bureaucracy he had created, abandoning, as well, his faith in paternalistic labor relations controlled by the government. Especially in the skilled trades, reformists ousted *pelegos* in election after election. By 1955, workers in São Paulo had declared their independence, rejecting the old system and establishing a new one, made up of autonomous labor institutions, free from government pressure.

Perhaps because of Vargas's deep-seated conservatism, the PTB failed to become the institutional heir to *getulismo*. For one thing, it never became a truly national party, since the middle class distrusted it and the bosses who controlled voting in the rural states were too powerful and wily. In many ways, moreover, Vargas's bureaucratic apparatus outweighed in influence the "Getulist" speeches and slogans and massive rallies orchestrated by Workers' Party organizers. After Vargas's death, the PTB further weakened itself by becoming involved in fractional disputes at the state level and in its willingness to ally with politicians of all stripes, from Communists, who moved to the PTB because their own party remained illegal, to members of the conservative PSD.[19]

Despite the limited nature of his prolabor measures and his lack of interest in expanding benefits to unskilled workers, Vargas's major political base always remained in the organized labor movement, even though opposition within labor ranks grew swiftly. By 1953 there were massive work stoppages and a new tactic, the multiple-category strike, to increase pressure by spreading the power of individual unions objecting to government control. Labor agitation had grown so much and pressure from industrialists and investors against his nationalistic policies had become so threatening that Vargas doubled the minimum wage in early 1954, seeking to bolster support for his government among workers. This act infuriated businessmen, who considered it the last straw, following on earlier restrictions on remissions of profits abroad, the creation of the Petrobrás and Electrobrás (effectively nationalizing the petroleum and energy industries), and other nationalist measures. Getúlio's May Day speech announcing the wage increase inflamed conservatives. "Today, you are with the government," he told workers, "tomorrow you will be the government."

Vargas summarized his final design for Brazil in a speech to Congress early in 1953: he used all of the usual themes, but with added emphasis on the needs of the "less favored" and with sharp criticisms of "the spirit of easy profits and speculative fortunes." Housing was badly needed;

---

19. See Café Filho's interview with R. J. Alexander, Rio de Janeiro, June 8, 1966, in *The ABC Presidents* (Westport, Conn.: Praeger, 1992), 104–108.

tens of thousands of migrants from the Northeast were arriving in the South every month. He also warned of the need to stabilize prices; inflation was undermining the postwar economy. But in the same speech, Vargas congratulated himself for his loyalty to corporatism: "I have always sought, since the beginning of my government," he affirmed, to "structure a corpus of organic measures" for the national good. Opposition to his government, he professed, came from those arrayed against the "social hierarchy."[20] Ignoring the fact that most urban Brazilians had gained little from his social reforms, he promised to extend to rural workers and the legions of landless squatters and migrants the minimum wage, accident insurance, protected employment, free medical and hospital treatment, and old-age pensions. Further, he vowed to distribute unproductive land to agricultural colonists for cultivation.[21] He began to speak nostalgically about the now-distant 1930 Revolution, which he said had sought to sweep away the formulas of the old order and create "something new, something viscerally Brazilian." At the same time, he drew his small circle of cronies and associates closer to him, cutting himself off from public opinion.

Confronting the realities of the changing international scene and rising domestic expectations brought about confusion. Many of his former allies began to distance themselves from him. In compensation, he drew closer to his family, relying on his daughter Alzira for advice and stubbornly refusing to remove his brother Benjamim ("Beijo") as federal police chief, despite his unsavory reputation. The officer corps remained bitterly divided among "legalists," committed to honoring the Constitution, leftist nationalists, and right-wing anti-Communists seeking to undermine Vargas's authority. On the civilian side, the industrial sector fared well, since depressed wages contributed to an upward turn in the real industrial product index between 1952 and 1954. Inflation and high prices, as well as the bloated bureaucracy and the prevalence of corruption at all levels of government, eroded many of the gains made by the urban employed. A group of junior military officers protested to the war minister in February 1954 that they could not afford to live on their shrunken military salaries. Recognizing the complaints, Vargas dismissed the man widely considered his protégé. For the time being, the military command remained loyal, although other officers issued a state-

20. "A Mensagem do Presidente Vargas," O Observador Econômico e Financeiro, 18:206 (March–April 1953), 38–45.
21. O Governo Trabalhista do Brasil, 2:313.

ment attacking the government for corruption and for its neglect of professional soldiers, and in April 1954, the UDN initiated impeachment proceedings against Vargas for allegedly negotiating with Perón as well as with the Chileans to create an anti-U.S. bloc in the hemisphere.

The final unraveling of Vargas's authority came on August 5, 1954, when a presidential-palace-inspired assassination plot against Vargas's nemesis Carlos Lacerda in Rio de Janeiro's Copacabana failed. In the attempt, which came to be known as the Toneleros case (for the street on which the shooting took place), a member of Lacerda's entourage, Air Force Major Rubens Vaz, was killed and Lacerda wounded. Anti-Vargas demonstrations erupted across the country. More than five thousand people lined the streets from the Aeronautical Club to São João Batista Cemetery in Botafogo to watch Major Vaz's funeral cortege. Lacerda was lifted up and carried on the shoulders of air force men. Opponents blamed Vargas for the crime; one large banner contained the words of Brigadier Eduardo Gomes: "For our nation's honor we will see that the crime does not go unpunished." When the marchers passed Monroe Palace, the home of the Senate, cries broke out to change the line of march to pass by the presidential residence at Catete. Outside the building, the mobs shouted "Down with Vargas! Death to Vargas!" Getúlio watched from a distance, from a second-story window, where he was meeting with Aranha.[22]

It was later determined that the gunman had been hired by Gregório Fortunato, the chief of Vargas's bodyguard squad (and the only black man in his inner circle). Lacerda, heir to an influential planter family, had been a radical as a youth but had turned staunchly conservative; as publisher of Rio's *Tribuna da Imprensa,* his opposition to Vargas had become insatiable. When the civil police moved slowly to investigate the crime, the air force carried out a massive dragnet involving helicopters, airplanes, airborne flares, and dogs, until it captured the gunmen, members of the palace guard. When they named Fortunato as having given the orders, he confessed. He denied, however, that the president or his family had been involved. The disavowal was rejected when it was revealed that Manuel Vargas, Getúlio's son, had transferred to Fortunato the deed to one of his father's properties in Rio Grande do Sul. Getúlio maintained his ignorance of the sale and seemed shaken, telling confidants that he felt as if he was sinking into a sea of mud. The shot that

22. Araken Távora, *O dia em que Vargas morreu* (Rio de Janeiro: Editora Brasiluso, S.A., 1966), 34–36.

killed Major Vaz, he said, "entered my back as well." His justice minister, Tancredo Neves, told a press conference that he would find the guilty
parties no matter who was involved.

On August 14, more than fifteen hundred military officers, led by former *tenente* heroes Eduardo Gomes and Juarez Távora, met at the Military Club and demanded Vargas's resignation. Conservative politicians
and spokesmen for business and industrial groups agreed. At a visit to
Rio's haughty Jockey Club Vargas was booed lengthily. By contrast, soon
afterward he was cheered by working-class spectators at the Vasco da
Gama soccer stadium. The lines had been drawn; he remained the hero
of the people but the elite had abandoned him. A few military men remained loyal, demonstrating on his behalf at the Vila Militar barracks,
and a sole Rio newspaper, *Ultima Hora*, defended him against the rising
crescendo of newspaper attacks. On August 22, nearly thirty general officers issued a public ultimatum demanding that Vargas step down. At a
crisis cabinet meeting on the night of August 23 and well into the early hours of the next day, Vargas told his ministers that if it were necessary to maintain order, he would step aside. He proposed a meeting with
Lacerda to iron out a compromise over political matters.

At 6:00 A.M. Police Chief Benjamim Vargas received an ultimatum
from the armed forces to appear at the Galeão air base to testify about
the Toneleros assault. Getúlio remained in his bedroom. At 7:45 he
spoke one more time with his brother, then asked his barber, Pedro
Lourenço Barbosa, who had come to shave him, to let him get a bit more
rest. Sitting up in his bed with his pistol in his right hand, he shot himself through the heart at 8:41 A.M. Rio's O Dia, having learned of the
events the evening before but not of Vargas's death, published a head-
line story in its morning edition stating that Vargas had resigned from
the presidency.[23]

The public reacted with violence in the streets when word of
Getúlio's death was announced. In Rio, angry mobs looted and burned
the Farroupilha and Difusora radio stations, both formerly unfriendly to
the president. Vargas's opponents saw advantage in making the man
they had reviled into a martyr, and the cryptic wording of the suicide
note (which blamed "foreign interests" for Brazil's crisis) made many assume that the United States was responsible for Vargas's death. Crowds
attacked the American Consulate and the First National City Bank.
The offices of Importada Americana S.A., an import firm in Rio, were

23. O Dia, August 24, 1954, 1.

set afire. American consulates across Brazil were stoned, with the greatest damage occurring in Porto Alegre, in Vargas's home state, where more than a dozen people were killed in the rioting and scores injured. The country entered into a state of shock unparalleled in its history. In response, the new chief of state, former vice-president João Café Filho, a man with honorable progressive credentials, ordered the arrest of hundreds of Communists and labor militants lest the military obstruct his continuing in office.

The government decreed eight days of national mourning. More than half a million residents of the capital thronged into Santos Dumont Airport to watch the plane with Vargas's coffin and immediate family take off for the South. Fights erupted as the plane lifted off the runway, and several dozen people were injured. The opposition *Estado de São Paulo* conjectured that "no one could have expected that Getúlio Vargas, so much in command of his life, would sacrifice himself just because of a [political] defeat."[24] The Brazilian Embassy in Washington, which subscribed to several American newspapers including the communist *Daily Worker*, sent home clippings of editorials wondering whether Vargas's death would "loosen up" Brazil's economic nationalism and open up the nation for investment.[25] The act of suicide silenced Vargas's critics and solidified permanently his image as protector of the poor, fighting to the end.

While we will never know what actually went on inside the seventy-three-year-old Vargas's mind in driving him to suicide, it seems likely that a compelling reason was his knowledge that opposition (UDN) politicians and their military supporters were plotting for a coup to install a new dictatorship, not simply to oust Vargas. On the day before his death, the president was told in a cabinet meeting by War Minister Zenóbio that nothing could be done to prevent a military coup if one occurred. Vargas told João Goulart, who visited with him at nine o'clock the evening before his death, that he would resist being deposed. Sandbags had been piled up in front of Catete Palace on the morning of August 24, anticipating an armed attack.[26] Suicide was the form of resistance he chose, a calculated political act. It was, Tancredo Neves argued much later, a solemn protest. Getúlio had been forced into a corner; he felt isolated and abandoned (although his family and friends still surrounded him).

24. *O Estado de São Paulo*, August 25, 1954, 1.
25. *New York Times*, August 28, 1954, 1; *Washington Post*, August 28, 1954, 1.
26. Vinícius Torres Freire in *Folha de São Paulo*, August 21, 1994, 8–9.

He thanked those faithful to him. Days before his death, he had uncharacteristically sent warm personal notes to some of them.[27] They considered his death as his last act of resistance against the world closing in on him. Just as Lincoln's bloody shirt made possible the presidencies of the seven men who followed him, Neves argued, Getúlio's death made possible the presidencies of Kubitschek, Quadros, and Goulart.[28]

A typed "testimonial letter" in two copies was found beside his body. It began ominously: "Once more the forces and interests against the people have organized themselves anew, and have broken out against me. . . . I have fought month after month, day after day, hour after hour, resisting constant, incessant pressures. . . . I have struggled against the pillaging of Brazil. . . . My sacrifice will keep [the people] united and my name will be your battle standard." "Serenely," it concluded, "I take the first step on the path to eternity, departing life to enter history." His words were dramatic, but they were not Vargas's usual language, and his close aide, journalist J. S. Maciel Filho, admitted privately that he had made changes in the typed version.[29] In 1978, Vargas's daughter Alzira produced a draft in Getúlio's hand on presidential stationery, more likely written in response to the move to oust him, not as a suicide note. It was bitter, lashing out at "hypocrites and traitors" and the failure of his friends to come to his aid, but it lacked the wide range of conspiratorial accusations of the typed version. "I have become dangerous to the powerful interests and the privileged castes," he wrote. "I thank those who have comforted me with their friendship, whether from near or afar."[30]

For decades, Vargas's suicide remained the single most momentous event recalled in the lives of most Brazilians. In 1990, novelist Rubem Fonseca, in *Agosto*, revisited the setting played out in the events surrounding the suicide. Taking his epigraph from James Joyce – "History, Stephen said, is a nightmare from which I am trying to awake" – Fonse-

---

27. See, for example, Interview, Vicente Rao, November 1984, in CPDOC/Fundação Getúlio Vargas, Archive, Rio de Janeiro SP/SP E-27.
28. Tancredo Neves, quoted in Rocha Lima, *Getúlio: Uma História Oral*, 262. See also Interview, João Goulart with Robert J. Alexander, June 5, 1972, in *The ABC Presidents*, 155. Vicente Rao describes his note from Vargas in Rocha Lima, *Getúlio*, 264; see also the statements by Barbosa Lima Sobrinho and João Cleofas, 264–265.
29. Maciel Filho conceded this to the author in an interview on March 26, 1965. The interview, however, was not recorded.
30. Interview with Alzira Vargas do Amaral Peixoto in the *Estado de São Paulo*, July 16, 1978, 6.

ca interwove fiction and fact to explore the corrupting influences of the day, including numbers gambling (the *jogo de bicho*), assassination attempts, homosexuality – themes rarely brought to the surface in pre-1954 Brazil. For Fonseca and many others, Vargas's death represented an awakening from innocence, the end of an era.[31]

Even though João Goulart was forced out of the cabinet by the military upon Vargas's death, the old politics continued, at least for a while. The man who abruptly ascended to the presidency was João Café Filho, the former legislator and lawyer who had fought against the imposition of the Estado Novo dictatorship in 1937 and who had been driven into exile in Argentina. In 1946 he had been a member of the Constituent Assembly and had worked on the section of the 1946 Constitution on economic and social affairs. After 1946 he became known as an opponent of the more conservative Eurico Dutra, and therefore became close to Getúlio, whose outlook he had come to share as Vargas became more personally progressive. He became president constitutionally upon Vargas's death and remained in office for another year and a half, devoting most of his efforts to completing Vargas's unfinished projects and conforming to a policy of transition. For labor minister, he selected PTB Senator Napoleão Alencastro Guimarães, a close friend to Vargas and the man who gave his funeral oration on the Senate floor. The UDN pressured him to cancel the upcoming elections and to govern by decree, but he refused. He did agree to call for the cancellation of congressional elections scheduled for October 1954, but Vargas partisans protested vehemently, and he permitted them to proceed.

That Café Filho had been willing to become a close political ally of a man who had driven him and many others into exile testifies not only to his own flexibility but to Vargas's capacity to win over persons whom his actions had wronged. Only a man for whom everything was political could have accomplished this, because he conveyed to his opponents that his hostility was not personal. Although obscured somewhat by his ability to seem enigmatic and not to reveal his motives, this trait explains Getúlio's longevity in power. Café Filho, asked about this later, said that he had decided to forgive Vargas because of the man's sensitivity to the people's needs. Vargas, he pointed out, had worked diligently to avoid conflict in relations between capital and labor; that he

31. See Carmen Chavez Tesser, "The Contexts of Rubem Fonseca's *Agosto:* The Fall of Vargas and the 1990s," paper presented at the Latin American Studies Association meeting, March 1994, Atlanta.

did not accomplish more Café Filho attributed to the "difficult economic and financial situation of Brazil."[32] This softening of memory may say more about the willingness of the Brazilian left to step back from severe judgments – after all, most of the left-wing members of the elite like Café Filho came out of the same background as their conservative opponents – but it is consistent with Getúlio Vargas's uncanny ability to seem to be many things to many people, and, like Franklin D. Roosevelt, come away with the respect of most of those who served with him, even if his policies were not consistent with their personal goals.

To his enemies, Vargas's smiling populist face dripped with hypocrisy. His May Day 1945 speech to workers at Rio's Vasco da Gama Stadium attacked "opportunists and reactionaries" who for decades had support-ed the "policy of the police state. . . . to stifle by force the demands of the people and the workers, the true producers of the wealth of the nation."[33] What he did often contradicted his rhetoric. He borrowed his economic nationalism from the *tenentes*, but he did not explain how Brazil could court foreign economic assistance, yet maintain control. His outlook re-mained consistent, based on what he considered the collective national interest. He kept industrial workers at the center of his public expressions of his goals for economic independence: he did not initiate policies as much as he let competing interest groups fight over them, at which point he stepped in as a conciliator. This was a populism that relied on public support, which Vargas sought through speeches and public rallies, al-though he was neither a spellbinding speaker nor a leader able to win over his adversaries. He still placed considerable emphasis on patronage, building a school here and a road there, after behind-the-scenes negoti-ations with powerful interest groups. His presidential victory, in fact, was due in large part to his alliance with Adhemar de Barros, a notoriously corrupt populist who never disavowed the widely known joke that "He steals but he gets things done." As president, Vargas blurred the distinc-tions between the two political parties that backed him, the PTB and PSD, although his government's actions followed much more closely the moderate PSD platform than the militancy of the Labor Party.

Vargas's prewar apprehensions about hitching Brazil's economy more closely to the United States and to Western Europe proved to have been well founded. Vargas's political success, moreover, had depended on his close control of the apparatus of government, and this was much less possible under the democratic framework of his elected presidency. Even had he enjoyed his old dictatorial powers, the dynamic nature of the postwar world system would have left him few options. Before long, Vargas found himself backed into a corner. Radical nationalists attacked his acceptance of technical assistance and foreign aid from the United States. In response, Vargas had proposed to create state agencies, Petrobrás and Electrobrás, to achieve an independent energy policy. The armed forces argued internally over nationalist goals and Brazil's role in support of the United Nations' police action in Korea, which was opposed vehemently by young army nationalists who were heirs to the old left-wing *tenentes*. Members of this group, some of whom, like Appollonio de Carvalho, had fought as volunteers on the republican side in the Spanish Civil War, allied with Vargas's left-wing civilian backers until both groups were purged after the 1964 hard-line military coup.[34]

Ironically, the flaws in the post-1945 political system that permitted Vargas to be elected were the same that undermined his presidency. Vargas's PTB was a hollow shell, lacking a national base; the PSD was divided, and the UDN offered intransigent opposition. State machines demanded patronage and resources in exchange for the votes of their congressional delegations. Most military leaders were disgusted at his election and offered no support. Vargas had to step back from some of his goals for practical reasons, allowing his opponents to attack him for being inconsistent. Getúlio never appreciated the strength of his adversaries, and he did not trust his major ally, Adhemar de Barros.[35]

All of this exacerbated the brisk deterioration of Vargas's presidency. Carlos Lacerda accused the PTB of harboring Communists and chastised Vargas for giving in to the demands of the Eisenhower administration that foreign aid for Brazilian economic development be accompanied by concessions to United States companies and curbs on the power of Petrobrás. Vargas, unaccustomed to personal attacks and likely furious, turned up the volume of his nationalist rhetoric, although he did not win additional leverage in the increasingly volatile political atmosphere. UDN politicians formed alliances with right-wing military officers in reaction

34. *Cavalheiros de Esperança,* José Carlos Sebe Bom Meihy's oral history of five Brazilian Spanish Civil War veterans (São Paulo: Ed. Loyola, 1997).
35. See Maria Celina Soares D'Araujo, *O Segundo Governo Vargas, 1951–1954,* 2nd ed. (São Paulo: Editora Ática, 1992).

to the Communist threat – which was exaggerated. Civilians, including Lacerda, attended seminars at the National War College.[36] In August 1954, the attempt made on Lacerda's life that was traced back to Vargas's security chief proved to be the final straw, stripping Vargas of popular support and leading directly to the decision of the military command to depose him. His world closing around him, Vargas opted to take his own life rather than to face humiliation for the second time in a decade.

Vargas-style populism was not merely a device for Vargas to woo support and to permit him to further his personal ambitions. It was, as well, the means through which Vargas projected his genuine desire to cast off the restrictive influence of the pre-1930 Old Republic. Although he did not reject traditional ways of doing things – indeed, his political style was a product of his *gaúcho* background and his success as a political broker – he also brought to national leadership a clear and ambitious goal for the kind of progress that would affect the lives of all Brazilians. His populist appeals greatly broadened the psychological boundaries of citizenship, even if his vision of civil society distrusted democracy. His initiatives in encouraging intellectuals to make their work accessible, in promoting patriotism and a nationalistic interpretation of history, were unique.[37] He appealed in his speeches (and in his suicide letter) to "all Brazilians, especially the humble." Before 1930, this was unthinkable. By the time of Vargas's death, these Brazilians had been incorporated into the national polity.

Vargas had reshaped the old political culture, even if it did not give up the ghost until 1950, when millions of Brazilians voted in a presidential election in an open atmosphere never before seen. Brazilians for the first time in their history thought of themselves as a single people with a common destiny. During the 1930s, Vargas had rejected traditional economic liberalism in favor of corporatist state interventionism. He reversed the Republic's system of decentralized administration. During his long, twenty-one-year tenure as head of state, Getúlio Vargas not only appointed almost all the heads of a vastly expanded bureaucratic elite but his efforts to substitute a modern, national apparatus of government for the fragmented state-based system of the ousted "Old Re-

---

36. See the two-volume biography by John W. F. Dulles, *Carlos Lacerda, Brazilian Crusader*, 2 vols. (Austin: University of Texas Press, 1991; 1996).
37. See Daryle Williams, "Ad perpetuam rei memoriam: The Vargas Regime and Brazil's National Historical Patrimony, 1930–1945," *Luso-Brazilian Review*, 31:2 (Winter 1994), 45–76.

public" meant that he determined the decision-making path as well. As a result, he personally shaped the modern Brazilian state.

Vargas's death, of course, brought "Getulism" to a halt, rooted as it was in Vargas's personal aura. The suicide and the extended period of grief accompanying his public viewing and funeral in some ways revitalized "Getulism," and it provided the opportunity for political parties of all stripes to borrow from it for their own ends.[38] It had its greatest institutional impact, naturally, on the Labor Party. The PTB was left reeling by Vargas's sudden departure, which left its rank and file disoriented, not knowing where to turn. It never evolved into a national party appealing to all workers; rather, it remained a personal vehicle for Vargas.[39] The first indication of the PTB's inadequacy came in the October 1954 congressional elections, when PTB leaders ran a campaign based on Vargas's memory but gained only two deputies. In Rio Grande do Sul, where Vargas's memory should have been strongest, the party lost two key seats. João Goulart, the ex-labor minister and the president of the PTB's national directorate, lost his senate race; Alberto Pasqualini, considered the principal ideological force behind the labor movement on the national level and a powerful state politician, lost the governorship to a candidate backed by an alliance of PSD and UDN supporters. In São Paulo the PTB won only 17 percent of the vote, down from the previous two elections in 1945 and 1950. Even though Vargas's son was elected to Congress from the Federal District, on the whole the party simply was unable to capitalize on Vargas's martyrdom. Weak where state-recognized labor unions were weak, especially in the North and Northeast, the PTB remained insignificant outside of the industrial South, despite Goulart's popularity and the intense behind-the-scenes work of former Integralist and law professor San Tiago Dantas, who joined the party in 1955 and, especially after Alberto Pasqualini's death in 1956, who became its ideological and strategic pilot.[40] Owing in no small measure to Dantas's efforts, the PTB caught on in the early 1960s, raising its vote-getting potential, but it never won more than 30 percent

38. See Ángela de Castro Gomes, "Trabalhismo e Democracia: O PTB sem Vargas," Luso-Brazilian Review, 31:2 (Winter 1994), 115–136.
39. See Joel W. Wolfe, "Getúlio Vargas and His Enduring Legacy for Brazil," Luso-Brazilian Review, 31:2 (Winter 1994), 2.
40. See Antonio Lavareda, A Democracia nas Urnas: o Processo Partidário Eleitoral Brasileiro (Rio de Janeiro: IUPERJ/Rio Fundo, 1991), chap. 6; Ángela de Castro Gomes, A Invenção do Trabalhismo, 2nd ed. (Rio de Janeiro: Dumara Editora, 1994).

of the vote at any level. It remained too sectarian and too narrowly identified with Vargas to permit it any greater degree of success.

During the nervous days following Vargas's suicide, his political heirs
sidestepped military intervention and maintained control, but much of
the apparent social harmony of the Estado Novo period had dissipated.
When compared with the legacy of Roosevelt's New Deal, which survived
long after FDR's death, Vargas's appeal was much less tangible and therefore difficult to pass on. Juscelino Kubitschek, a skilled PSD politician
from Minas Gerais, launched Brazil on a developmentalist course that followed Vargas's policies, but he was a very different kind of politician, and
he downplayed Vargas's populist methods to win working-class support.
After Kubitschek came reformist Jânio Quadros and, after his abrupt resignation in the face of congressional intransigence, Vargas's protegé, rumored (without foundation) to be his illegitimate son, *gaúcho* João
Goulart, from a now-more-radicalized PTB. Goulart's government would
be ousted in a coup on March 31, 1964, when the armed forces, backed
by anti-Communists and entrenched industrial and landowning elites,
imposed a repressive dictatorship that would last nearly two decades. Vargas's incomplete revolution had made this possible. There were striking
parallels to the 1930s and 1940s. Constitutional freedoms were suspended in the wake of arbitrary arrests, exiles, and the widespread use of torture. Intellectuals and educators were smeared in a hysterical anti-Communist campaign, and the far left responded by launching a campaign of
kidnappings and bank robberies. Censorship and government decrees deprived Brazilians of the right to associate and to hear dissenting views, and
human rights abuses reached unprecedented levels. The armed forces imposed programs of civic awareness and patriotism in the schools and
through the media, exactly as the DIP had done a generation earlier.
There had been no meaningful land distribution, and patronage overshadowed civil service reform. Powerful family clans still controlled voters in the rural states, and much of the population remained excluded from
political participation.[41] Vargas worked enormously hard but he did not
delegate responsibility well, so outside of the Federal District politicians
did mostly whatever they pleased. There were few avenues for public crit-
icism, so administrators and public officials had little reason to fear being
exposed for corruption or challenged as incompetent.[42]

---

41. See Schneider, *Brazil*, 68–69.
42. Richard Bourne, *Getúlio Vargas of Brazil, 1883–1954: Sphinx of the Pampas* (Lon-
    don: Tonbridge and Knight, 1974), 215.

CHAPTER FIVE

DIFFERENT GETÚLIOS

Practically no one outside of Rio Grande do Sul knew anything about Getúlio Vargas when he sat in Washington Luís's cabinet or in the governor's mansion in Porto Alegre. Photographs in newspapers (and grainy black-and-white newsreel clips) introduced him to Brazilians during the 1930 presidential campaign and after he became head of state. Radio increased enormously his contact with the public, and, after the period during the middle 1930s when he dwelled on the Communist threat, his message turned patriotic and communicative. His advisors wanted Vargas's voice to be heard because they sensed, correctly, that the Brazilian people would respond to a personal touch. His image was not charismatic, like Mussolini or De Gaulle, but that of a sagacious, determined man, personally honest in a country where political corruption was assumed, and determined to accomplish his goals. Labor Minister Marcondes Filho called his chief "Brazil's number 1 worker" in a speech at Volta Redonda. This identification clearly helped Vargas win the presidency in 1950, since millions remembered him nostalgically, an indication that the Estado Novo for most had been benign. During the early 1950s, though, Vargas's image changed again, as things spun out of control. How one perceived Vargas, of course, depended on one's position in society.

THE HAVES

Vargas earned the respect of Brazil's privileged classes gradually but reluctantly. Even when he rose to treasury minister in the national cabinet, many considered him little more than a party hack who had been handed a position for which he was not qualified as patronage for his state. After 1930, most well-placed observers figured that it would be a matter of time before Vargas was edged out. Only after Vargas deftly seized dictatorial powers was he grudgingly afforded respect, and even then people continued to underestimate him, saying that he was a puppet of the military. His preference for dealing behind closed doors led even those who came to fear him to believe that others were using him for their own ends. To some degree, of course, this was correct.

Elites knew that Vargas was one of them, that, as a landowner and scion of a powerful and well-connected family, he shared the outlook of his class. They knew that his speeches were orchestrated for mass consumption and that he was a consummate politician. They respected him for that, although ultimately they felt he had gone too far. Yet over the years he was never hated in Brazil the way his contemporary Roosevelt was hated in the United States, because rich and powerful Brazilians knew that he would keep the common people in line by maintaining the controlling apparatus of government. "He's a great politician. He has contempt for man," a professional man sitting at a table in a Belo Horizonte café told a foreign visitor in 1943.[1]

Forward-looking industrialists supported Vargas because they understood that his policies would create favorable conditions for growth. Roberto Simonsen, the president of the *paulista* Industrial Association, was one of Vargas's key supporters in the 1933–1934 national Constituent Assembly. "The [1930] Revolution," he said, "proved how few statesmen we had and how profoundly ignorant we were of our real social situation."[2] Those who admired Vargas the most tended to be politicians and journalists who marveled at his political sagacity. They felt comfortable with his preference for brokered deals over partisan infighting. São Paulo businessmen and coffee producers, who raised armed insurrection against his government in 1932, were mollified when he bestowed a financial windfall on them by subsidizing prices as exports continued to plunge. Over time, however, Vargas phased out price supports in favor of nationalistic policies seeking to achieve economic integration and to build up the country's traditionally neglected regions. Old-line elites resented Vargas's assault on laissez-faire liberalism and what they considered to be his overly friendly relationship with labor. Constitutionalists were angered by Vargas's cavalier attitude toward the concept of checks and balances; intellectuals hated him for suspending civil rights and for his use of police methods to intimidate and to squelch dissent.

1. Waldo David Frank, *South American Journey*, 53.
2. Roberto Simonsen, *Rumo à Verdade* (São Paulo: Editora Limitada, 1933), 10.

Perhaps because he was himself from the geographic periphery, Vargas collected around him men of very different types. Aranha was "at home in troubled waters," as Waldo Frank said, frequently clashing with the fascist sympathizers in Vargas's inner circle. Assis Chateaubriand, another of Vargas's closest associates, was known for his explosive temper and his political shrewdness. Labor Minister Marcondes Filho was a lawyer and an ex-Integralist, known for his cynicism. What all of Vargas's supporters in the elite shared, perhaps, was their preference for statist, not democratic goals. Even progressives like Pedro Ernesto Baptista and João Café Filho trusted in the will of the state to distribute income and to carry out social reform.[3]

These allies aside, most *pessoas de categoria* ("important people") never embraced him fully, even though Vargas never betrayed them. Many distrusted Vargas's wooing of the poor, perhaps because it implied opening opportunities for nonwhites even when they knew that most jobs were held for members of the respectable urban middle class. Skilled factory jobs went to immigrants, not blacks and *mulatos*, who were relegated to the most dangerous, menial, and poorly paid jobs in the economy. After all, there had always been a strain of racial supremacism among some elite groups, such as the Sociedade dos Amigos de Alberto Tôrres during the 1930s. Others felt uneasy at Getúlio's habit of mingling with common people while traveling. This attitude was captured by a cartoon drawn by Canini during the 1950 election campaign: Getúlio stands smiling, watched over by an enormous, dark-complexioned scowling angel, holding one fist clenched and the other hand extended protectively over Getúlio's head.[4]

Contemporaries never successfully could explain either Vargas's mystique or his political longevity. Many cited Vargas's *gaúcho* background, but others resented Vargas's use of *gaúcho* props to give the appearance of a man of the people. If Getúlio was a "typical" *gaúcho* from that time, so was elegant Oswaldo Aranha and bellicose Flores da Cunha and Communist Luis Carlos Prestes. Rightists never forgave Vargas for flirting with the fascists during the mid-1930s and then turning against them. Centrists talked about his reluctance to govern democratically, but their model was more controlled than spontaneous. Respectable conservatives – the liberal constitutionalists of the 1930s who joined the opposition UDN in

3. Fernando Henrique Cardoso, "Challenges of Social Democracy in Latin America," in Menno Vellinga, ed., *Social Democracy in Latin America: Prospects for Change* (Boulder, Colo.: Westview Press, 1990), 279.
4. Reprinted in Ivar Hartmann, *Getúlio Vargas* (Porto Alegre: Tchê!, 1984), 17.

the 1940s – saw Vargas in a banal light, devoid of complexity.[5] Leftists hated Vargas for his ties to industrialists, his alliance with the hard-line military command, and his construction of a labor apparatus that crushed the old anarcho-syndicalist unions and promised benefits only to workers willing to sign away their militancy. Intellectuals frowned on Vargas, especially when they were affluent enough not to need government employment. They also knew about the fate of intellectual fellow travelers who were arrested and imprisoned during the Estado Novo for being considered dangerously socially conscious. Brazil's cultural elite remained sharply divided between far right and far left during the Vargas period, and he did little to nurture the center, if that is where his own inclinations lay.

Those close to Vargas, on the other hand, praised his tenacity and his political skills. They agreed with his immigration policy, which made entry difficult for Asians, non-Aryans, Jewish refugees from Hitler, and others considered undesirable.[6] Vargas's supporters also liked his sarcastic sense of humor. When he was warned that his stubborn refusal to replace *tenente* João Alberto as São Paulo's interventor was making *paulistas* so angry that someone might shoot his appointee, Vargas replied: "Well, this could solve the problem."[7]

THE HAVE-NOTS

What exactly do we mean when we use the term "people"? Surely not this coarse horde of illiterate, diseased, shrivelled, malaria-ridden half-castes and niggers. . . . People means race, culture, civilization, affirmation, nationhood – not the dregs of a nation.
– *JOÃO UBALDO RIBEIRO, VIVA O POVO BRASILEIRO*

Throughout the Vargas years, the unmistakable division separating the social classes remained essentially untouched by government reforms. Brazil's haves, in fact, employed more maids and domestic servants than any country in the Western world, because labor was so cheap. Whether remaining in the rural interior or as migrants to urban areas, these men and women were barely above subsistence level, hidden, in a sense, from

---

5. See Roberto Schwartz, *Misplaced Ideas: Essays on Brazilian Culture*, ed. John Gledson (London: Verso, 1992), 47.
6. Jeffrey Lesser, "Immigration and Shifting Concepts of National Identity in Brazil during the Vargas Era," *Luso-Brazilian Review*, 31:2 (Winter 1994), 23–44.
7. Moisés Velinho, cited in Valentina da Rocha Lima, *Getúlio: Uma História Oral* (Ria de Janeiro: Ed. Record, 1986), 86.

the everyday world of the affluent. That the have-nots on the whole tended to accept their lot caused them to be treated as if they were children, a by-product of the paternalistic legacy of Brazilian society.[8] They used good-naturedness and resignation as coping mechanisms, although when they snapped, mobs smashed and burned streetcars (*quebra quebra*) or looted storehouses for food. The lower classes, Spanish journalist Ricardo Baeza pontificated, are a "garrulous and laughing people, who do not yet know the poison of thought or the curse of work."[9]

Vargas maintained a sharp distance in his mind between himself and the people he called *populares* in his diary. They loved him nonetheless. During the 1930 election campaign pro–Liberal Alliance crowds overturned streetcars in Salvador. After the Liberal Alliance triumph, thousands lined the tracks to watch Vargas's train proceed from the South to Rio de Janeiro, where he would take office. Street poets called Getúlio the *defensor dos marmiteiros*, the protector of the workers who carried their tin lunch boxes of rice and beans with them to their jobs.[10] At the same time, the growing migration of rural families to the cities of the coast in desperate search for jobs spawned ever larger slums: foul *mocambos* on the river banks of Recife, shanties in Salvador and Porto Alegre, *favelas* sprouting in São Paulo for the first time, between 1942 and 1945, and a proliferation of new and larger *favelas* on the hillsides of Rio de Janeiro.

Carolina Maria de Jesus, an indigent black girl in rural Minas Gerais living at the lowest rung of poverty, scorned by the "good families" in her small city and condemned to deprivation, describes in her autobiographical memoirs what the 1930 Revolution meant to her:[11]

One day I awoke confused to see the streets filled with soldiers. It was a revolution. I knew only revolutions of ants when they moved

8. For more discussion of this theme, see the author's *Brazilian Legacies* (New York: M. E. Sharpe, 1997).

9. Ricardo Baeza, *Bajo el signo de Clio: Reminiscencias del Brasil* (Madrid: Cia. Interamericana de Publicaciones, 1931), 305–308, translated by G. Harvey Summ, in *Brazilian Mosaic: Portraits of a Diverse People and Culture* (Wilmington, Del.: S R, 1995), 101.

10. See Lêdo Maranhão de Souza, *Classificação Popular da Literatura de Cordel* (Petrópolis: Ed. Vozes, 1976), esp. 81–83.

11. Carolina Maria de Jesus, *Diário de Bitita* (Rio de Janeiro: Nova Fronteira, 1986). It is telling that, although in 1960 Carolina became the best-selling author in Brazilian history with the publication of her diary, *Quarto de Despejo*, her writings about her childhood elicited so little interest in Brazil that the diary was first published in France, then in Argentina, and only then in Brazil.

about. Revolutions by men are tragic. Some killing others. And the people only talked about Getúlio Vargas and João Pessoa. It was the union of the State of Paraíba with the State of Rio Grande do Sul. And the *tenentes* asked people to arm themselves, that men shouldn't be absent in the hour of their country's litigation. These seditions occur because of the arrogance of those who want to govern the nation. With Getúlio Vargas we will have more work.

The soldiers spread through the streets with green, yellow, and white banners with Getúlio's face in the center. Those who saw the portrait liked him and said: "Now Brazil will be watched over by a man!" This will move the country forward. We are a country without a leader. We have to wake up. Countries cannot lie down eternally in a splendid cradle. Our country is very backward. The girls who were domestic servants didn't leave their employers' houses. I was working in Dona Mimi's house, the wife of the *gaúcho*. He was happy it was his state [Rio Grande do Sul] that would bring order to Brazil. I walked the streets. I heard the soldiers sing:

Long live our Revolution
Brazil will ascend like a balloon
With Getúlio, Brazil moves ahead
With Getúlio, Brazil won't fall.

Let's have more bread on the table
Getúlio is a friend of the poor.

When she was eighteen or nineteen, in the early 1930s, Carolina was hospitalized at the Santa Casa de Misericordia in Ribeirão Preto. She wrote:

In the ward the women only spoke about the [1930] Revolution, that it was beneficial for the people. That it had changed the rules of the game for workers. Salaries were better; they now were able to have bank accounts and other benefits from the working-class legislation. A worker is able to retire when he is old and be paid for full-time work. Workers were content with the laws. And Getúlio was becoming known as the "father of the poor." The people were disciplined.

Carolina, who wrote her memoirs during the last years of her life in the mid-1970s, did not remember that Vargas's social legislation came into effect only over decades. Unskilled workers were initially excluded from benefits, and Vargas's lectures about the need for a disciplined work force dated from the Estado Novo, not from his first years in office. Still, Carolina (or Bitita, as she was known) remembered that Getúlio gave young men the opportunity to join the army and therefore leave the hardscrabble interior. Many of them got jobs in São Paulo, she said; in their letters home to their relatives they convinced them to come to São Paulo also. They came to believe that São Paulo was the paradise for poor people. This was the moment in which she decided that when she could, she would go to São Paulo herself, a place that for her, in her words, was "heaven's waiting room."

Men in rural Minas Gerais, Bitita said, when they got together, started to speak about Getúlio being the great protector of the poor. She later wrote that she thought "Will this be the politician who is going to improve Brazil for the Brazilians? . . . He had reanimated the people, that people who were lukewarm, apathetic, leave it for tomorrow, idealistic dreamers, now moving into action because they believed that this government would not deceive them." Planners, she claimed, said that they were going to São Paulo to get a loan from Getúlio and open a plant with fifty workers because Getúlio said that if workers have jobs they won't have time to go astray. "Not only does he give us loans," she wrote, "but his goal is to make workers the beneficiaries. Industry in São Paulo brings immediate profits."

Almost from the outset of his arrival in the public eye, millions of these men and women revered Vargas as a father figure. One reason for this was the importance of fictive kinship in Brazilian society. The descendants of slaves became kin of African tribal ancestors through initiation into spiritist cults. Landless peasants traditionally took powerful figures as godparents for their newborn children – in the northeastern backlands in the late nineteenth century, for example, parish birth records list the Virgin Maria as *madrinha* for thousands of baby girls, and the northeastern charismatics Antonio Conselheiro or Father Cícero as *padrinhos*. Many more families elicited permission of the local landlord to godfather (and therefore protect) their offspring. In the same way, Getúlio Vargas, the first national politician to reach out to all Brazilians, became the nation's *padrinho*. For ordinary people, Getúlio was accessible, all-powerful, demanding of their loyalty, and willing to intervene on their behalf if they proved him worthy.

Many lower-class Brazilians, including Carolina de Jesus, mixed spiritism with the penitential Roman Catholicism prevalent in the hinterlands. For people with such beliefs, Getúlio was a miracle-working saint, one with whom one could commune spiritually. They decorated personal shrines with his photograph, and asked him for personal intervention, as they did to clay statues for Father Cícero, the miracle-working defrocked priest whose backlands Ceara religious community in Joaseiro coexisted with Vargas's government during the 1930s and who exerted considerable influence in state politics.[12]

The life histories of ordinary Brazilians who reached adulthood during the 1930s and 1940s demonstrate incontestably that the Vargas era was pivotal in changing their lives, even if the new opportunities for mobility were more incremental than dramatic. Consider the case of Maurílio Tomás Ferreira, born in 1915 in rural Espírito Santo:[13]

> I had six brothers, most of them older. I even have a photograph of them. Three were drafted into the Guard (Tiro de Guerra), all at once, and they had to go even though they were married and had small children. . . . Before the Vargas government things were out of hand. . . . We lived on my father's land he had bought. . . . everyone in the family had a little house and a small plot. . . . He distilled *cachaça* [rum] from sugar cane. . . . I had four sisters also. My father was angry because he now had to take care of his three daughters-in-law and their kids. My father had to pay for their uniforms, shoes – in the countryside you had to provide everything yourself.
>
> I went to a rural school, very rudimentary. After primary school I studied with a teacher my father hired for all of us. Getúlio regulated lots of things. Before that things were disorganized. I was now the oldest boy living at home. My father decided to send me to the army too, to get it over with, so I lied about my age. . . . I served in the army in 1930 when I was fifteen. . . . I was sent first to Vitória and then to Rio, to the Praia Vermelho barracks. I got out in December. I returned to work with my father and when I was twenty-two I married, in 1937. I grew corn and potatoes and

12. See Ralph della Cava, *Miracle at Joaseiro* (New York: Columbia University Press, 1970), and David J. Hess, *Samba in the Night* (New York: Columbia University Press, 1994).
13. Maurílio Thomas Ferreira, interview conducted by Marieta de Moraes Ferreira, Rio de Janeiro, May 2, 1994.

coffee beans and raised pigs. There was no place to sell things, so I had to transport my produce, and this was expensive. We made very little money. Things grew well; my father sometimes harvested ten thousand sacks of coffee. But we had too little land for all of my brothers and their families. All of my family were *crentes* [evangelical Protestants]. There was a church in Córrego Rico. We went. I directed a choir. We were baptized. I met my wife there, when she was twelve years old.

[In 1942] I decided, overnight, to leave. We had two children already. We went to [the town of] Muniz Freire and bought a house with my savings. I had no job, nothing. I worked as a barber but didn't make very much; the town was too small. I worked for the mayor's office. I got one job through one of my brothers-in-law who was a driver for an Arab. I became foreman on his farm but he didn't pay me. I stayed for a year and then left for another foreman's job. Then I got a job with the railroad. I got it [in 1945] when I went to Cachoeiro to sell chickens. A fellow I sold them to told me to try and get a railroad job, that they were hiring many people. He introduced me to some officials of the Leopoldina Railroad. They hired me. I liked the idea of living in Cachoeiro because there was a school there my kids could attend. My children all studied, one as far as the fifth grade, the others to high school. And railroad workers were eligible for pensions; [we were] one of the first. . . . When I started working they registered me in the railroad pension institute. There was an enormous union building in Cachoeiro. The union sold provisions and merchandise to us at cheaper prices. Later on the union gave a scholarship for my youngest son to study at high school.

Starting in 1945 my wife and I always voted in elections, every year. . . . I joined the PTB. . . . and became active in the union. . . . I admired Getúlio Vargas, always voted for him. . . . He named the state interventors. . . . He was leading Brazil forward. . . . When he killed himself it was an enormous shock. . . . I kept his photograph [the union had given to us] and a copy of his suicide letter, to remind me of what he did for poor Brazilians. . . . He was the chief organizer of this country.

Looking back on his life nearly a half century later, Maurílio recognized that this was the turning point in his life. Employment by a state agency meant school for his children, a future. To have a government job meant security and a pension. Perhaps because he understood that so few other workers received these benefits, Maurílio idolized Vargas, considering him his personal benefactor. He would have scoffed at social scientists writing that Vargas's labor measures were enacted to control the labor force, because he knew that he and his family benefited. As long as he belonged to the union, his wife would receive food at reduced prices at the union-run store. He would receive a pension, and his children would be eligible for scholarships available to families of union members. He considered voting for Vargas a natural obligation and something that gave him satisfaction. The union allowed him to advance: when Maurílio started, he was an apprentice brakeman. When he retired in 1970, he held the position of "chief of the train." Such upward mobility would have been impossible before 1930.

The People's Adulation

Visitors from the coast and from abroad looked at the people of Brazil's hinterland as if they were foreigners in their own land. Newspapers and magazines devoted almost no attention to the interior, whose residents were seen in simplistic ways, emphasizing their backwardness. But backlanders knew much more than they were given credit for, learning quickly that the *gaúcho* in the presidential palace thought about them. In addition, aided by the construction of new roads, families increasingly migrated to places where they believed they would find work: not only to the industrial cities of the South but to the rubber fields of the Amazon and Acre.[14]

What seems obvious about the way needy men and women saw national politics during the 1930s is that their outlook shared very little in common with the worldview of Brazil's Communists and antifascists. Newspapers like *A Plebe, a Manhã,* and others voicing the position of the left used excited language denouncing imperialism, racism, *latifundia,* foreign monopolistic controls. These were slogans couched in a stylized vocabulary far too distant from the day-to-day lives of the lower classes they were attempting to rally. Where the ANL did touch at least some men and women – thousands but not tens or hundreds of thousands – was when it complained about the failure of the 1930 Revolution, low wages, police brutality, and racial discrimination. It should also be remembered that the men who risked their lives to topple Vargas's government in 1935 were sergeants, corporals, and common soldiers;

14. See Frank, *South American Journey,* 320.

and in Recife, the rebels were mostly enlisted men who had been sent to São Paulo in 1932. These soldiers would have been shocked had they heard Vargas's New Year's radio broadcast to the nation, in which he warned that "forces of evil and of hate have overshadowed the lovable spirit of our land and our people."[15] As far as they were concerned, they had been fighting to rid Brazil of these very elements.

Before censorship tightened during the Estado Novo, some expression of popular ambivalence about Vargas surfaced. The regime paid subsidies to composers of Carnival sambas to write lyrics endearing Getúlio to the people, with mixed results. The hit samba of 1931 was Lamartine Babo's "Ge-gê" (Seu Getúlio [see Appendix]). But Lulu Parola, a Bahian samba composer, wrote lyrics in 1934 explaining how he felt about things:

Carnaval desanimado
tem-se logo a explicação
é que com a Revolução
tudo está desmascarado

(Down-in-the-dumps Carnival
is that way for a reason
It is the Revolution
that is unmasked)

Six years later he wrote about Getúlio's failure to keep the lid on prices:

Carnival está na porta
A vida cara que importa?

(Carnival is at the door
Who cares about the high cost of living?)

This undercurrent of skepticism was not lost on state authorities. In 1940 Rio de Janeiro's police chief banned the use at Carnival of masks or half masks, on the street or inside, and also prohibited the use of any

15. Robert M. Levine, *O Regime de Vargas* (Rio de Janeiro: Nova Fronteira, 1980), 172; Aspásia Camargo et al., *O Golpe Silencioso: As Origens da República Corporativa* (Rio de Janeiro: Rio Fundo, 1989), 48–49.

military items (hats, boots, and so on) in costumes. The prohibition was only lifted in 1946. The police also banned parades of men dressed as women, an old Carnival tradition, but under Vargas considered an affront to family morality.[16]

Although there were exceptions, the further one went from Rio de Janeiro, the more watered down was Vargas's popularity. Many retained a healthy suspicion of Vargas's motives, especially those who had been members of nongovernment-sanctioned unions or who saw that Getúlio's legislation would not benefit them. Poor people desperately struggled to gain the government's attention: in 1941 four raft fishermen from northeastern Ceará heroically sailed their tiny balsawood raft all the way around Brazil's Atlantic bulge to ask Vargas personally to help their village. Newspapers reported on their journey, and when they arrived in Rio de Janeiro harbor they were taken, their clothing still wet, directly to Catete Palace, where Vargas embraced them and promised aid. Nothing ever came of his pledge, however, and one of the four sailors drowned tragically in a reenactment of their voyage filmed by Orson Welles for a movie he was making for the OIAA.

Waldir dos Santos, born in 1916, was a lifelong employee of the English-owned Morro Velho gold mine in Minas Gerais. His father was an alcoholic actor who died when his son was an infant; his mother, in Waldir's own words, was "a very sexually active mulata" who also worked in theater, although as an amateur.[17] Both performed in a local theater company, which remained active throughout the 1920s – a fact that gives pause to stereotypes about the backwardness of rural Brazil held by many on the coast. Their life was hard, filled with poverty, and they lived in a shack with a floor of pounded earth. But their lives were buoyed by the frequent religious festivities on the many saints' days in the region. Waldir spent six years in school, two of them in the third grade, which he had to repeat. Fellow classmates provided his uniform, his books, his pens and pencils, although, as he remembers, the items were "lent" to him, not given. When the rich children misbehaved, they were ignored; when he did, he was beaten severely by the teacher.

In 1928 his mother took him and his surviving brother to Belo Horizonte, the state capital. He and his brother found jobs. He remembers

16. Quoted in Rogério Menezes, *Um Povo a Mais de Mil* (Salvador, BA: Scritta Editorial, 1994), 64–72.
17. Waldir dos Santos, interviews with Andréa Casa Nova Maia, Nova Lima, Minas Gerais, August 1994–September 1995.

the 1930 Revolution. When it broke out, the police cut off the water supply to the neighborhood where he lived because it was close to an army barracks. There was gunfire and general chaos. Dead animals were left in the street for days, until they began to rot. The army regiment surrendered.

A poor boy, Waldir nonetheless held strong opinions about politics. He believed that Vargas was named head of the revolutionary forces because he was thought to be easily manipulated. But he sensed that the Revolution was a popular uprising, that through it ordinary people would be able to play their part. For this reason he always supported Vargas fervently, although at the age of sixteen he had no other option but to sign up for work in the Morro Velho gold mine. The work was so hard that at the end of the day he sobbed with exhaustion. There was no chance to complain; miners died of lung disease. He worked in the tunnels on one of the three daily eight-hour shifts with boys as young as fourteen.

His brother died and his mother found work as a street sweeper. On the side she sewed to supplement her meager wages. But as a mine employee, Waldir ultimately was able to move into company-owned housing. He received a better job. In his spare hours he went with women and considered himself a "Bohemian" of the neighborhood. When World War II came, immigrants from Germany and Italy who lived in Nova Lima were treated harshly; their houses were stoned. Waldir did not understand why Brazil entered the war, believing that the Americans took advantage of Getúlio's "naiveté" to force Brazil's hand. Waldir continued to work in the mines, retiring in 1952.

Waldir's story illustrates a different Brazilian trajectory from that of workers employed by the state. Although his work was backbreaking, he appreciated the benefits provided by the mining company as a private enterprise: chiefly workers' housing but also (in cooperation with the local Catholic Church) religious festivities. There was also music, samba, Carnival. Waldir's recollections are cheerful, and he considered his salary acceptable, although by international standards it was woeful. For him, Getúlio was no hero because he did not provide anything personally for him, but he was concerned that foreigners would take advantage of his president, and he became a nationalist. After the war, Waldir noted, Brazil improved its condition in the world economy "and our fiscal reserves got healthy because Brazil was making lots of money in those days. But unfortunately once again the Americans knew how to take advantage of the Brazilians." Dutra and his cronies, he says, traded the nation's fiscal reserves "for yoyos and other junk made in Europe and in the U.S. They inundated us with plastic junk that they always do when they want to get rid of things they don't want." True or not, being a mine worker from a background of poverty in the interior of Brazil did not mean that one remained oblivious to things of the world.

THE LEGACY

Brazilians acknowledge their trust and affection for political figures by referring to them by their first name or a nickname, except when they are stuffy, like Rui Barbosa, or widely disdained, like the military generals who ran Brazil after 1964. Getúlio Vargas during much of his public life was known simply as "Getúlio," or "seu Gê," something like "Mr. G." This was, as has been noted, a mark of respect, a sign that people were comfortable with him. He cultivated this image: his daughter tells the story of a visit from the Papal Nuncio who told Vargas that he had proof that the Vargas ancestors were descended from Italian princes. Vargas replied: "Look, Mr. Nuncio, in Brazil we don't look for such things, because the search usually ends up in the jungle or in the kitchen."[18]

More than a decade after Vargas's death, Getúlio Vargas's memory remained warm in the hearts of working-class Brazilians. Consider this interview with a steelworker during the 1960s, a man named "Zé Maria." Among Zé Maria's recollections are these:

I think [I] would feel comfortable with the late Getúlio [Vargas]. I think I even would have enjoyed chatting with him – but, of course, this is no longer possible, right? . . . Getúlio was different. Every time he came here to Belo Horizonte I was right there to see him. I liked him a lot. I don't know why, but I had a special liking for him. I thought he governed well. He was a good man. [He] . . . mixed right in.

I saw Getúlio conversing with the people. He wasn't too proud to speak with any kind of person – even the "lowliest." He appeared honored talking with even the poorest of men – and, it seems he was a very humble man, y'know? – a man who was both humble and intelligent. . . . I was there when he was speaking with a man who was all crippled up – first he put his hand on the man's

18. Alzira Vargas do Amaral Peixoto, quoted in Rocha Lima, *Getúlio: Uma História Oral*, 26–27.

head, then he gave him an *abraço*. Wherever he went he behaved this way, y'know? I had a tremendous affection for him. . . . When [he] was our president – for some fifteen years – it seems that life was much better, much calmer, more balanced, y'know?[19]

The next chapter contains excerpts from telegraphs and letters sent by ordinary Brazilians to Vargas and his officials. They illustrate several things. First, the survival of the traditional Brazilian custom of personal requests, seeking, as it were, to cut through red tape and the cumbersome regulations of government. Second, they show the extent of the burdens of everyday life in a society increasingly modernized but in so many ways unchanged from the past. And they point to the frustration caused by promises of attention to the needs of the poor clashing with the reality of the magnitude of the problem. "Not a single Brazilian is ignorant of the assistance that your humane government offers to the disadvantaged classes," a widowed farmer with eighteen children, fourteen of them minors, wrote to Vargas in 1944, "and especially your efforts to protect families."[20] Unable to pay back taxes, the petitioner asked that the debt be excused. Other letter writers explained that they had passed the civil service examination but had not received appointments to public jobs; others lamented that the buying power of their pension checks had been eroded by the rising cost of living. To what extent should Vargas be faulted for promising more than he could deliver?

19. Robert S. Byars, "Culture, Politics, and the Urban Factory Worker in Brazil: The Case of Zé Maria," in Robert E. Scott, ed., *Latin American Modernization Problems: Case Studies in the Crises of Change* (Urbana: University of Illinois Press, 1973), 71–72, reprinted in John Charles Chasteen and Joseph S. Tulchin, eds., *Problems in Modern Latin American History: A Reader* (Wilmington, Del.: SR Books, 1994), 119–120.
20. Letter, Zenon Belmiro Alves da Cunha, Bonito, Bahia, February 21, 1944, in Brazilian National Archives, Rio de Janeiro, "Pedidos" file.

CHAPTER SIX

VARGAS'S INCOMPLETE
REVOLUTION

Vargas was, in Gramsci's phrase, a "passive revolutionary from above." His revolution was partial, one in which new constituencies and new rules were grafted onto traditional political practices. Although his career spanned three constitutions and enormous changes in the political climate, his pragmatism always prevailed. He always was willing to take risks, a trait that explains not only his political longevity but the miscalculations that led to his ouster in 1945 and that drove him to suicide. He was able to adjust to changes in national and international circumstances but he fundamentally left unaltered much of the fabric of Brazilian life. Some things endured throughout his decades in power, including the readiness of the armed forces to intervene and the elite's tenacious hold on privilege. Brazil's distribution of income remained among the least equal in the world, but Vargas did not perceive this as a problem that needed to be solved.

In 1930, he had stood at the center of forces united in their demand for change and sharply divided over what results they sought. Because of this, Vargas needed to devote almost all of his energy to negotiating among factions and keeping himself in power. Only in 1932, when São Paulo revolted to restore the old system, did he show that he could act decisively and with the use of force. He believed in granting regulated citizenship without disharmony and, therefore, without freedom to dissent. Putting a good face on Vargas's regime in the early 1940s, a visiting political scientist called it "despotism mitigated by sloppiness." Corruption remained a national institution; little could be accomplished without bribes to expedite action, and, "how big businessmen flaunt[ed] the tax laws [was] a story in itself."[1] He was more concerned with staying in power than in holding to any firm purpose.

---

1. Karl Loewenstein, *Brazil under Vargas* (New York: Macmillan, 1942), 98–99.

His assiduous shifting, moreover, produced different revolutionary streams. This was possible because for Vargas practicality came first, and, as such, he was able to play political poker by dealing from different hands. He reorganized civil society, bringing benefits to many (but not all) urban employees and workers although he ignored the countryside. The 1930 Revolution ended the more blatant abuses of the old "politics of the governors" by renewing interventionist powers that the national executive had lost in 1889, but it placed patronage and coercive powers in the hands of his interventors and, after 1945, under a hybrid form of backroom brokering involving partisan politics. The regionalist dimension of politics might have survived even more than it did had not the *paulistas* been pragmatists, suppressing their resistance to Vargas because they agreed with Vargas's social corporatism and his measures to intervene in the economy.[2] In the other outlying states, Vargas's interventors replaced the clans in power before 1930, but in most cases new oligarchic alliances emerged, so that in the decades after Vargas's death prominent local elites continued to dominate state politics in the old ways.

LIMITED CITIZENSHIP

Democracy for the man from Rio Grande do Sul to whom most things had come easy was a luxury he felt Brazil could not afford. For him, the rights of citizenship were not inalienable, but to be awarded in exchange for loyalty and docility. "The right to vote cannot stifle hunger," he said in a speech during the Estado Novo, "nor can the right to assemble educate your children."[3] Nor were people his primary goal. Spending for public works outstripped everything else, including the armed forces. During Vargas's final term, Brazil spent less than one-fourth on public health per capita than the United States. Public works projects were necessary for economic development, but they did little to address so-

2. Joseph L. Love, *Crafting the Third World: Crafting Underdevelopment in Rumania and Brazil* (Stanford: Stanford University Press, 1996), 146–147. See also Randal Johnson, "The Dynamics of the Brazilian Literary Field, 1930–1945," *Luso-Brazilian Review*, 31:2 (Winter 1994), 5–22, esp. 7. Also see Joan L. Bak, "Cartels, Cooperatives, and Corporatism: Getúlio Vargas in Rio Grande do Sul on the Eve of Brazil's 1930 Revolution," *Hispanic American Historical Review*, 63:2 (May 1983), 255–275; Susan K. Besse, *Restructuring Patriarchy: The Modernization of Gender Inequality in Brazil, 1914–1940* (Chapel Hill, N.C.: University of North Carolina Press, 1996), 4–5.
3. Cited by Frank D. McCann Jr., *The Brazilian-American Alliance, 1937–1945* (Princeton: Princeton University Press, 1973), 333.

cial needs. One obstacle faced by Vargas was that, unlike the United States with its strong traditions of local self-government (and the ability to raise funds through municipal bonds), the Brazilian system limiting the ability of states and localities to raise revenue required almost exclusive reliance on federal initiative.

The law-and-order side of Vargas's social legislation brought workers under forms of social control unheard of in the industrial democracies. Employers detested Vargas's reforms as much as Republicans hated Roosevelt's New Deal, although Vargas's were far more controlling. All Brazilians under Vargas's labor legislation had to carry a work folder (*carteira de trabalho*); to obtain one of these, they needed to show a birth certificate and a document from the police stating that they had a clean record. All job records were entered in the folder, including transgressions and firings. Once a worker had a *carteira* with bad entries he would likely never get a job again. If he threw it away, or simply never registered for identity documents, he would be a nonentity, ineligible for medical treatment or on-the-books employment. Migrants distant from the places of their births and usually illiterate and fearful of bureaucracies found it nearly impossible to get the papers necessary for work.

Vargas's style was rooted in the tradition in which supplicants sought personal intervention from officials to cut through red tape or to bestow favors. An irony of Vargas's legacy, therefore, was that although he championed a merit-based civil service program, the old style of personal favors not only survived in the states but increased at the national level as a result of the government centralization. Brazilian archives are filled with personal requests to cabinet ministers (and to Vargas himself) for jobs for relatives, favorable treatment in granting contracts, overruling regulations – all in violation of what Vargas said he was trying to accomplish. The more government bureaucratized state employment, moreover, the more power individual administrators accumulated, and it was never certain that they would act in the interest of their constituencies. As a result, many of Vargas's reforms ended up – intentionally or not – *para inglês ver* ("for the English to see"). Vargas's corporatist framework, moreover, encouraged authoritarian decisions, because he believed that otherwise the needy would continue to be ignored.[4]

In making himself the chief of state of all Brazilians, Vargas limited the potential for rivals to emerge. His fame spread by word of mouth,

4. See Philippe C. Schmitter, *Corporatism and Public Policy in Authoritarian Portugal* (London: Sage, 1975), 9–10.

even through the guileless popular poetry of backlands cordel poets.[5] As a result of his unrivaled popularity, after 1945 the Communists had to ally with Vargas and the political organizations he left behind but, at the same time, to compete with them.[6] Vargas also confounded his enemies by continually experimenting: during the to-be-dashed 1937 presidential campaign, for example, Labor Ministry officials trucked in workers from government-sponsored unions to political demonstrations.

He did not hide his admiration for persons secure in their wielding of power. Pedro Ludovico recalled an encounter between Vargas and a Carajás chieftain during an excursion to a reservation in Goiás. When the tribesman presented Vargas with a petition, Vargas asked him by what authority he spoke for his people. "Because I have the most power," came the reply. When Vargas asked him, affably, how long he would continue to hold this power, the chief replied, "As long as I'm alive." Vargas laughed, because this was his outlook as well.

Brazilians forgave Vargas for delivering less than he promised, in part because they were so grateful for his reaching out to them. Despite his image as father of the poor, well less than half of the adult population in 1945 could read and write, and many more were functionally illiterate. Vargas's personal diaries reveal him as colorless, dutiful to routine, and lacking in curiosity (although they also reveal the tedium of office holding: day after day receiving delegations, "parades of complaining congressmen," and other numbing obligations). He also was personally insensitive. At the height of the wave of arrests carried out under the regime's National Security Law, the day following the imprisonment of Interventor Pedro Ernesto, one of his closest lieutenants and a member of the inner cabinet, Getúlio wrote that his conscience had bothered him when he signed the arrest order, and that he was not convinced of his friend's guilt. But that was the end of it; he quickly turned to writing in his diary about a *churrasco* (barbecue) he attended in someone's house.[7]

5. Michael Conniff, introduction to section on Orígenes Lessa, in John Charles Chasteen and Joseph S. Tulchin, eds., *Problems in Modern Latin American History: A Reader* (Wilmington, Del.: SR Books, 1994), 113.

6. Carlos Estevam Martins and Maris Hermínia Tavares de Almeida, "Modus in Rebus: Partidos e Classes na Queda do Estado Novo" (mimeograph copy, 1984), 18–19, cited by John D. French, *The Workers' ABC: Class Conflict and Alliances in Modern São Paulo* (Chapel Hill, N.C.: University of North Carolina Press, 1992), 290, n. 44.

7. Getúlio Vargas, *Diário*, vol. 1, *1930–1936* (Rio de Janeiro: Siciliano/Fundação Getúlio Vargas, 1995), entry for April 3–4, 1936.

His most far-reaching goal was to modernize the country while pre-serving its national independence. This aim evaded him, but his achievements in turning Brazil into a more modern country yielded more "revolutionary" change than any other policy. The effort also usurped great resources. Government centralization was costly: funds for such massive projects as the Paulo Affonso hydroelectric station on the São Francisco River, for example, could never have been raised by states, given their constant bickering and their depleted credit ratings. As a re-sult of the war, just as Vargas and other nationalists had feared, Brazil had become more dependent on the United States and influenced by its culture – through advertising, movies, consumer goods, and the direct influence of the behavior of the thousands of American servicemen sta-tioned at Brazilian bases during the war.

A New Dealer?

Vargas displayed tough-mindedness and tactical skill as head of state. Like Franklin D. Roosevelt, who in a moment of diplomatic flattery had called Vargas one of the inventors of the New Deal, Getúlio was an as-tute and dexterous political operator, and, also like Roosevelt, a politi-cal chameleon. Vargas's and Roosevelt's measures imparted to ordinary citizens, in most cases for the first time, the premise that government cared about them and would defend their interests.[8] The New Deal reached broader sectors of American society than the Estado Novo did in Brazil, but Vargas faced a more daunting task. Vargas was a skilled ad-ministrator who understood how to keep his own counsel, how to use delay and flattery, and how, like Roosevelt, to act with guile and sinu-ousness. Whereas the New Deal was ferociously attacked by business in-terests, Vargas's legislation drew a mostly passive response. Like Roo-sevelt's successor, Harry S Truman, Vargas's values were clear, fixed, and traditional. Both men came from small towns, disliked city glitter, and preferred the company of cronies. Vargas was personally honest, but paradoxically, like Truman, he got his start with the backing of a pow-erful political machine.[9]

8. Fredrick Pike, *FDR's Good Neighbor Policy* (Austin: University of Texas Press, 1995), 152.
9. See David Oshinsky's review of Alonzo L. Hamby, *Man of the People: A Life of Harry S Truman* (New York: Oxford University Press, 1995), in *New York Times Book Review*, October 29, 1995, 10–11.

There were great differences between the Vargas regime and the New Deal as well. Vargas, unlike FDR, did not work to synthesize opposites. Unlike the New Deal, Vargas's Estado Novo did not appeal to Brazil's social conscience. Roosevelt attacked "economic royalists" and greedy plutocrats; Vargas stayed silent. The *paulistas* still held grudges because they considered him an unsophisticated southerner – and his employment of nationalistic and corporatist measures went against the grain of the *paulista* tradition that considered politics as a tool to further their business interests. Most other Brazilians did not seem to care as much, and over time many became nostalgic for Vargas's paternalism.

In the United States, nationalism during the Roosevelt administration took the form of isolationist feelings in Congress, although most Americans remained neutral in their opinions. During wartime, the United States government created internment camps for citizens of Nisei origin, and some private citizens and small-town officials harassed Americans of German origin. In Brazil, nationalism as well as discrimination against foreign nationals came from the state. For example, the government required all holders of German passports to report weekly to police stations. Some of these were Jews who had fled the Nazis, and the police looked away while the non-Jewish Germans taunted and sometimes physically abused the refugees. The Estado Novo closed foreign-language schools, banned the importation of school books written in foreign languages, and, in 1942, rounded up and sent Axis-country nationals to internment camps in several locations, including a harsh Amazonian penal colony at Tomé-Açu in Pará.

William E. Leuchtenburg has termed Roosevelt's New Deal a halfway revolution because although it achieved a more just society by recognizing groups that had been previously unrepresented, it passed over many others, including sharecroppers, slum dwellers, and most non-whites.[10] Vargas's drive for national integration and modernization created an entrenched bureaucracy made up of functionaries and managers, but he refused to give this emerging interest group any political voice. He bypassed them in the 1950s when he addressed his populist slogans to the working class. Relatively well educated and always upwardly mobile, the urban middle class might have become a source of political support, but Vargas pushed it aside, benefiting the old elite in his actions

---

10. William E. Leuchtenburg, *Franklin D. Roosevelt and the New Deal* (New York: Harper & Row, 1963). See also his *The Supreme Court Reborn: The Constitutional Revolution in the Age of Roosevelt* (New York: Oxford University Press, 1995).

while appealing to blue-collar workers in his speeches and public statements.

Vargas left many institutions untouched, including Brazil's 1916 Civil Code, a conservative legal document that reinforced patriarchal social relations, declaring husbands the legal heads of their households and leaving married women virtually without rights. He left charity work in the hands of the private sector, although he turned charitable organizations into semipublic agencies by giving them subsidies. During the 1920s, a number of *paulista* factories had pioneered the concept of the "workers' villages" (the Vila Operária Maria Zélia, for example) in which workers were given housing and provided with a comprehensive program of social benefits, including schools, infant-care centers, chapels, and soccer teams. The archdiocese of São Paulo maintained a Metropolitan Catholic Workers' Central, with local agencies in the working-class neighborhoods of Moóca, Penha, Bras, Barra Funda, Itaquera, Ipiranga, and Lapa. The organization built children's playgrounds, showed films, and sponsored classes for women in hygiene and domestic skills. The city of São Paulo established a bureaucratic agency responsible for children's recreation; in January 1935 it came under the jurisdiction of the new Department of Culture and Recreation.

Foremost among the traditional institutions was the Santa Casa de Misericordia, long the sole source of medical assistance for the urban poor, especially in the cities of the hinterland. By the end of the war, the Santa Casa had become essentially a state charity. Other welfare organizations included the Legião Brasileira de Assistência (LBA), the Serviço Social da Indústria (SESI), and a similar agency for commercial workers (SESC). The last two, established under Dutra in 1946, were funded by a 2 percent payroll tax levied on employers. Such institutions on such a broad scale would have been inconceivable a generation before. The cost of social legislative programs to employers ranged from 20 to 26 percent of payroll expenses, not including payment for public holidays and weekly rest days, an additional 22.8 percent.[11] Even though salaries remained very low by European or North American standards, these percentages still were high. On the other hand, the degree to which employers evaded payment of social security taxes, or diverted funds from pensions and welfare institutes (as happened brazenly during the morally bankrupt Collor administration during the early 1990s), or

---

11. George Wythe, *Brazil: An Expanding Economy* (New York: Twentieth Century Fund, 1949), 243.

excluded employees from the coverage by one ruse or another, cannot be determined and likely was high.

The Estado Novo was porous enough to permit some mobilization in the form of private associations. In 1942, for example, neighborhood associations emerged in several São Paulo cities, promoting urban improvements. After 1945, more private groups organized, challenging the notion that only the state could propose change. The newly legal Communist Party established "Democratic Committees" as alternatives to official *sindicatos*, first in Belém and then in other cities. Worker committees were organized in several industries to sidestep the official unions, which continued to be controlled by the government. The year 1946 saw the creation of the Popular Campaign against Hunger, which published lists of merchants who charged excessive prices for basic food. After Vargas's election in 1950, a wave of strikes, marches, and other protests demanded that the president raise wages and combat inflation and soaring prices. Three hundred thousand workers struck in São Paulo in 1953, and nearly half a million marched in rallies in São Paulo and Rio de Janeiro. In cities people enlisted in the national Campaign against the High Cost of Living.[12]

Men benefited more than women under Vargas's legislation. The laws were written by male bureaucrats for the good of male wage earners and their dependents. It was always assumed that men headed families and that families were natural; legislation aimed at helping women who were not part of families, or even who worked to supplement family income, never was considered, although women held more than three-quarters of all teaching positions and dominated white-collar commercial and retail jobs.[13] Although Vargas's decrees were color-blind, persons of mixed race (if not pure blacks) were more likely to gain government employment than in the private sector, where hiring practices openly excluded non-Caucasians. Many citizens of color came to owe their higher economic status to the changes ushered in by Vargas's programs, if not to any conscious effort by Vargas to assist persons of color. Still he became a hero to many of them. Photographs show that blacks participated in Vargas-era rallies and activities, but typically not in any significant number.

12. Maria da Glória Cohn, *História dos Movimentos e Lutas Sociais: A Construção da Cidadania dos Brasileiros* (São Paulo: Loyola, 1995), 84–93.

13. See Theda Skocpol, *Protecting Soldiers and Mothers: The Political Origins of Social Policy in the United States* (Cambridge, Mass.: Harvard University Press, 1992), 525–526; Instituto de Economia, *Pesquisa sobre o Padrão de Vida do Comerciário do Distrito Federal* (Rio de Janeiro, n. p., 1949), 70.

The Estado Novo, as Susan K. Besse shows, borrowed from fascist practice when it empowered the state to mediate between conflicting interests within civil society. After 1937 the regime issued many new laws and decrees governing women in the work force, training, marriage, the family, social security, health, reproduction, and employment.[14] More women than men were employed as textile operatives, and as noted, most teachers, retail employees, and semiskilled workers were women. Women were ignored both by Vargas's official *sindicatos* and by independent unions both on the left and on the right (although rightist organizations tended to offer auxiliaries and other associations for women, emphasizing the woman's role in the family). When women did express their views collectively, they tended to protest work-related grievances, especially in the factory commissions that bypassed the *sindicato* system through the early 1950s, and were less political than male unionists and union leaders.

Vargas was the first Brazilian head of state to place women on his political agenda. He gave them the vote; however, this was a hollow gesture since there were no direct elections between 1933 and 1945. The regime did little to enforce regulations prescribing work conditions for women. The DIP paid homage to motherhood and the role of women as homemakers, but the government's lipservice to women and the traditional value system tended to smother impulses to mobilize feminist activities. As a result, Brazil failed to develop a women's movement of any significance. Vargas drew legitimacy from accepted assumptions about the naturalness of social hierarchy and paternal authority embodied by his role as benevolent and dependable father.[15]

Vargas's reforms principally affected people who in the United States or Western Europe would fall into the lower middle class: salaried employees to whom the government extended, for the first time, job security, pension rights, and better working conditions. Workers in this group lived under constant economic pressure, were much less economically comfortable

14. Susan K. Besse, "Crimes of Passion: The Campaign against Wife Killing in Brazil, 1910–1940," *Journal of Social History*, 22:4 (Summer 1989), 653–666, esp. 662; Baptista de Melo, "Política da família," *Arquivo Judiciário (Supplemento)*, 56 (November 5, 1940), 37–40; "Decreto-Lei N. 1.764 de 10 de Novembro de 1939: Cria a Commissão Nacional de Proteção à Família," *Boletim do Ministério do Trabalho, Indústria e Comércio*, 64 (December 1939), 92–93; Cândido de Moraes Leme, "Dos Crimes Contra a Assistência Familiar," *Anais do 1º Congresso Nacional do Ministério Público* (Rio de Janeiro, n.p., 1943), vol. 4, *Comentários ao Código Penal*, Parte Especial, 292–325.
15. Besse, *Restructuring Patriarchy*, 202.

than groups above them, and lacked a safety net to keep them from falling, in times of trouble, into the lower-class mass below them. Scorned as lacking taste and old-fashioned – public functionaries and small property owners in particular came in for mockery – they held on tenaciously to the fact that they were still considered superior to people who worked with their hands. Increased demands for specialized skills, accompanied by higher levels of professionalization across the country, prompted the creation of the civil service, which administered nationwide competitive examinations to fill many job vacancies. Moreover, a good proportion of the population did not earn the minimum wage, and it was pegged lower outside of the Center-South. On the other hand, Vargas used his wage policies to lessen traditional reliance on the export sector, strengthening the hand of the industrial elite and urban workers. The minimum wage affected both supply and demand in a complementary way.[16]

Employers regularly ignored the rules, claiming that they would have to close if they could not do so. More than anything else, this is why Vargas's sweeping social and labor legislation failed to change very much, although Vargas remained popular among the working-class Brazilians he so ardently courted. They, in turn, became the basis of his successful run for the presidency in 1950. Industrialists and employers did not care whether Vargas's rhetoric was progressive or corporative: they simply intended to block any reform that interfered with their profits. Virtually all of the strikes between 1931 and 1936, from Rio Grande do Sul to Pará, and all of the limited strikes and work stoppages that took place between 1936 and 1940, were to win rights and conditions guaranteed by law but not provided.[17] The Companhia de Tecidos Paulista, in Pernambuco, forced workers – large numbers of them women and children – to work twelve-hour days in spite of the eight-hour-day legislation. The same was true for many mills in São Paulo, where fourteen-hour days were not uncommon.[18] There were many ways of getting around regulations. Anthropologist Janice Perlman tells the story of a sixty-year-old migrant who waited six months to obtain his folder, only to be told by a manager that he could have the job if the work card was not

16. See M. C. Tavares, *Acumulação de Capital e Industrialização no Brasil*, 2nd ed., (Campinas: UNICAMP, 1986), 111.
17. Maria Célia Paoli, "Os Trabalhadores Urbanos na Fala dos Outros," in *Movimentos Sociais e Democracia no Brasil* (São Paulo: Ed. Marco Zero, 1995), 86.
18. See Stanley J. Stein, *The Brazilian Cotton Manufacture: Textile Enterprise in an Underdeveloped Area, 1850–1950* (Cambridge, Mass.: Harvard University Press, 1957).

signed, so that the firm would not have to pay social security benefits, pensions, sick-leave, and overtime rates. The man accepted the job, working a twelve-hour shift, four hours over the legal maximum, at half the minimum wage, and without any worker protection.[19] Those without any papers fared worse. Police regularly stopped buses, raided shantytowns, and otherwise demanded to see documents; those without them were charged with vagrancy.

Vargas's pragmatism allowed him to prevail in situations where others might have floundered. Unlike Mexico's Lázaro Cárdenas, who slapped foreign investors in the face by nationalizing Mexican oil, Vargas courted foreign investment, being very careful to meet debt payments, even in Depression years, because he did not want to prejudice coffee producers. Under Vargas Brazil incorporated a host of corporatist elements rooted in the country's own history and its conservative Roman Catholicism, and guided by the influence of intellectuals such as Francisco José de Oliveira Vianna, who rejected liberal democracy as weak and lacking discipline. Much of the regime's legislation was limited in effectiveness to the federal capital of Rio de Janeiro, directly under the eye of the national government. Rural and distant areas fared the worst: with the exception of public health and other hygienic programs implemented by the Americans as part of the effort to increase wartime rubber production, the lives of Brazilians in the hinterland were touched by Vargas's measures far less than in the populated cities of the coast, and in most cases not at all.

The urban and rural poor comprised about half of the Brazilian population during all of Vargas's tenure as head of state. Lacking skills and unable to work except as menials, they played only marginal roles in Vargas's new Brazil. The rural poor languished at the very bottom of the social ladder, treated in ways much like the untouchable castes in India or the Japanese Burakumin. In 1935, Sir William Seeds, the British ambassador, in a report to London, noted with anger that General Góes Monteiro had said, in his presence, that most of the Brazilian people were "like vegetables" and the rest "given to indiscipline and anarchy."[20]

19. Janice E. Perlman, *The Myth of Marginality: Urban Poverty and Politics in Rio de Janeiro* (Berkeley: University of California Press, 1976), 158.
20. Confidential Report, Petrópolis, Sir William Seeds to Sir John Simon, Foreign Office, March 1, 1935, 2002/3761/18655/3893, Public Record Office, London. See also John Ogbu, *Minority Education and Caste* (New York: Academic Press, 1978).

Sociologists contend that only external efforts to equalize the status of such castelike groups can elevate them to equal status, and clearly this did not occur in Brazil. Rural education lagged, minimum wages were not enforced in the countryside, and economic realities dashed chances for upward mobility.

Most rural Brazilians lived in thatched mud huts without plumbing or electricity. They frequently received wages below the minimum while prices for goods and supplies were high. Rural residents barely participated in the market economy. They were not consumers, and their life expectancy did not exceed four decades. The rural infant mortality rate was among the highest in the world. Insufficient diet and endemic disease, including debilitating parasitic infections, took their toll on physical stamina. The minimum rate of pay fixed by Getúlio Vargas, Stefan Zweig complained, "has not yet been able to penetrate to the interior, into the forests of Matto Grosso and Acre, parts of the world as far removed from a street as they are from a railway."[21] The earlier decades saw a flurry of attention given to rural problems, including such powerful novels as José Américo de Almeida's A Bagaceira and José Lins do Rêgo's Menino de Engenho, about life in the dying sugarcane region of the Northeast, but after the mid-1930s virtually no new socially conscious writing appeared.[22]

In the towns and villages of the hinterland, conditions were only marginally better. Pigs wandered the unpaved streets foraging for garbage. Emaciated dogs roamed the streets; dogs as well as bats carried rabies. Buildings rarely exceeded two stories and for the most part were cinderblock shells without glass windows. These towns had small numbers of educated and well-to-do people but rarely if ever a physician or a dentist. Ambitious young men from the "better families" (as they were known) of these towns and small cities often migrated to the state capital or to Rio de Janeiro to pursue their careers. Young women rarely did, because even if they could find housing with distant relatives, a young woman living away from her immediate family in a big city would be considered unsuitable for marriage or worse. Vargas's legislation had little impact in the interior. The regional agencies provided jobs but patronage overshadowed the new civil service apparatus. The lack of op-

---

21. Stefan Zweig, Brazil: Land of the Future (New York: Viking Press, 1941), 150.
22. For a treatment of urban proletarian life, see Patrícia Galvão's 1933 novel, Industrial Park, trans. Elizabeth Jackson and K. David Jackson (Lincoln: University of Nebraska Press, 1993).

portunities for employment hindered any real progress attributable to government programs. Since there was rarely any industrialization, there were no labor unions. Vargas's biggest outlay of revenue was always for transportation, but it could be said that these projects provided the biggest impact in most of the hinterland since they built the roads that permitted families to flee.

Vargas's goals were cautious. His commitment to industrialization was gradual and not without vacillation. By 1942, he had fully committed himself to using state interventionism.[23] Much of the infrastructure change accomplished by 1945 at least was the result of United States aid during the war: modern airfields, rebuilt railroads, mining and port improvements, and the new steel plant at Volta Redonda.[24] Many of Vargas's other programs came up short because he did not commit sufficient resources to carry them out and because he lacked any nationwide plan for implementation. His social legislation, much of which would remain in place through the middle 1990s,[25] was limited in scope and uneven. When the minimum wage was introduced in 1940, eligible workers in Rio de Janeiro received the equivalent of $131 a month. This was a generous amount, although workers continued to stay out of official *sindicatos*, which not only guaranteed the minimum wage but which added benefits. The national monthly minimum wage rose to the equivalent of $252 by 1954 but thereafter went into free fall, bottoming out at $120 a month in 1992.[26] Moreover, most of the population earned less than this.

Vargas's social and welfare legislation transformed not only the state's role in society but it redefined Brazilian citizenship. The Estado Novo bureaucracy, for example, required that applicants for its new public housing projects for industrial workers had to be "regulated citizens," tax-paying, wage-earning persons with all of their documents in order and approved by the board of the Institute for Retirement and Social Welfare of Industrial Workers (IAPI). These requirements were not unlike the ones set by Henry Ford's screening process for company housing in Dearborn, Michigan, except that Ford's regulations were privately im-

23. See Love, *Crafting the Third World*, 148–149.
24. See Frank D. McCann, "Brazil and World War II: The Forgotten Ally," *E.I.A.L.*, 6:2 (1995), 35.
25. Stephen Hugh-Jones, "A Glass Half-Full," *The Economist* (London), 334 (April 29, 1995), "Survey Brazil," 4.
26. Biblioteca Isaac Kertenetzy, Centro de Documentação e Disseminação de Informação do IBGE, *Revista CIDE* (April–June 1992), 14.

posed whereas the IAPI's were set by the state. In the end, Vargas's housing programs yielded a few model apartment complexes here and there but did nothing to alleviate the critical (and growing) housing shortage that afflicted all of the major cities.

Vargas's regulated citizenship was based on occupational stratification defined by legal norm, and under this system only as wage earners in good standing could workers gain access to their citizenship rights and duties.[27] Pensions, a cornerstone of Vargas's social program, were so eaten away by inflation that by the 1950s in many cases it was not worth the cost of the bus fare for pensioners to pick up their retirement checks. Traditional qualifications for voting were bent to accommodate this concept. In 1932, for example, a new ex-officio voter registration system enacted under the auspices of Vargas's first labor minister, fellow *gaúcho* Lindolfo Collor, permitted illiterates to register to vote for the Constituent Assembly if they were members of official *sindicatos*. Vargas was clearly seeking to create a pliant working-class bloc, loyal to the state and especially to his government.

Many of Vargas's initiatives produced little more than paperwork and moral self-congratulation. He lauded public school teachers as the "little, overshadowed heroes of daily life,"[28] but he did little to improve their wages. Almost all teachers were underpaid and underqualified; most lay teachers were paid little more than manual laborers. Their salaries sometimes were paid months late. At the secondary level, Brazil had fewer than a dozen no-tuition secondary schools. Vargas's educational reforms varied enormously from state to state, although Vargas's National Educational Plan, which called for free and semi-mandatory public education, was made part of the 1934 Constitution. In Rio de Janeiro, Anísio Teixeira took dramatic steps to professionalize education, expand matriculations, and to improve schools, but he was fired as being too liberal after the ANL was closed in 1935, during a wave of antiintellectualism. São Paulo achieved progress mostly under its own auspices, under the unwritten arrangement its elite had made with Vargas after 1932 to let the state carry out its own programs. The drive to modernize Brazil led Vargas to create free, comprehensive universities, but few nonelite youths who did not attend private sec-

27. See Wanderley Guilherme dos Santos, *Cidadania e Justiça* (Rio de Janeiro: Editora Campus, 1979).
28. See Vargas's 1940 speech honoring educators in the *Revista de Educação Pública*, 1:4 (October–December 1940), 472.

ondary schools could hope to pass the rigorous *vestibulários* (entrance examinations).

The state of Goiás, in the country's central plateau, epitomizes how the rest of Brazil fared. In 1930, illiteracy stood at 83.3 percent with many towns having no schools at all. The state government eagerly endorsed Vargas's educational initiatives, hoping that emphasis on education would help integrate Goiás into the national economy. But lacking resources, most of the state's educational reform initiatives took the form of regulations, creating a Potemkin village effect. Goiás adopted one of the most rigorous curricula in the nation for secondary schools, for example, but there were only a handful of secondary schools in the state. Education was declared to be essential for promoting the mentally and physically robust "new man," and the government published an educational journal; it also provided a list of approved films about Goiás, to be used in the classroom to instill positive values and to show "the blissful and abundant quality of agricultural life." But there were no projectors, and many schools lacked electricity. Goiás's interventor Pedro Ludovico made a heroic try, allocating as much as a quarter of the state budget for education between 1930 and 1937, but to little avail. By 1940, literacy had improved a scant 3.6 percent from 1920 levels.[29]

At best, Vargas's system created a framework of agencies and institutions that rationalized government services and provided a delivery system for benefits to designated recipients. We have seen that the government reached only so far. In Brazil's immense hinterland, the labor system shared features with Parchman Farm, the Mississippi prison colony created in 1904 to put inmates to work to produce profit.[30] The analogy goes only so far, but wages were so low that most Brazilians lived in austere poverty. Vargas's paternalism was severe, and because of the racial character of Brazilian privation, greater subordination was demanded from nonwhites than from whites who were poor, especially immigrants.

The contention that Vargas's reforms actually accomplished little – that programs were shallow and limited in their impact – is borne out by examining the allocation of fiscal resources under Vargas's tenure. De-

---

29. Maria de Araújo Nepomuceno, "A Illusão Pedagógica, 1930–1945: Estado, Sociedade e Educação em Goiás" (Ph.D. diss., Universidade Federal de Goiás, 1991), esp. 101, 140.
30. See David M. Oshinsky, *Parchman Farm and the Ordeal of Jim Crow Justice* (New York: Free Press, 1996).

spite his constant and growing emphasis on the need to elevate the condition of the poor, the fact is that while the government claimed to allocate between 5 and 10 percent of the national budget for public education during Vargas's tenure, it is likely that a good portion of the funds were either never delivered to needy school systems or, worse, stolen. Nor did the government encourage individuals to help. There were few taxes on income or on inherited wealth, and charitable philanthropy remained very limited. Nor did the Roman Catholic Church, historically relatively poor and socially very conservative, have a major impact in social relief. Banks never were given incentives to provide credit for small lenders to start businesses or to build housing. The federal government established an independent monetary authority, with limited powers, only in 1946, and Brazil's Central Bank was only fully established in 1964.[31]

Determining to what degree the improvements in the lives of ordinary Brazilians came about from government action rather than evolutionary change is of course elusive. During the 1930s and 1940s, many countries with different kinds of governments acquired social security systems of approximate scope. Vargas never eliminated the role of the states, many of which, especially São Paulo but also Minas Gerais and Rio Grande do Sul, initiated or maintained social programs of their own. In the stagnant municipality of Cunha, in São Paulo's Paraíba Valley, the state during the 1930s built schools, a health service, a pediatric center, an agricultural station, judicial and police facilities, a state bank, statistics and records agencies, and a meteorological station – all entities that affected the lives of its citizens in direct and indirect ways every day.[32] World War II boosted exports, brought in hard currency reserves, and increased the power of industrial labor unionists. Import substitution stimulated manufacturing, although the interruption of shipping made it nearly impossible to obtain needed tools and metals.

What must be kept in mind when evaluating the legacy of the Vargas era is the fact that most reforms were concentrated overwhelmingly in the country's two largest cities, São Paulo and Rio de Janeiro. After all, during Vargas's time all other Brazilian cities were commercial and

31. Gail D. Triner, "The Formation of Modern Brazilian Banking, 1906–1930," *Journal of Latin American Studies*, 28:1 (February 1996), 49–74.
32. See Robert W. Shirley, *The End of a Tradition: Culture Change and Development in the Município of Cunha, São Paulo, Brazil* (New York: Columbia University Press, 1971), 105–106.

service emporiums, not centers of industry. Outside the Center-South, government reform benefited producers' profits through regional agencies like the Sugar and Alcohol Institute (IAA) but gave workers neither rights to bargain in defense of their interests nor any forum to express their grievances.[33] Brazil had virtually no rural labor unions, for example, until the 1960s. Gains occurred in some places but not in others. During the 1920s and early 1930s in Minas Gerais, for example, militant workers in Belo Horizonte, the state capital, were constantly defeated when they struck for resolution of their grievances because industrialists and employers worked closely with the police and officials of the state, but in Juiz de Fora, in the same state, the success of industrial workers in allying with service workers and artisans in a common bloc and their unions' close ties to unions in Rio de Janeiro resulted in important gains.[34]

Analysis of social and economic conditions can reveal unexpected findings. Of 1,000 students entering first grade in 1942 only 155 completed three years of primary school. In 1995, sixty-five years after Vargas swept into power at the head of a victorious coup d'etat that soon declared itself to be revolutionary, and forty-one years after Vargas's death, Brazil's infant mortality rate stood at 51.6 per thousand, almost ten times worse than Spain's, a country surpassed by Brazil a decade earlier in aggregate economic output.[35] That conditions were even worse in preceding decades, when Vargas's social legislation was enacted, hints at the magnitude of the problems faced by government planners and at the shallow impact of the Vargas-era programs. At the end of World War II, life expectancy in southern states was eight years higher than the national average and sixteen years more than in the long-depressed Northeast. Vargas had done little for the poor regions of the country.

Vargas's Role

Vargas's suicide in 1954 produced outpourings of grief that matched in intensity and scope the heartfelt shock felt by most Americans at the death of Franklin D. Roosevelt in 1945. Even though Vargas had not

33. Anthony W. Pereira, *The End of the Peasantry: The Rural Labor Movement in Northeast Brazil, 1961–1988* (Pittsburgh: University of Pittsburgh Press, 1997), 26–27.
34. Eliana Regina de Freitas Dutra, *Caminhos Operários nas Minas Gerais* (São Paulo: HUCITEC Editora, 1988), 196–197.
35. *Brazil News*, March 8, 1995, 1.

provided very much, and even if the archaic hierarchical structure of the Brazilian oligarchy had remained completely intact, he was the first politician to extend dignity to the Brazilian people. The contrast between the political spirit of the Old Republic, which despised the common people, and the uplifting rhetoric of Vargas's radio broadcasts and speeches and public appearances, which reached even to the most remote reaches of the vast country, was striking. Vargas really had become the father of the poor in the minds of the mass of the population. And for nationalists, the stridency of his admonition against imperialism and foreign interests that dominated his suicide letter confirmed that he was a prophet and seer. In some ways Vargas's alarm paralleled his contemporary Dwight D. Eisenhower's warning to Americans about the "civil-military complex," but whereas Eisenhower was ignored, in Vargas's case his campaign against foreign domination galvanized a certain sector of public opinion, even though it yielded to the developmentalism of Kubitschek and of the military regime of the 1960s and 1970s.

Vargas left his mark on Brazil during his entire career, but it was especially the Estado Novo that left a lasting influence. Its inheritance was not of laws and degrees but of individuals. Many of the Vargas-era players remained on the stage for years after his death.[36] Francisco Campos, the author of the 1937 Constitution, played a major role in the 1964 military coup, and Felinto Müller, the detested chief of police, sat during the most repressive years of the dictatorship in the Senate as president of ARENA, the hard-line party. Amaral Peixoto, Vargas's son-in-law, became the governor of Rio de Janeiro, and Adhemar de Barros, fired as interventor of São Paulo by Vargas in 1941, surfaced as a Vargas ally during the 1950s famous for his cynical label, "He steals, but he gets things done."

Vargas, as well as the populist presidents who followed him, raised public expectations precariously. Vargas oversaw the expansion of the electorate to unprecedented levels of participation, and the 1946 Constitution, in what for some was a fit of idealism (but for others was a cynical manipulation), made voting a required act, a risky business in a country with one of the worst public school systems in the hemisphere. The long periods of authoritarian rule under Vargas and again under the post-1964 military dictatorship ill-equipped new generations of voters

36. On the inheritance of the Estado Novo, see Kurt von Mettenheim, *The Brazilian Voter: Mass Politics in Democratic Transition, 1974–1986* (Pittsburgh: University of Pittsburgh Press, 1995), 79–81.

to handle open electoral campaigns. By the 1980s, when all Brazilians over *sixteen* were required to vote, electoral politics became a contest fueled by advertising agencies, sound bites, and fifteen-second television spots. The raised expectations of the populist years carried forward to the Carnival-like atmosphere of the 1950s campaigns. The proliferation of personality-based political parties and shifting electoral alliances based on deal making, culminated in the election of Fernando Collor in 1990, who would be impeached and forced to resign from office for blatant corruption.

It is speculative at best to distinguish between changes attributable specifically to Vargas and his government and those brought about automatically by the evolving and modernizing government structure. All Western governments became increasingly bureaucratized during the twentieth century, providing state administrators at all levels with the power to share and select state policy.[37] In democracies, one of the ways new policies are weighed is in terms of the success or failure of previous policies. In the Brazilian case, however, the sharp and abrupt transitions from one kind of regime to another after 1930, and the wholesale substitution in the cast of administrators and political appointees, made this much less the case. Nor were Estado Novo technocrats particularly interested in the successes of previous governments, since their endorsement of corporatism gave them a ready guide by which to administer. The same was true for Dutra in 1945 and Vargas in 1950 and, to a lesser degree, Kubitschek in 1956; each plunged ahead with new initiatives although at the same time tacitly preserving the old hierarchies and power framework, resulting in very little change actually being undertaken. Vargas's social security system lasted for decades – only in the mid-1990s did private pension funds begin to supplement the universal state-run system to any real extent[38] – even though the state system was almost always considered inadequate.

In the mid-1950s, nearly four in ten Brazilians still lived below the poverty line, equal in number to Brazil's entire population in 1930. Given large expenditures in the public sector for improving sanitation, health, and water supply in the 1970s, and given the growing diversification of the urban economy after 1950, it is apparent that during Var-

---

37. Robert Hanneman and J. Rogers Hollingsworth, "Refocusing the Debate on the Role of the State in Capitalist Societies," in Rolf Torstendahl, ed., *State Theory and State History* (London: Sage, 1992), 42, 38–61.
38. James Brooke, in *New York Times*, September 10, 1994, 17, 25.

gas's time the percentage must have been much higher. Poverty in rural areas has always been pervasive, and before 1955 the national population was much more rural than it is today. From 60 to 65 percent of all northeasterners were living below the poverty line in 1994; the figure may have been double that in earlier decades. Of all areas of life badly affected by public policy deficiencies, researchers identified housing and education, finding housing infrastructure rapidly deteriorating.[39] This summarizes Vargas's social legacy as well: his reforms almost never reached those who needed it the most.

Vargas's laws were never intended to close the vast gap between rich and poor. Only laws based on concepts of redistributive justice could have brought real change, but this was alien in concept to Vargas and the upper classes. Vargas's reforms raised the quality of life for millions but distanced the lives of millions even further from the affluent. They modernized Brazil, but they did not do much to enlarge the domestic market, or to deal with underemployment, or to facilitate the acquisition of land, or to provide technical training, or to remove the pariah status of men and women doomed by lack of opportunity to grinding poverty. The period between 1939 and the early 1970s yielded increased real wages for industrial workers (industrial wages rose 60 percent between 1939 and 1975) but witnessed a decline in real wages and living conditions for unskilled workers, the vast majority.[40]

Many Brazilians had concrete reasons to revere Vargas. He gave benefits to salaried workers and he instituted the minimum wage. Employees of the new government cartels (in the steel industry, in cement, in petroleum refining, among others) genuinely gained in many ways. But most Brazilians did not work for Petrobrás or Electrobrás[41] or Volta Redonda. The manipulation of Vargas's image, however, extended even to his suicide letter, the published version of which was edited by someone else, probably J. S. Maciel Filho. The letter was too self-serving, too political, to be consistent with Vargas's lifelong ability to distance himself from events. "After years of domination and looting by international economic and financial groups," the letter claimed, "I made myself chief

39. See Lúcio Kowarick, ed., Social Struggles and the City: The Case of São Paulo (New York: Monthly Review Press, 1994).

40. J. Wells, "Industrial Accumulation and Living Standards in the Long-Run: The São Paulo Industrial Working Class, 1930–1975," Journal of Development Studies, 19:2–3 (1985), two parts; Paul Cammack, "Brazil: The Triumph of 'Savage Capitalism'," Bulletin of Latin American Research (1984), 117–130.

41. The petroleum and electric power cartels created by Vargas in the 1950s.

of an unconquerable revolution. I began the work of liberation and I in-stituted a regime of social liberty. I had to resign, but I returned to gov-ern in the arms of the people." Perhaps, but the words were not his, and the self-pity too pointed. Vargas never created a regime of social liberty, and his revolution proved to be less than unconquerable because it was not taken seriously by many of its own makers.

Structural changes introduced by Vargas's provisional government increased the number of government workers significantly, and, as the result of the introduction of civil service methods for hiring bureaucrats later in the decade, public employment became possible for legions of persons lacking traditional patronage connections. Although these jobs often did not always pay very well, government employment, especially as *funcionários* – the generic term for functionaries – became very desir-able. For one thing, while commercial white-collar employees had to work twelve hours a day, government workers often only worked five or six hours a day, leaving time for other activities – including second jobs.

Why did Fernando Henrique Cardoso after his election in 1994 an-nounce that his presidential administration would represent "the end of the Vargas era" in Brazilian history?[42] What Cardoso meant was that he hoped to terminate the interventionist nature of Brazil's government and its corporatist framework. At the same time, Cardoso's efforts were accompanied by a Vargas-like personal political style: meeting in private with a handful of prominent people and cutting backroom deals (al-though, unlike Getúlio, having reports of the negotiations leaked to the press).[43]

Economic development under Vargas created work for engineers, economists, accountants, and managers. Because it was tied more than ever to international factors beyond its control, in the postwar years fluc-tuating conditions sometimes caused skilled craftsmen and artisans to lose their independence and to sink into the industrial work force. White-collar employees were poorly paid but they enjoyed higher status than industrial workers, many of whom earned more. Starting in 1923,

42. See Luiz Werneck Vianna, "O coroamento da Era Vargas e o fim da História do Brasil," *Dados*, 38:1 (1995), 163–172.
43. Cardoso understands the irony of attacking Vargas's legacy while preserving his style. He told William C. Smith in 1983 that he had found that politics has a "different logic" than academics, and referred to Max Weber's essay "Politics As a Vocation." In 1996, Cardoso targeted inertia and favoritism as remnants of the past that needed to be exorcised from government (*Jornal do Brasil*, April 3, 1996, 1). Courtesy of William C. Smith.

with the creation of a pension and retirement bank for railway workers, and stretching through the 1930s (when the government centralized social welfare administrative units), Vargas's social security system on one hand never achieved universal coverage and was mired in bureaucracy, but on the other hand by the end of the Vargas era it rivaled or excelled the principal Latin American countries in terms of coverage.[44] Whether one sees the Brazilian glass as half-filled, taking into consideration the sheer size of Brazil's needs, or half-empty, dwelling on its failings, depends on what one is looking for.

The rules changed after 1950 when Vargas won the presidency combining support from traditional machine politicians (in Minas, especially, and from the corrupt personalist Adhemar de Barros machine in São Paulo) and labor unions. But it was one thing to govern by decree and by private negotiations with industrialists, hand-picked interventors, and generals. The press, smarting from the years of censorship, celebrated its new freedom by creating a circuslike atmosphere and by refusing to give Vargas, as elected president, the deference that had been calculatingly demanded under the Estado Novo. Most leading newspaper publishers distrusted his populist bent. Popular support for Vargas ebbed in reaction to a new economic predicament – high inflation – that Vargas inherited for the most part from the Dutra government's fiscal policies in its last years when it abandoned its moderate stance and printed currency in response to deficits. To win $300 million in United States economic aid in late 1952, Vargas raised taxes, a step demanded by the Joint Brazil–United States Economic Development Commission but one that permitted opposition politicians to pillory him. During 1952 and 1953, only half of the promised funds were made available, and, although Vargas prevailed on Washington ultimately to make good on most of its promises, he had been embarrassed publicly. His enemies attempted to impeach him and remove him from office.

"My adversaries, in the heat of their attacks," he told his audience on Labor Day, 1952, "continue to assail me for being, at the same time, 'Father of the Poor' and 'Father of the Rich.'" This was his paradox, and he never was able to overcome it. He wanted to aid the working class, but he knew that employers would not stand for far-reaching reform, and he always pulled back. Ultimately his pragmatism alienated many. His op-

---

44. Maurício C. Coutinho and Cláudio Salm, "Social Welfare," in Bacha and Klein, *Social Change in Brazil: The Incomplete Transition* (Albuquerque: University of New Mexico Press, 1989), 238.

portunistic about-face in 1951, when he allied himself with rank-and-file workers against the *pelego*-run *sindicatos* he had created, rankled his enemies, who called him a man lacking in principles. So did his habit of making up with former enemies. It had been easier to get away with this as authoritarian head of state. Now, the contradictions in his political style caught up with him. Industrial employers bridled at the wage increases and other concessions to workers and happily abandoned him in 1945; leftists called him "father of profit-making sharks."[45]

Vargas's developmentalist goals were stymied by wartime realities and by the fact that unrestricted imports wiped out Brazil's foreign exchange reserves, although Brazil did gain considerable technology transfer, new equipment, and improved infrastructure as a result of its alliance with the United States. After the 1950 election, his government provided direct subsidies for industrialization in an effort to shake off reliance on imports, to enlarge the domestic market, and to provide jobs. This policy was embraced even more aggressively during the late 1950s by Juscelino Kubitschek, who extended subsidies to private investment in favored sectors, especially automobile manufacturing.

Analysis by economists of structural breaks in Brazil's economy during the Vargas period suggests that Vargas had an important (but not pervasive) effect on Brazil's economic development. Brazil moved from being a largely agrarian society with some light industry to a largely urban, industrial society with major heavy industry. The changes accomplished under his long tenure, most of which were implemented between 1950 and 1954, were not substantial enough to lead to significant structural change in the overall index of manufacturing output. Vargas's economic policies stimulated Brazil's recovery from the Depression while they enabled him to diversify the economy by stressing industrialization.[46] The stimulus provided to both public and private steel firms had long-term effects, and Volta Redonda remains a showcase model community in terms of its benefits for its employees and their families, despite its high levels of environmental pollution.

The Estado Novo's industrial relations system was based on forced harmony. The struggling organized labor movement was deprived of its

45. See Limeiro Tejo, *Brasil: Problema de um Continente* (São Paulo: Edições Arquimedes, 1964), 28.

46. Hassan Arvin-Rad, Maria J. Willumsen, and Ann Dryden Witte, "Brazilian Industrialization under Vargas: Structural Breaks and Continuities," forthcoming in the *Journal of Development Economics* (1998).

independence by the state control that was imposed in exchange for state paternalism.[47] The Labor Ministry could easily find "irregularities" in any part of the union apparatus it desired to repress. Elections could be nullified, union officials fired, and bank accounts seized.[48] In theory, both labor unions and employers' associations became *sindicatos*, amicably negotiating contracts, wages, and working conditions without recourse to strikes or harassment. True to the corporatist model, decisions would actually be made on a tripartite basis, with the state as the third party. The regime's technocrats believed that this system would boost productivity and avoid conflict. Labor *sindicatos* were expected to act in a dual fashion: as representatives of their membership but also as representatives of the state. There was a strong nationalist dimension to this model. In 1931, Vargas had issued the law of the Nationalization of Labor, decreeing that all firms have a work force at least two-thirds Brazilian-born, and under the Estado Novo only Brazilian citizens could apply for *sindicato* membership or file claims with the Estado Novo's conciliation commissions and labor courts.[49]

When intellectuals considered Vargas's legacy they tended to dwell on sweeping theories, not the struggles (and small triumphs) of the lives of ordinary people. Writers saw what they wanted to see, underestimating the attractiveness of Vargas's favors for employed workers, expecting that the working class as a whole would band together in enthusiastic solidarity to fight for their grievances. Few intellectuals understood or acknowledged the compelling power of traditional interpersonal relations, the enduring paternalistic ties, for example, between workers and employers, the underemployed and their patrons. They ignored – or possibly did not know about – the existence of the vast unofficial (underground) informal economy, which complicated worker–employer relations. Labor relations in Brazil had always been highly personalized. This, more than many other factors,

47. Barbara Weinstein, "The Model Worker of the Paulista Industrialists: The 'Operário Padrão' Campaign, 1964–1985," *Radical History Review*, 61 (1995), 92.
48. Biorn Maybury-Lewis, *The Politics of the Possible: The Brazilian Rural Workers' Trade Union Movement, 1964–1985* (Philadelphia: Temple University Press, 1994), 1–2.
49. George Reid Andrews, *Blacks and Whites in São Paulo, Brazil, 1888–1988* (Madison: University of Wisconsin Press, 1991), 147. In Cuba, Gerardo Machado's Law of the 50 Percent, requiring that half of all employees of commercial and manufacturing firms be Cuban-born, led to a wave of riots against immigrants, especially Jews. See Robert M. Levine, *Tropical Diaspora* (Gainesville: University Press of Florida, 1993).

may explain the failure of the Vargas government's labor unions to attract more than a handful of members despite the benefits they conferred.[50]

There were other reasons for the failure of Vargas's unions. Many of them had almost as many bureaucrats as rank-and-file members. During the early 1940s the labor minister paid cash bonuses to bring new members into the fold. Only Brazilian citizens were permitted to join unions, excluding large numbers of foreign-born workers in the southern states, but no steps were taken to change this policy. The way the government unions operated also drove away potential members. The Labor Ministry hand-picked union leaders; dissidents were thrown out. Anyone who wished to speak at union meetings had to show his identity cards. Strikes were outlawed after 1937. Since unions were financed by the obligatory union tax, labor officials had no incentives to enlarge membership because this would stretch resources. And although all workers paid the union tax, to join a union they had to make a small additional dues payment, a burden for heads of families struggling to live on their incomes, always extremely low. Members enjoyed benefits not offered to others (vacation colonies, sports teams, food cooperatives, medical clinics, subsidized bars inside their headquarters), but these incentives were apparently not attractive enough to recruit new members.

Vargas's civil service reforms attempted to curb patronage but in the end the old system stubbornly survived, although in a more limited form. Persons seeking bank jobs, for example, customarily had *apadrinhos* (godfathers) to help them get hired, promoted, and otherwise advance in their careers. These patrons were sometimes members of landholding families or, especially as time passed, important clients of the bank whose economic weight gave them leverage. In the 1930s, banks began to hold competitive examinations when jobs opened, although patronage still mattered when decisions came down to selection among many well-qualified applicants. Still, many Brazilians for the first time were able to aspire to jobs never before open to them. Most did not make it to become lawyers, physicians, or engineers, but the public sector provided white-collar jobs that carried with them the desired status of the nonmanual trades.[51]

---

50. See Mark Dineen, *Listening to the People's Voice* (London and New York: Keegan Paul International, 1996), 154–158.
51. Leticia Bicalho Canedo, *O Sindicalismo Bancário em São Paulo* (São Paulo: Ed. Símbolo, 1978), 30. See also the novel by Sra. Leandro Dupré, *Eramos Seis* (São Paulo: Companhia Editora Nacional, 1943), on the aspirations of urban middle-class family members in São Paulo.

The weak foundations of Brazilian democracy during Vargas's final term were Vargas's own legacy, but one man cannot be blamed entirely for the changes of the postwar world. Indeed, Vargas's efforts to transform Brazil from a collection of twenty semiautonomous states to a modern nation could not have succeeded had there not been an accompanying revolution in technology and in the delivery of information – from passenger airplanes to network radio to publishing chains to the integrative influences of professional sports. Even if Vargas's reforms had less of a permanent effect on Brazilian life than the bureaucratic planners of the 1930s and 1940s had hoped for, by the decade of his death, the 1950s, many aspects of life had been radically altered. The expanded complexity of government and the economy, accelerated by the enhanced role given to central government agencies but probably inevitable regardless of the regime in power, accompanied a new free-market atmosphere in which traditional status designations had yielded, in most cases, to the idea of acquired status. Outsiders, then, for the first time enjoyed access to positions of importance, in contrast to earlier times, when jobs were filled almost exclusively through personal connections. Still, some forty thousand federal positions were withheld from civil service postings, giving the executive tremendous leverage to broker patronage deals.

For years Vargas's propagandists attempted to portray him as larger than life, but this effort never rang true, and most Brazilians preferred to see him as a homespun man who liked to ride horses, someone who was like them. It is interesting that although he did nothing specifically for nonwhite Brazilians, black and mixed-race people cherished his name, just as American blacks loved President Roosevelt, although he accepted racial segregation. Vargas mastered the art of addressing ordinary people, and he never drew a line in the sand between the "people" and the upper classes. Nor did Vargas call for the redefinition of property rights, or for redistribution of wealth, as did Juan Perón in Argentina. Vargas's language, puffed up and moralistic, put people to sleep. His government, despite its trappings of nationalistic theater, like Salazar's Portugal, Franco's Spain, and France's first Vichy government, never imposed a strong ideological framework, and it relied on simplistic propaganda that few educated Brazilians took seriously.

Why he ultimately opted to kill himself, of course, can never be known. Given that Vargas hid his emotions even from himself – his diaries reveal this clearly – he may, when his world started to fall in on him, have been no longer able to suppress his innermost feelings of disappointment. A guarded and self-involved personality, Vargas was probably more driven by his need to achieve his unrealistic goals than he ever showed. Such persons, if they cannot strike back at their adversaries, are capable of harming themselves when thwarted. All leaders are confronted with the need to rationalize when their policies go awry, and in Vargas's case – unlike the case of Richard Nixon, who imagined that his enemies were out to get him – his opponents in the military were on the verge of physically ousting him for the second time in a decade.[52] His suicide letter implies that deep down he may have been far more consumed by the need to achieve his goals, by then wholly unattainable, than has ever been suspected.

Affluent Brazilians understood that the government's propaganda machine, in the words of Hernane Tavares de Sá, had "inflated outrageously" the concrete accomplishments being claimed; they also knew that their problems had not been solved, nor had their standard of living risen as far as the broadcasts and speeches promised.[53] But Vargas had made them aware of Brazil's vulnerable place in the world, and from the first days of his Liberal Alliance presidential campaign in 1930 he had let them know that he cared about all Brazilians, not just the powerful. To the lower half of the population with barely enough to eat, this mattered little, although many of these men and women nostalgically considered Vargas the "father of the poor" anyway. It was enough that he had spoken in their behalf. If Vargas was Brazil's "father," he treated his children differently, ignoring those with darker skin and who lived in the countryside with benign neglect, favoring those of his "children" who he considered to have the potential to carry out his dreams of national construction. Yet that he did not treat his fellow Brazilians equally did not diminish the adulation that millions held for him. When confronted with these facts, ordinary people would shrug and say: O presidente sempre lembrou da gente ("the president always remembered us").

---

52. The psychoanalyst Blema S. Steinberg makes this point about Lyndon Johnson and Richard Nixon in her penetrating *Shame and Humiliation: Presidential Decision-Making on Vietnam* (Pittsburgh: University of Pittsburgh Press, 1996).
53. Hernane Tavares de Sá, quoted in the *Washington Post*, August 28, 1954, 1.

CHRONOLOGY

1883   (April) Getúlio Vargas is born in São Borja, Rio Grande
        do Sul.

1898   Vargas enlists in the 6th Army Battalion in São Borja.

1900   Vargas enters military school at Rio Pardo.

1904   Vargas leaves the military and enrolls in law school in
        Porto Alegre.

1909   (March) Vargas is elected to Rio Grande do Sul Chamber
        of Deputies.

1911   Vargas marries Darcy de Lima Sarmanho.

1916   Vargas is elected to state senate and in the following year
        is named majority leader.

1921   Carlos Chagas Reform Law of 1921 offers health care for
        some municipal workers.

1923   Eloy Chaves Law creates a national labor council, estab-
        lished to advise on matters relating to railway workers. Leg-
        islation is passed mandating creation of funds for retire-
        ment and survivors' pensions. Covered are railroad workers
        with ten years' service with exclusions for serious miscon-
        duct or *force majeure*. No other workers are covered.

(May) Vargas is seated in the federal Chamber of Deputies. Civil War erupts in Rio Grande.

1924   Vargas becomes a leader of the state congressional delegation.

1925   The National Labor Council (Conselho Nacional do Trabalho) starts operation, made up of five persons each representing employers, workers, officials, and economists. Their job was to recommend labor policy on workmen's compensation, pensions, and worker vacations. Sunday rest and the eight-hour workday become legal norms, although most employers ignored them. Protection is extended to dock workers a year later.

1926   (March) Vargas is named finance minister.

            Limits are imposed on right of factories to use workers under sixteen for more than six hours a week but are rarely enforced.

1927   Vargas resigns, then runs unopposed for president (governor) of Rio Grande do Sul.

            Federal Code of Minors is enacted to protect children under eighteen in the work force but is not enforced.

1928   (January) Vargas takes office in Porto Alegre.

1929   After Wall Street Crash, coffee exports plummet, unemployment rises, and imported goods become much more expensive.

            Vargas accepts the Liberal Alliance nomination for presidency.

1930   (January) Vargas calls for legislation for urban and rural workers to guarantee education, health, housing, vacations, leisure, minimum salary, consumers cooperatives, pensions, social security, and protection for women, children, the infirm, and the elderly. Specifics are vague.

(March) The presidential election is won by Júlio Prestes de Albuquerque.

(March) Vargas's vice-presidential candidate, João Pessoa, is assassinated.

(October) The Liberal Alliance launches an armed uprising against government.

(November) Vargas takes power as chief of the provisional government.

Union membership nationwide totals 270,000, with 4,000 more in illegal Communist groups and 2,000 in illegal anarcho-syndicalist cells. The largest single union represents Rio de Janeiro's white-collar workers, some 30,000 strong.

1930–1931   The Labor and Education Ministries are created.

Educational reforms are advanced in Rio de Janeiro under Anísio Teixeira.

The impact of Great Depression is severe.

1931   "Two-thirds" law, requiring two-thirds of a firm's employees to be native-born, is decreed.

Public service employees are eligible for pensions.

1932   Work booklets (*carteira de trabalho*) for all employees are required.

(July) São Paulo revolts but then surrenders within two months.

The Instituto de Previdência do Funcionário Públicos da União (to aid federal employees) is created.

1933   Miners become eligible for pensions.

           Members of the Constituent Assembly are named.

1934   (July) Constitution is approved; Vargas is given a four-year term as president.

           Bank employees and commercial workers become eligible for pensions.

           Hora do Brasil radio broadcasts begin.

1935   Labor Ministry issues national codes for union organization and sets forth the obligations of union members. Compensation for dismissal without just cause is promised. Government receives right to intervene if unions engage in political activity or illegal strikes. Employers are forbidden to refuse to negotiate with recognized unions, which were to receive benefits only for their members.

           (November) Communist-led insurrections occur in Natal, Recife, and Rio de Janeiro.

1935–1936   An industrial spurt occurs.

1936   (September) The National Security law makes Brazil a police state.

1937   (November) The Estado Novo dictatorship ends state autonomy, suppresses independent labor unions, and outlaws strikes.

           Federal institutes to aid regional production and sales of sugar, alcohol, salt, maté tea, and pine products are established.

1938   Health clinics are instituted for members of officially sanctioned unions.

Industrial workers in government unions become eligible for pensions.

Public Administration Department (DASP) is established.

Brazil defaults on foreign debt (again in 1939).

(May) After Integralist *putsch,* the party is banned, as are all other political parties. Foreign languages are prohibited in schools and the press.

1939   Nationalistic laws under Estado Novo make foreign investment more difficult; industrial development becomes the leading goal of the regime.

Syndicalist Law dissolves all nonrecognized unions. Unions are prohibited from engaging in politics or from affiliating with international labor organizations or foreign labor unions. Only one union is allowed each job category or craft.

World War II begins in Europe.

1940   (May) Minimum wage legislation goes into effect, but is weakened by loopholes by which individual workers – and sometimes all workers in a given industry – could be excluded from coverage.

New penal code is established.

The national adult illiteracy rate is 65 percent.

A federal agency is created that later would become the National Steel Commission (CSN). Construction is started on Volta Redonda steel mill.

U.S. Army–funded Special Service for Public Health (SESP) extends sanitation works to regions in the hinterland, especially rubber-producing areas of the Amazon.

1941   (December) Japanese attack Pearl Harbor, bringing United States into war.

1942   (January) Brazil breaks relations with Axis powers.

            (August) Brazil declares war on Reich.

1943   New labor code provides for Sunday vacations, paid vacations, old-age compensation, accident insurance, low-cost meals at work, housing loans, vocational training schools, severance pay, and the eight-hour day, but all are selectively enforced, if at all, in most parts of Brazil.

            (May) Vargas agrees to call elections after the war ends.

1944   Brazilian Expeditionary Force leaves for Italy.

1945   (February) Rio's *Correio da Manhã* defies censorship and publishes article calling for elections, and Vargas agrees.

            (June) Brazil declares war on Japan.

            (July–August) PSD and UDN select Generals Dutra and Gomes as candidates.

            (October) Vargas is ousted.

            (December) Dutra is elected president. Vargas is elected senator by two states and federal deputy by seven.

1946   (September) A new constitution is established. Estado Novo is ended. Suffrage is broadened and made compulsory.

            Steel production begins at Volta Redonda.

1947   Ministry of Education, aided to a small extent by private initiative, claims to be providing classes for more than 500,000 pupils. Social security covers 3,000,000 full-time workers. Also, 2,760 free rural schools are ready for use but many have no teachers due to lack of funds for teacher salaries.

The Communist Party is declared illegal.

1948 SESP sprays Amazonian sites against malaria.

Commission of the Valley of São Francisco funds the construction of forty-three hospitals with a total of eighteen hundred beds in rural places lacking hospitals.

1950 (October) Vargas is elected president with 48.7 percent of the total vote.

1951 (January) Vargas assumes office. The CNPq, the Brazilian equivalent of the National Science Foundation of the United States, is created. The CNPq funds atomic energy research.

1952 Banco Nacional do Desenvolvimento Econômico (BNDE) and the Banco do Nordeste Brasileiro are established.

1953 The state petroleum agency, Petrobrás, is created.

1954 A federal agency to construct hydroelectric power plants in the São Francisco region is created, and a second steel refinery at Volta Redonda opens.

(August) Vargas commits suicide on the eve of a military coup to oust him. João Café Filho is sworn in as president.

CONTEMPORARY SOURCES

DOCUMENTS

"THE SOCIAL QUESTION"
(FROM THE PLATFORM OF THE LIBERAL ALLIANCE, 1930)

One cannot negate the existence of a social question in Brazil as one of the problems that will have to be dealt with seriously by public authorities. The little that we have in terms of social legislation either is not applied or only in tiny measures, sporadically, in spite of the promises that have been made by us as signers of the Versailles Treaty and of our responsibilities as members of the International Labor Organization, whose conventions and regulations we fail to observe. . . . The activities of women and children in factories and commercial establishments in every civilized nation are subject to special conditions which we, up to now, unfortunately do not heed. We need to coordinate activities between the states and the federal government to study and adopt measures to create a national Labor Code. Both the urban and rural proletariat require instructional measures, applied to both, to address their respective needs. These measures should include instruction, education, hygiene, diet, housing, protection of women and children, of invalids and old people, credit, salary relief, and even recreation, including sports and artistic culture. It is time to think of creating agricultural schools and industrial training centers, of making factories and mills safe, bringing sanitation to the countryside, constructing workers' villas, granting vacations, a minimum salary, consumer cooperatives, and so forth.[1]

---

1. Translated by author from flyer handed out on street corners, Porto Alegre, 1930 (Robert M. Levine collection).

GETÚLIO VARGAS'S FIRST DIARY ENTRY
OCTOBER 3, 1930

. . . Everything is ready, all steps have been taken. It should be for 5:00 P.M. today. What will be the fate of this uncertain adventurous step? It is impossible to summarize what has happened so far. During the morning, I met with the secretary to the president [governor] of Rio Grande do Sul, with whom I dictated the day's correspondence and gave him a draft of the revolutionary manifesto to type in final form, to be distributed tomorrow. I wrote it last night, reading it to Oswaldo Aranha and Flores da Cunha. . . . At 11:30 . . . I prepared for the day, lunched quietly with my family, and went to play a game of ping-pong with my wife as we do every day at this time . . . 4:30. The hour is growing near. I examined myself and found myself to be with the tranquil spirit that one has when he has thrown down a gauntlet because he finds no other dignified departure from the state in which he finds himself. I do not care about my own fate, but am concerned about the responsibility I have for an act that will decide the destiny of the collectivity. This group supports entering into struggle, at least its most healthy, vigorous, and active elements. Will deception follow? How can a government whose function is to maintain order turn revolutionary? And if we lose? I will be assigned the blame, as one who was ambitious, who knows? I feel that only the sacrifice of one's own life can rescue one from the error of failure.[2]

VARGAS'S MANIFESTO TO THE PEOPLE OF SÃO PAULO,
1932, IN THE MIDST OF THE CIVIL WAR

São Paulo is isolated. All of the attempts to bring others in to the sedition against the government have failed. Every day the federal troops are closing the circle around the *paulista* forces. . . . There is no desire to annihilate or humiliate São Paulo, only to bring it back into the national union. . . . Personally, as chief of state, this does not make me feel good, and I have no feelings for any need for vengeance. At the front of the Provisional Government, installed by the 1930 Revolution, I cannot abide any reactionary movement that attempts to seize power under the pretext of a false call for constitutionalism. . . . The government will

2. Getúlio Vargas, *Diário*, vol. 1, *1930–1936* (Rio de Janeiro: Siciliano/Fundação Getúlio Vargas, 1995), 3–4.

never refuse to listen to appeals for peace. . . . The primary objective of my serene and conciliatory message is to avoid further bloodshed by our brothers and the material sacrifices caused by the rebellion. It is consuming great fortunes, and causes deep wounds in the soul of the national spirit.[3]

DIARY ENTRY
NOVEMBER 26–27, 1935

I was awakened early and informed of the [insurrection]; I got up at 4 A.M. and followed things via telephone. At dawn, many friends, especially members of Congress, came to the palace. The news was inexact, and there were so many people I couldn't work. I decided to visit the zones where fighting had taken place to see for myself. I went first to Praia Vermelha . . . I went to the hospital, spoke with some of the police investigators, and returned; then I went to the headquarters of the War Ministry. . . . [At the end of the day] I returned to Catete to take care of routine business. I kept receiving many visitors, deputies, and senators. I have the impression that the prestige of our government has really increased.[4]

VARGAS'S EXPLANATION OF THE NEED FOR THE ESTADO NOVO
APRIL 1938

We never have had a truly Brazilian constitution, one that deals with the scope of our vast problems. We have an immense and underpopulated territory with a poorly fed, undereducated, and badly served population. . . . We have periodic droughts and flooding, problems of providing sanitary services that challenge our engineers. Perhaps I erred in not fighting more to make the executive more than simply the figurehead on the bow of a ship. . . . For months and months we have had emergency laws to rescue agriculture from its crisis, to resolve vital problems, or to avoid public calamities. . . . The conditions, whether economic or financial or political, were not there to give us the luxury of pretending to be a democracy. Do you appreciate the costs of an election, not only in money but in time, in personal attacks, in prejudicial costs to a people seeking to move forward? We will have in a short time

3. Translated by author from leaflet, São Paulo, 1932 (Robert M. Levine collection).
4. Diário, 1:446–447.

to confront a very serious situation, perhaps a war, and to take difficult steps belying the poetic supposition that we are free in our own house. . . . The 1937 Constitution is only a trial, a transitory experiment, to take us through the storm that is approaching with a minimum of sacrifice possible.[5]

LETTER FROM NORBERT A. BOGDAN
AN AGENT FOR THE J. HENRY SCHROEDER BANKING CORPORATION
STATIONED IN BRAZIL, 1938

Of all living statesmen of the world today, [he] is without a doubt the coldest, most rational, and cynical one. Emotion of any kind he does not know. . . . He is a man for whom the words "Loyalty" and "consideration" have no meaning. . . . What we today see in Brazil is a dictatorship which is naturally a highly [authoritarian] one but which is neither truly fascist nor totalitarian. . . . In fact it is no system at all and there is no clear or preconceived ideology or doctrine back of it. Vargas had none and still doesn't have any. It is simply Getúlio Vargasism supported by the armed forces and now engaged in picking from the various forms of government at present practiced in different parts of the world.[6]

LETTER FROM M. S. HULL, A FOREIGN RESIDENT, TO
GUSTAVO CAPANEMA, MINISTER OF EDUCATION AND HEALTH, RIO
APRIL 21, 1942

Will you permit me to express my appreciation of the way in which, in your reform of the educational system of Brazil, you have safeguarded, or rather, restored the old classical culture of this country, while providing for the increased needs of science and industrial development that a great modern state demands? In the process of transforming a rich, young country into the vast, intricate mechanism that a state is today, there is always a danger of neglecting the humanities as being decorative rather than useful. This danger you have perceived and avoided, and in the splendid future which Providence has indubitably destined for Brazil

5. Recounted by Alzira Vargas do Amaral Peixoto, *Getúlio Vargas, Meu Pai* (Porto Alegre: Globo, 1960), 366–371.
6. National Archives, Washington, D.C., Record Group 59, B, letter to U. S. Embassy, Rio de Janeiro, Copy sent to Dr. Herbert Feis and Secretary of State Sumner Welles.

through the energy and initiative of her sons in exploiting her great potential resources, you have taken care to preserve her links with the past, that ancient traditional culture which was so striking and so enchanting in Brazilians of the passing generation.[7]

VARGAS'S LABOR DAY ADDRESS

TO WORKERS IN VASCO DA GAMA STADIUM

1951

After nearly six years of political exile, during which time our long relationship never left my mind, I am here again at your side to speak with you about those days and to defend the legitimate interests of the people and to promote measures that are indispensable for the well-being of workers. This Labor Day celebration has a symbolic importance both for me and for you: it represents a new coming together of workers and the government. It is with deep emotion that we restore this relationship. In this atmosphere of national celebration, in which we bring back a government that speaks to the people as a friend speaks to a friend, in the simple, loyal, and frank language that we always used. Not only in the hours of glory and triumph but also in those of suffering and persecution, the working class always remained faithful, disinterested, and filled with valor. I can repeat today from my heart what I said once before: that the workers never disappointed me. They never came to me seeking selfish or private favors. They always spoke in the name of the collectivity to which they belong, for the recognition of their rights, for improvement in their living conditions, for redress of grievances of members of their class, and for the well-being of those sharing these difficulties. . . . I need you, workers of Brazil, my friends, my companions in our long journey, as much as you need me.[8]

VARGAS'S SUICIDE LETTER

AUGUST 24, 1954

Once more the forces and interests against the people are newly coordinated and raised against me. They do not accuse me, they insult me; they

---

7. Gustavo Capanema Papers, National Archives, Rio de Janeiro. Copy courtesy of José Carlos Sebe Bom Meihy.
8. Translated by author from copy in Brazilian National Archives, Rio de Janeiro, "Presidente da República" file.

do not fight me, they slander me and refuse to give me the right of defense. They seek to drown my voice and halt my actions so that I no longer continue to defend, as I always have defended, the people and principally the humble. I follow the destiny that is imposed on me. After decades of domination and plunder by international economic and financial groups, I made myself chief of an unconquerable revolution. I began the work of liberation and I instituted a regime of social liberty. I began the work of liberation. I was forced to resign. I returned to govern on the arms of the people.

A subterranean campaign of international groups joined with national interests revolting against the regime of workers' guarantees. The excess-profits law was held up in Congress. Hatreds were unleashed against the justice of a revision of minimum wages.

I wished to create national liberty by developing our riches through Petrobrás, which had scarcely begun to operate when the wave of agitation clouded its beginnings. Electrobrás was obstructed to the point of despair. They do not want workers to be free. They do not want the people to be independent.

I assumed my government during an inflationary spiral that was destroying the rewards of work. Profits by foreign companies reached as much as 500 percent annually. In declarations of goods that we import, frauds of more than 100 million dollars per year were proved. I saw the coffee crisis increase the value of our principal product. We tried to maintain that price but the reply was such violent pressure on our economy that we were forced to surrender. I have fought month after month, day after day, hour after hour, resisting constant, incessant pressures, unceasingly bearing it all in silence, forgetting everything and giving myself in order to defend the people that now fall abandoned. I cannot give you more than my blood. If the birds of prey wish the blood of anybody, they wish to continue to suck the blood of the Brazilian people. I offer my life in the holocaust. I choose this means to be with you always. When they humiliate you, you will feel my soul suffering at your side. When hunger knocks at your door, you will feel within you the energy to fight for yourselves and for your children. When you are scorned, my memory will give you the strength to react. My sacrifice will keep you united and my name will be your battle standard. Each drop of my blood will be an immortal call to your conscience and will uphold the sacred will to resist.

To hatred, I reply with forgiveness. And to those who think that they have defeated me, I reply with my victory. I was a slave of the people and today I am freeing myself for eternal life. But this people whose slave I was will no longer be slave to anyone. My sacrifice will remain forever in your souls and my blood will be the price of your ransom. I fought against the looting of Brazil. I fought against the looting of the people. I have fought bare-chested. The hatred, infamy, and calumny did not defeat my spirit. I have given you my life. I gave you my life. Now I offer you my death. Nothing remains. Serenely I take my first step on the road to eternity and I leave life to enter history.[9]

LETTERS FROM BRAZILIANS
(TO GETÚLIO VARGAS EXCEPT AS OTHERWISE NOTED)[10]

JOÃO LAUBA DO NASCIMENTO, CAETITÉ, BAHIA, TELEGRAM (ONE OF TWO) AUGUST 27, 1938

I ask for personal protection from an armed bully, José de Fóra, who has threatened my life in spite of my protests to local authorities. I am certain that you will help, Your Excellency, restore peace to the population of our town.

PEDRO UMBELINO, PRESIDENTE BUENO, MG, TELEGRAM, NOVEMBER 11, 1938

We workers in the Northeast corner of Minas Gerais offer solidarity with your government and on this anniversary of the Estado Novo. We implore you to protect us from the Syrian merchants in this region, who exploit the sweat of Brazilians, raising food prices for food and harming the well-being of the sons of our country.

TELES DA CRUZ, FORTALEZA, CEARÁ. CONFIDENTIAL TELEGRAM, OCTOBER 28, 1940

I am editor of the newspaper *Diário da Manhã* and a member of the Cearense Press Association and other organizations. I protest the DIP's order to suspend circulation of our newspaper. Everything has been done properly, and the DIP previously approved our registration with the Ministry of Justice. We seek your assistance. I am a great admirer of you and your great government. . . . But we cannot obtain newsprint.

9. Translated by author from copy in clipping file, Brazilian National Archives, Rio de Janeiro.
10. Translated by author from copies of letters and telegrams in Brazilian National Archives, Rio de Janeiro, "Pedidos" file.

VITOR MOREIRA AZEVEDO, MALACACHETA, MG, TELEGRAM,
DECEMBER 7, 1940

At the same time that Your Excellency works to make our country ever greater and ever richer through the exploration of the subsoil, other agents place obstacles in the way of mineral prospectors, already living in misery [explaining that he is a prospector who found a large crystal, nearly two hundred kilos, worth merely ten contos because of imperfections, but was denied permission to sell it because his license wasn't in order].

JOÃO BATISTA BOMFIM, FROM SAN JOÃO MARCOS, SÃO PAULO,
APRIL 11, 1941

Workers from the electric utility are bulldozing our city, and we ask you to intervene to stop them. Their actions have left hundreds of Brazilian families indigent. The company is attempting to frighten people to sell their properties to it for minuscule prices, and their construction poses physical dangers to us.

IVETTA GUERREIRO DANIEL, CAMPINAS, SÃO PAULO, SEPTEMBER 21, 1941

I have just received a letter from my mother in the capital of the State of Piauí saying that terrorist elements are setting fire to houses in that city. On one street there have been more than two hundred incidents. I ask that you guarantee protection for my mother, who is "old" but who has young children and lacks resources.

HOMEOWNERS ON TWO STREETS, DEODORO, RIO DE JANEIRO, TELEGRAM,
DECEMBER 28, 1941

Please arrange for us to have increased pressure in our water supply.

PADRE FERNANDO VASCONCELOS [A CATHOLIC PRIEST], CAXIAS,
MARANHÃO, TELEGRAM, MARCH 17, 1943

For more than two months, the mayor of this town has forced *thousands* of local poor rural residents to work without pay for the administration. They are told they have to work two days a month, but because of travel distances it often adds up to service for up to twelve days. I've complained to the interventor and others but nothing has been done. I ask for your assistance to stop this exploitation of these impoverished *caboclos*, who leave their families and walk up to twenty leagues to do this work, for fear of being jailed if they refuse. If they have them, they are obliged to bring mules and oxen with them. Yesterday nine men were arrested when they refused to work without pay. Today six more were put into jail.

HELENA FERNANDES ALVES DE BARROS, RIO, MARCH 31, 1943

I pray, Your Excellency, with all my heart and on bended knees, for you to receive the wisdom of God's mercy [claiming that she is a penni-less widow asking for tax relief before her house is seized by local au-thorities for nonpayment, and referring to an earlier letter, sent express four months earlier, that received no reply nor prompted any interven-tion on her behalf].

AVELINO FRANCISCO DO CARMO, MUNIZ FREIRE, ESPÍRITO SANTO, FEBRUARY 11, 1944

I am a Brazilian citizen, fourty-four years old, a reservist, a carpen-ter, and live in Muniz Freire. (1) I am poor with seven children; (2) I am in great difficulty because I do not have tools with which to work; (3) there has been illness in my family; (4) I know that Your Excellen-cy has spoken for the need to help families with more than seven chil-dren. Therefore with great respect I ask for the following tools: a small saw, a large saw, two hammers, three planes (nos. 4, 5, and 6), screw-drivers. . . .

ANTONIO JOSÉ DE SOUZA, CITY OF SÃO PAULO, FEBRUARY 16, 1944

I was born in Pernambuco, and am married with two children. I in-jured my right hand while working at an agricultural station in Paraná. I received a small pension but it is only half of what I expected, and I cannot sustain my family. The cost of living has gone up 100 percent in the past two years. Please order the Pension Institute to pay more in cas-es like mine.

RAFAEL SARAIVA, TRAIPÚ, ALAGOAS, MARCH 1, 1944

"Ask and you shall receive" are Christ's words, and I pray on the al-tar of our Country to you our exalted leader, the President of the Re-public, Dr. Getúlio Vargas. I humbly implore you to protect us from the calamitous times in which we live. . . . I know that the distance between Traipú and Rio de Janeiro is very great. I am married, thirty-four years of age, and live as a peddler. There are no jobs. I am an orphan, and re-sponsible for my sainted and dear mother. I beg for relief from the mis-ery in which I live. I ask for compassion. Please name me as an interim notary in any federal tax collection agency in the country.

LUDOVICO IANCHUCKI, PONTA GROSSA, PARANÁ. MARCH 4, 1944

I am Brazilian, married, one child, in the army reserves, and have worked twenty-six years on the Paraná-Santa Catarina Railroad. In 1942 I sent you a petition asking that you tell the railroad administration to promote me, when I was passed over. I waited but nothing happened. I have a wife and seven children at home, and am bitter at the fact that my children cannot attend school but have to walk the streets looking for ways to earn money to evade the hunger that stands at our door. Please grant me the promotion.

EDGARD DE ARRUDA BARBOSA, PAREIRAS, SÃO PAULO, OCTOBER 30, 1944

[The mayor of Pareiras] is a businessman who has abused his office, using it for personal profit, dealing on the black market and selling rationed goods (salt, gasoline, sugar) to the public for absurdly high prices. He owns a gas pump and has recently received a large shipment of precious gasoline. We are a small place, six kilometers from the railroad, and we have no doctor. People come here in trucks to buy fuel from the mayor, making him rich. [This report of "grave accusations" came with its signature notarized and affixed with three revenue stamps.]

RIVAURA DANTAS BANDEIRA, SABAINA, PARAÍBA, DECEMBER 20, 1944

May the generosity of your heart encourage you not to refuse my humble request. I am a poor girl, my widowed mother's only support. I worked hard to prepare for the DASP [Civil Service] typist examination and I passed it. I received my certificate, but have not been offered a position yet. I ask for your intervention so I can care for my poor mother. I would be willing to accept any job in Paraíba or Pernambuco.

MARTA TEIXEIRA, LAVRAS, MINAS GERAIS, DECEMBER 21, 1944

I read about penicillin in a magazine and ask for you to help me obtain some. My father is dead and my mother has been paralyzed and bedridden for years. If my mother had penicillin she would be cured of her unceasing martyrdom.

GASTÃO FIGUEIRA DE ARAUJO, BELO HORIZONTE, MINAS GERAIS, DECEMBER 22, 1944

I have been a machinist on the Central do Brazil railroad since I was young, and working on such a dangerous and physically demanding job, night and day, has left me in poor health. I want to retire but can only do so if I am promoted to "Category J."

JOÃO JOSÉ DE OLIVEIRA, CUIETÉ, MINAS GERAIS, DECEMBER 23, 1944

Knowing your generous heart, Your Excellency, I ask for help so that we are not jewed [sic] by the police. [They intimidate us without reason.] I am a father and head of a family. . . . Please look into our situation.

AMÉLIA NOGUEIRA DA SILVA, QUELUZ, MINAS GERAIS, TO DONA DARCY VARGAS, DECEMBER 28, 1944

I wish you a Happy New Year. The church of São João Batista in Queluz needs major reconstruction costing thousands of cruzeiros. I ask for help . . . because I know the reputation of our First Family of Brazil and of Dr. Getúlio Vargas for simplicity, charity, and wishing to satisfy [even] the smallest desires of your countrymen!

LUIZ AUGUSTO VIERIA, NILÓPOLIS, STATE OF RIO DE JANEIRO, JANUARY 4, 1945

I can only explain what really happened if I can communicate with you [President Vargas] in person. Your Excellency's protection of the Brazilian worker, especially in cases of injustice, are well known [in asking Vargas to intercede to force his employer to make restitution after being forced out of his job after two years and ten months on the job].

PETITION SIGNED BY FOURTEEN PEOPLE, SERRINHA, BA, DECEMBER 10, 1945, TO PRESIDENT JOSÉ LINHARES

People are living enormous anxiety these days because of social problems, and here and in many regions of our country there is begging and stark poverty [in asking, following Vargas's ouster, for construction of an Asylum and Hospital for the Poor in their city].

TESTIMONIES

LAFAIETE CASSIANO DOS SANTOS
BORN IN SÃO JOSÉ DO ALÉM PARAÍBA, MINAS GERAIS, 1921

My name is Lafaiete. I grew up in the interior of Minas Gerais. I grew up in the countryside, outside of the town. . . . We couldn't attend school; as a child I worked on the land with my parents. Our food came from the fields. If you didn't cultivate, you didn't have beans. My father and his father were sharecroppers. . . . I always wanted to go to the city. My father was suspicious. He didn't like *quillin* [dried food bought in shops]. When I was twenty I left. I had a girlfriend in São José . . . then I went to Volta Redonda. . . . I heard about the Company (CSN) [Volta Redonda Steel

Agency] through some propaganda about it, perhaps a poster. I heard there were lots of jobs there, jobs that would pay the minimum wage. At that time, the minimum wage was good, very good. You could live on it.

I decided to take the risk of leaving my family, my friends, my girl-friend, to go there. Getting there from Minas wasn't easy. You had to get permission to travel. In the countryside the local boss [*coronel*] had to like you . . . without a "safe conduct pass" you couldn't go anywhere. If the boss didn't send a note to the police, you didn't get one. . . . And you had to have a good health record. The Company didn't want workers who were undernourished or unhealthy. The first thing they did when you arrived was give you an inoculation . . . every time you went on a vacation, when you got back they gave you another one.

I went there by train. There were no busses; the roads were unpaved. I arrived in Volta Redonda in 1941. When I got off, there was nothing there. I slept on the ground. At 5 A.M. the Company agents came to get us. We lined up. The work started right away. The construction was start-ing. . . . we built the place from the ground up. . . . There were 22,000 of us, living in the midst of the machinery and the building materials.

Working for the CSN was the best job in Brazil. Everything was guar-anteed: work papers, holidays, a bonus at the end of the year. And the government paid us on time. I think it's the best job even today. I think that the CSN is the best place to work in South America, along with Petrobrás [the state petroleum cartel].

In 1947 I married my old girlfriend from São José. . . . My children were born in Volta Redonda and went to school. . . . two of them went to work for the Company although one left to start his own mechanic's shop. Company employees always get preference. . . .

. . . We have an excellent hospital. . . . the Company gives Christmas presents. We have a sports club. . . . I retired after twenty-three years and went on my own to do construction. My retirement salary is good but I have always liked to work. I am seventy-four but I still do carpentry.[11]

ABEL LOPES DE AZEVEDO
BORN IN MARQUÉS DE VALENÇA, RIO DE JANEIRO STATE, 1931

My father was a street cleaner in Barra do Pirai and my mother a do-mestic servant. They had so many children I can't remember the num-

11. Lafaiete Cassiano dos Santos, interview with Juliano Spyer, Volta Redonda, September 1994.

ber for sure, but I think there were twelve – but only three survived. . . .
My sisters were sent to work in the textile factory in Barra. At twelve I
became a shoeshine boy. Then I got a Saturday job in a factory cutting
soap into bars and counting them. I also bottled liquor at a distillery and
was a street vendor. I was called up for military service; after that, I became a waiter. Only in 1945 did I obtain working papers. Up to then,
the work I did was illegal – children cannot work without authorization
and only for regulated hours. . . . I bartered most of my salary for goods.
Only a little was left; we spent it on fooling around – eating something
on the street, going to the movies, these things. I never got through el-
ementary school. In 1953 I went to work for a company that did contract work for the Volta Redonda Steel Plant (CSN), doing manual labor. When the work was finished we were to be fired, but the boss agreed
to transfer his best workers to the CSN at the lowest work category. The
initial contract was for a trial period of 120 days. . . . I slowly worked my
way up, from carrier to helper to machine operator to electric cart driver, then (finally) as a full-fledged industrial worker and administrator.
I spent twenty-nine and a half years with the CSN and retired in 1982
for reasons of health. I was able to study two and a half hours a day in a
company school and earned my equivalency degrees through high
school. Some of what I studied was vocational, linked to my work at
CSN. You were tested, and if you passed you could move up to higher
jobs. The CSN always gave preference to its own employees who were
studying. . . . Getúlio? He was an excellent head of state. . . . In fact, I
got to see him personally when he visited once to open a new steel fur-
nace. . . . He gave the impression of being a modest man, and he min-
gled with us. His big Negro bodyguard Gregório tried to stop him but he
didn't listen, and he shook hands with the workers, mine too.[12]

IRENE GUIMARÃES MOTA
BORN IN MERCÊS, MINAS GERAIS, 1941

I lived in Mercês until I was fifteen. I had seven brothers and sisters. My
father was a tailor and my mother a seamstress. . . . My grandparents
took me to Volta Redonda to work. My uncle was one of the first employees in Volta Redonda, in 1946. I was a clerk and had worked in Mes-
bla [a department store]. . . . I took a bookkeeping exam at the CSN. I

12. Abel Lopes de Azevedo, interview with Juliano Spyer, Volta Redonda, Sep-
    tember 1994.

passed it and was accepted. That wasn't easy – it was really difficult! Everyone had studied and only the best were hired. . . . We had to be tested on mathematics, Portuguese, stenography, geography. . . . I didn't type well and had to take the exam twice. The Company was expanding so I got it, although it took six months.

Although the bosses are all men, I never felt discrimination. . . . At the cafeteria everyone eats together: men, women, bosses, blacks . . . everyone! The food is all the same too. . . . When you retire, however, the pension isn't much. . . . it's just as bad as for anyone else who retires on a pension in Brazil. And they calculated my pension incorrectly, so I am protesting. . . . In all, though, the CSN was everything for me: it was like a mother. . . . I was even able to buy some shares when I retired.[13]

Popular Music[14]

"GE-GÊ" (LAMARTINE BABO), JANUARY 1931

Only with revolution
Thanks to the radio and telegraph
We will transform
This green and yellow Brazil. . . .

"É NEGÓCIO CASAR!" [IT IS WISE TO MARRY!]
(ATAULFO ALVES COM FON-FON AND HIS ORCHESTRA)
OCTOBER 1941

Watch out!
My life is changing
I'm not the old person
Who crawled home at dawn
Do what I did
Because life is for those who work
I have a sweet home
I am happy with my wife
The Estado Novo

---

13. Irene Guimarães Mota, interview with Juliano Spyer, Volta Redonda, September 1994.
14. Song lyrics translated by author from copies in Brazilian National Archives, Rio de Janeiro.

Is given to lead us in the way
In Brazil there is nothing that we lack
But it is necessary that we work
We have coffee, petroleum, and gold
No one can doubt this

It is for those with four children
The President pays honors
It is wise to marry!

"BRASIL BRASILEIRO!"
(SEBASTIÃO LIMA AND HENRIQUE DE ALMEIDA)
AUGUST 1942

My heart is small
But large enough fit within it
My tan-colored Brazil
Brazil that the poets
Serenade in their ardor. . . .

Brazil! My Brazil of green seas
A Giant that is awakening
From a secular dream
Brazil! Brazilian pride. . . .

Consecrated hero, leader of my people
Brazil! My Brazil so loved
Shines to the world through the Estado Novo. . . .

"AI, GEGÊ!"
(JOÃO DE BARRO AND JOSÉ MARIA DE ABREU)
MARCH 1950

Ai Gegê! . . . What longing
We have for you

Beans have gone up in price
Coffee has gone up as well
Dried beef goes up too
No one can afford things

Everything goes up, up, up
Every day on the message boards
Only our poor currency
Goes down every day.

Ai, Gegê . . .

"SIXTY-ONE YEARS OF THE REPUBLIC"
(*SILAS DE OLIVEIRA AND MANO DÉCIO DA VIOLA*)
MARCH 1951

We present the most important parts of our history
If our memory doesn't fail us . . .

Today we have justice
In glorious opulence
October 3, 1950
Brought to us the person
Who always rescued our country
In bitter times
The eminent statesman
Getúlio Vargas
Elected by the people
His important and elevated victory
Will mark for certain
A new chapter
In the history of the Brazilian Republic.

"HYMN TO GETÚLIO VARGAS"
(*JOÃO DE BARRO*)
SEPTEMBER 1958

Getúlio Vargas
You will live in history
In the arms of the common people
You climb to the altar
Getúlio Vargas
Your audacious and masculine spirit
Will remain forever
in Brazil's heart . . .

Photographs

Photographs convey historical information as much as any conventional written document. The photographs reproduced here capture the flavor of the Vargas era.

1. *Getúlio Vargas, at the side of Oswaldo Aranha, leaving Porto Alegre railroad station en route to Rio de Janeiro, October 11, 1930. CPDOC/Fundação Getúlio Vargas (FGV). Arq. Getúlio Vargas.*

Sobrenome — Alves de Oliveira

Nome — Francisco

Vulgo —

Idade 30 annos — Nascido em 30 de março de 1905

E. Civil Solteiro — Nacionalidade Brasileira — Natural de São Gonçalo - Rio Grande do Norte — Filiação: pai José Vicente de Oliveira

Mãe Maria Felismina de Oliveira

Instrucção Assigna o nome

Profisssão Agricultor

Residencia Mareana - São Gonçalo - crespos

Notas Chromaticas . . { Côr Morena Cabellos Cast.esc.e Estatura: 1 m. e 56 cts. { Barba Feita Bigodes Aparados Olhos Castanhos escuros

Preso em 25 de janeiro de 1936 Identificado em 28 de fevereiro de 1936

SIGNAES PARTICULARES

OBSERVAÇÕES
Suspeito communista

Photographia tirada em 28 de fevereiro de 1936

ASSIGNATURA DO IDENTIFICADO
Francisco Alves d. Oliveira

O Official Manoel Borges de Lima

REGISTRO GERAL N.

INDIVIDUAL DACTILOSCÓPICA Serie 2333 Secção 3122

SERIE

POLICIA DO ESTADO DO RIO GRANDE DO NORTE

Gabinete de Identificação e Estatística Criminal

SISTHEMA DE VUCETICH

REGISTRO GERAL Nº

SERIE MÃO DIREITA

SECÇÃO MÃO ESQUERDA

| Polegars | Indicadores | Medios | Annulares | Minimos |

SECÇÃO

2. Arrest document, "Suspected Communist" Francisco Alves de Oliveira, Rio Grande do Norte, February 28, 1936. Gabinete de Identificação e Estatística Criminal, Natal.

3. *Rural harvest, Ijuí, Rio Grande do Sul, 1938. Caxias do Sul Municipal Archive. Despite Vargas's goal to modernize Brazil, agriculture remained as primitive in the late 1930's as it had been for decades. Men and women shared the task of planting, maintaining the fields, and harvesting.*

4. Integralist Wedding of Angelo Duso and Ada Andreazzana.
Caxias do Sul Cathedral, mid-1930s. Caxias do Sul Municipal
Archive. Not only most of the wedding party but the groom himself
wears the full Integralist uniform, complete with the Σ emblem on the
sleeve. The bride and bridegroom are of Italian origin; Integralism was
very strong among German and Polish-Brazilians as well.

5. Pro–Estado Novo demonstration, Caxias do Sul, circa 1940. The banner on the church reads "The people of Caxias welcome the eradication of extremism under the New State." Caxias do Sul Municipal Archive. It is ironic that the Estado Novo, rooted in corporatism with a dose of fascism thrown in, urged the population to resist "extremism." The message likely referred to the banning of the Integralist and Nazi parties.

6. *Barefoot rural men and women in mayor's office waiting room,
rural Minas Gerais, 1941. The photograph illustrates the time-
honored Brazilian tradition of taking requests personally to officials.
Photograph by Genevieve Naylor.*

7. *Portraits, place unknown, circa 1941. Photograph by Genevieve Naylor. The framed official presidential portrait of Vargas sits surrounded by smaller family photographs in what appears to be a studio display. There is a second Vargas photograph on the wall, suggesting that the studio not only was honoring Vargas but selling his images. One or more of the smaller photographs may also be of Getúlio when he was young. Some of the framed photographs seem to have been taken long before this picture was shot. All were studio poses, even the young girl atop a horse.*

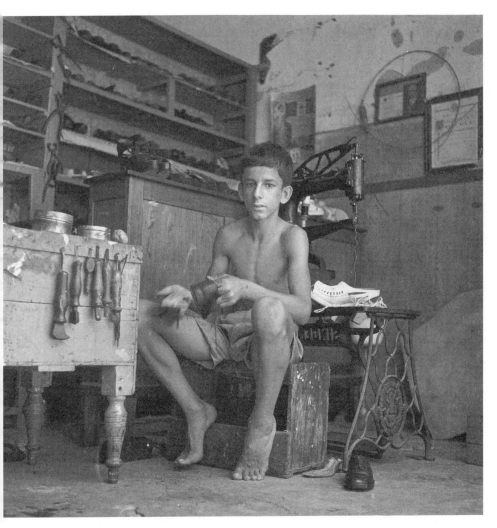

8. *Child at his cobbler's workbench in violation of government social legislation, place unknown, circa 1941. Photograph by Genevieve Naylor.*

9. *Factory workers using no protective devices, Evaristo de Antoni Carpentry Shop, Rio Grande do Sul, mid-1930s. Caxias do Sul Municipal Archive.*

10. *Orphanage children, mid-1930s, Rio Grande do Sul. Caxias do Sul Municipal Archive. Vargas did little to improve conditions in state-run institutions. These orphans were dressed as if they were in prison; they received little or no schooling. When they reached adolescence they were made "apprentices" to local firms or agricultural properties under conditions that in many cases amounted to indentured servitude.*

11. *Migrants fleeing drought receiving food, São Francisco River region, 1941. Photograph by Genevieve Naylor. Vargas's regional agencies did little to improve conditions in drought-prone areas. The New Deal changed California's desolate Imperial Valley into rich farmland by introducing irrigation, but in the Brazilian Northeast, refugees from poverty could do little but migrate to other parts of the country in search of work.*

12. Men and boys, Congonhas, Minas Gerais, 1941. A government anti-leprosy campaign poster is on the wall of the church. Photograph by Genevieve Naylor.

13. *Government union officials (pelegos), Rio de Janeiro, 1941.*
Photograph by Genevieve Naylor.

14. Vargas campaigning for the presidency, Ponta Grossa, Paraná, 1950. CPDOC/FGV. Arq. Getúlio Vargas.

15. *Getúlio Vargas in Uberaba, Minas Gerais, 1950.*
CPDOC/FGV. Arq. Getúlio Vargas.

16. *Vargas lying in state at presidential palace, August 1954.*
CPDOC/FGV. *Arq. Getúlio Vargas.*

17. Waiting for the funeral procession, Rio de Janeiro, August 1954.
CPDOC/FGV. Arq. Getúlio Vargas.

18. *Watching Vargas's funeral cortege pass by from the presidential palace to Santos Dumont Airport, Rio de Janeiro, August 1954. CPDOC/FGV. Arq. Getúlio Vargas.*

BIBLIOGRAPHIC ESSAY

Bibliographical references are confined to English-language sources. Most of the books and articles listed, however, extensively cite the Portuguese-language literature, which may also be found in bibliographic guides at research libraries and, in a preliminary way, on the Internet.

For background, see E. Bradford Burns's *A History of Brazil*, 3rd ed. (New York: Columbia University Press, 1993); Charles Wagley's *Introduction to Brazil*, rev. ed. (New York: Columbia University Press, 1971); T. Lynn Smith's *Brazil: People and Institutions* (Baton Rouge: Louisiana State University Press, 1972); Ronald M. Schneider's *Brazil: Culture and Politics in a New Industrial Powerhouse* (Boulder, Colo.: Westview Press, 1996). Also, Fernando de Azevedo, *Brazilian Culture: An Introduction* (New York: Macmillan, 1950); and Thomas W. Merrick and Douglas H. Graham, *Population and Economic Development in Brazil, 1808 to the Present* (Baltimore: Johns Hopkins University Press, 1979). See also Peter Flynn, *Brazil: A Political Analysis* (London: Ernest Benn, 1978). Stefan Zweig's *Brazil: Land of the Future* (New York: Viking Press, 1941) and Waldo David Frank's *South American Journey* (London: Victor Gollancz, 1943) are wartime paeans to Brazil's potential. A more comprehensive analysis is presented by Karl Loewenstein's *Brazil under Vargas* (New York: Macmillan, 1942). G. Harvey Summ offers interesting sketches in *Brazilian Mosaic: Portraits of a Diverse People and Culture* (Wilmington, Del.: SR Books, 1995). See also Joseph A. Page, *The Brazilians* (Reading, Pa.: Addison-Wesley, 1995).

The transition from the Old Republic to the Vargas era is dealt with by Joseph L. Love, *Rio Grande do Sul and Brazilian Regionalism, 1882–1930* (Stanford: Stanford University Press, 1971), and his *São Paulo in the Brazilian Federation, 1889–1937* (Stanford: Stanford University Press, 1980), as well as companion volumes by John D. Wirth on

Minas Gerais (Stanford: Stanford University Press, 1977) and Robert M. Levine on Pernambuco (Stanford: Stanford University Press, 1978). Also see Eul-Soo Pang, *Bahia in the First Brazilian Republic* (Gainesville: University Presses of Florida, 1979), and Teresa A. Meade's *"Civilizing" Rio: Reform and Resistance in a Brazilian City, 1889–1930* (University Park: Penn State University Press, 1997). Michael Conniff's *Urban Politics in Brazil: The Rise of Populism, 1925–1945* (Pittsburgh: University of Pittsburgh Press, 1981) analyzes populism in Rio de Janeiro. Agricultural issues and benefits to workers are addressed in Thomas H. Holloway, *Immigrants on the Land* (Chapel Hill: University of North Carolina Press, 1981). See also Maxine L. Margolis, *The Moving Frontier* (Gainesville: University Presses of Florida, 1973), and Mauricio A. Font, *Coffee, Contention, and Change in the Making of Modern Brazil* (Cambridge, Mass.: Basil Blackwell, 1990).

Overviews of the Vargas period are provided by Robert M. Levine, *The Vargas Regime* (New York: Columbia University Press, 1970), and "Perspectives on the Mid-Vargas Years, 1934–1937," *Journal of Interamerican Studies and World Affairs*, 22:1 (1980), 57–80; Thomas E. Skidmore, *Politics in Brazil, 1930–1964* (New York: Oxford University Press, 1967); John W. F. Dulles, *Vargas of Brazil: A Political Biography* (Austin: University of Texas Press, 1967); Ronald M. Schneider, *"Order and Progress": A Political History of Brazil* (Boulder, Colo.: Westview Press, 1991); and Michael L. Conniff and Frank D. McCann Jr., eds., *Modern Brazil: Elites and Masses in Historical Perspective* (Lincoln: University of Nebraska Press, 1989). Joel W. Wolfe edited a special issue of the *Luso-Brazilian Review* (31:2, Winter 1994), "Getúlio Vargas and His Legacy." The issue includes essays by Randal Johnson on Brazilian culture during the 1930s, by Jeffrey Lesser on immigration and shifting concepts of national identity during the Vargas era, by Daryle Williams on Brazil's national historical patrimony, and by Dain Borges on Brazilian social thought of the 1930s. Wartime Brazil is examined in Robert M. Levine, *Brazil in the 1940s through the Photographs of Genevieve Naylor* (Durham, N.C.: Duke University Press, 1998). The Portuguese and European fascist experience, useful for comparison, is described in Antonio Costa Pinto, *Salazar's Dictatorship and European Fascism* (New York: Columbia University Press, 1995). See also Richard Graham, "Dilemmas for Democracy in Brazil," in Lawrence S. Graham and Robert H. Wilson, eds., *The Political Economy of Brazil* (Austin: University of Texas Press, 1990), 7–25, and Werner Baer, *The Political Economy of Brazil* (Austin: University of Texas Press, 1990).

For Vargas's role, see Joan L. Bak, "Political Centralization and the Building of the Interventionist State in Brazil: Corporatism, Regionalism and Interest Group Politics in Rio Grande do Sul, 1930–1937," *Luso-Brazilian Review*, 22:1 (Summer 1985), 9–25, and John D. Wirth, *The Politics of Brazilian Development, 1930–1954* (Stanford: Stanford University Press, 1970). For opposition to Vargas – a subject infrequently studied – see John W. F. Dulles, *The São Paulo Law School and the Anti-Vargas Resistance* (Austin: University of Texas Press, 1986). Frank D. McCann Jr., *The Brazilian-American Alliance* (Princeton: Princeton University Press, 1973), and Stanley E. Hilton, *Brazil and the Great Powers, 1930–39* (Austin: University of Texas Press, 1975), deal with trade policy and Brazil's entry in World War II. McCann's "Brazil and World War II: The Forgotten Ally. What Did You Do in the War, Zé Carioca?" in *Estudios Interdisciplinarios de America Latina y el Caribe* (Tel Aviv), 6:2 (1995), 35–70, provides an excellent summary of the larger picture. For Brazil's role in the Third International, see Manuel Caballero, *Latin America and the Comintern, 1919–1943* (Cambridge: Cambridge University Press, 1986), as well as Stanley E. Hilton's *Brazil and the Soviet Challenge, 1917–1947* (Austin: University of Texas Press, 1991), and John W. F. Dulles's *Anarchists and Communists in Brazil, 1900–1935* (Austin: University of Texas Press, 1973) and its sequel, *Brazilian Communism, 1935–1945: Repression during World Upheaval* (Austin: University of Texas Press, 1983). Richard Bourne's breezy *Getúlio Vargas of Brazil, 1883–1954: Sphinx of the Pampas* (London: Tonbridge and Knight, 1974) offers interesting detail about Vargas's life.

For conservative ideology as well as the role of the Roman Catholic Church, see Scott Mainwaring, *The Catholic Church and Politics in Brazil, 1916–1985* (Stanford: Stanford University Press, 1986); C. F. G. de Groot, *Brazilian Catholicism and the Ultramontane Reform, 1850–1930* (Amsterdam: CEDLA Incidentele Publications, 1996); Jeffrey D. Needell, "History, Race, and the State in the Thought of Oliveira Vianna," *Hispanic American Historical Review*, 75:1 (February 1995), 1–30; and Dain Borges, "Brazilian Social Thought in the 1930s," *Luso-Brazilian Review*, 31:2 (Winter 1994), 137–150. Also, W. E. Hewitt, "Catholicism, Social Justice, and the Brazilian Corporative State since 1930," *Journal of Church and State*, 32:4 (Autumn 1990), 831–850; Margaret Todaro Williams, "Church and State in Vargas's Brazil: The Politics of Cooperation," *Journal of Church and State*, 18:3 (Autumn 1976), 443–462; and Kenneth P. Serbin, "Brazil: State Subsidization and the Church since 1930," in Satya Pattnayak, ed., *Organized Religion in the*

Political Transformation of Latin America (Lanham, Md.: University Press of America, 1995), 153–175. See also Jeffrey Lesser, *Welcoming the Undesirables: Brazil and the Jewish Question* (Berkeley: University of California Press, 1995).

Economic issues are treated in Stephen Haber, ed., *How Latin America Fell Behind: Essays on the Economic Histories of Brazil and Mexico* (Stanford: Stanford University Press, 1997); Warren Dean, *The Industrialization of São Paulo* (Austin: University of Texas Press, 1969); Joseph L. Love and Nils Jacobsen, eds., *Guiding the Invisible Hand: Economic Liberalism and the State in Latin American History* (New York: Praeger, 1988), especially Steven C. Topik's essay in that volume, "The Economic Role of the State in Liberal Regimes: Brazil and Mexico Compared"; and Topik's seminal essay, "The State's Contribution to the Development of Brazil's Internal Economy, 1850–1930," in the *Hispanic American Historical Review*, 65:2 (1985), 203–228, as well as his *The Political Economy of the Brazilian State, 1889–1930* (Austin: University of Texas Press, 1987). Also see Richard M. Morse, "Manchester Economics and Paulista Sociology," in John D. Wirth and Robert L. Jones, eds., *Manchester and São Paulo: Problems of Rapid Urban Growth* (Stanford: Stanford University Press, 1978), 7–34; Carlos F. Diaz-Alejandro, "Latin America in the 1930s," in Rosemary Thorp, ed., *Latin America in the 1930s* (New York, 1982), 17–49; and Joseph L. Love, *Crafting the Third World: Theorizing Underdevelopment in Rumania and Brazil* (Stanford: Stanford University Press, 1996). Thomas E. Skidmore compares Vargas with Perón in Working Paper No. 3 of the Latin American Program of the Wilson Center, Smithsonian Institution, Washington, D.C., 1977. See also Stanley E. Hilton, "Vargas and Brazilian Economic Development, 1930–1945," *Journal of Economic History,* 68 (December 1975), 754–778.

The first part of Gil Shidlo's *Social Policy in a Non-Democratic Regime: The Case of Public Housing in Brazil* (Boulder, Colo.: Westview Press, 1990) discusses Brazil's need for public housing after 1930. Lucio Kowarick's *Social Struggles and the City: The Case of São Paulo* (New York: Monthly Review Press, 1994) offers retrospective data on the city during the 1930s. For a political scientist's overview, see Frances Hagopian, *Traditional Politics and Regime Change in Brazil* (Cambridge: Cambridge University Press, 1996). For labor, see Barbara Weinstein, "The Industrialists, the State, and the Issues of Worker Training and Social Services in Brazil, 1930–50," *Hispanic American Historical Review* 70 (August 1990), 379–404, and her monograph, *For Social Peace in Brazil* (Chapel Hill:

University of North Carolina Press, 1996); Joel W. Wolfe, *Working Men, Working Women: São Paulo and the Rise of Brazil's Industrial Working Class, 1900–1955* (Durham, N.C.: Duke University Press, 1993). See also John D. French, "The Populist Gamble of Getúlio Vargas in 1945," in David Rock, ed., *Latin America in the 1940s* (Berkeley: University of California Press, 1994), 141–165; Michael L. Conniff, "Voluntary Associations in Rio, 1870–1945: A New Approach to Urban Social Dynamics," *Journal of Interamerican Studies and World Affairs*, 17 (1975), 64–81; Hobart A. Spalding Jr., *Organized Labor in Latin America* (New York: New York University Press, 1977), and Kenneth Paul Erickson, *The Brazilian Corporative State and Working Class Politics* (Berkeley: University of California Press, 1977). Useful also is Marshall C. Eakin's *British Enterprise in Brazil: The St. John d'el Rey Mining Company and the Morro Velho Gold Mine, 1830–1960* (Durham, N.C.: Duke University Press, 1989).

Joseph L. Love's article "Political Participation in Brazil, 1881–1969" in the *Luso-Brazilian Review*, 7:2 (1970), 3–24, remains a classic. See also his article with Bert J. Barickman, "Rulers and Owners: A Brazilian Case Study in Historical Perspective," *Hispanic American Historical Review*, 66:4 (November 1986), 743–765. A longer view is provided by Kurt von Mettenheim, *The Brazilian Voter: Mass Politics in Democratic Transition, 1974–1986* (Pittsburgh: University of Pittsburgh Press, 1995). On sports, see Joseph Arbena, ed., *Sport and Society in Latin America* (New York: Greenwood Press, 1988); Janet Lever's *Soccer Madness*, 2nd ed. (Chicago: Waveland Press, 1995), is very helpful. See also Jerry Haar, *The Politics of Higher Education in Brazil* (New York: Praeger, 1977), and Fay Haussman and J. Haar's *Education in Brazil* (Hamden, Conn.: Archon Books, 1978). The classic monograph on education is still Robert J. Havighurst and J. Roberto Moreira, *Society and Education in Brazil* (Pittsburgh: University of Pittsburgh Press, 1965).

Social dynamics and women's issues are explored in Sonia E. Alvarez, *Engendering Democracy in Brazil: Women's Movements in Transition* (Princeton: Princeton University Press, 1990); Susan K. Besse, *Restructuring Patriarchy: The Modernization of Gender Inequality in Brazil, 1914–1940* (Chapel Hill: University of North Carolina Press, 1996); and June E. Hahner, *Emancipating the Female Sex: The Struggle for Women's Rights in Brazil* (Durham, N.C.: Duke University Press, 1990). For race relations, see George Reid Andrews, *Blacks and Whites in São Paulo, 1888–1988* (Madison: University of Wisconsin Press, 1991); Thomas E. Skidmore, *Black into White* (New York: Oxford University Press, 1974); Michael George Hanchard, *Orpheus and Power* (Princeton:

Princeton University Press, 1994); and Robert M. Levine and José Carlos Sebe Bom Meihy, *The Life and Death of Carolina Maria de Jesus* (Albuquerque: University of New Mexico Press, 1995). Also see Robert M. Levine, "The First Afro-Brazilian Congress," *Race: A Journal of Race and Group Relations*, 15:2 (1973), 185–194; and Dain Borges, "The Recognition of Afro-Brazilian Symbols and Ideas, 1890–1940," *Luso-Brazilian Review*, 32:2 (Winter 1995), 59–78. See also David J. Hellwig, *African-American Reflections on Brazil's Racial Paradise* (Philadelphia: Temple University Press, 1992), and Florestan Fernandes, "The Negro in Brazilian Society: Twenty-Five Years Later," in Maxine L. Margolis and William Carter, eds., *Brazil: Anthropological Perspectives: Essays in Honor of Charles Wagley* (New York: Columbia University Press, 1979), 96–113. Elizabeth and K. David Jackson have published a translation of Patricia Galvão's 1933 proletarian novel, *Industrial Park* (Lincoln: University of Nebraska Press, 1993), with a very useful afterword by David Jackson. See also Susan K. Besse, "Pagú: Patricia Galvão – Rebel," in William H. Beezley and Judith Ewell, eds., *The Human Condition in Latin America* (Wilmington, Del.: SR Books, 1987), 103–117. Assorted social issues are examined in Edmar L. Bacha and Herbert S. Klein's *Social Change in Brazil, 1945–1985: The Incomplete Transition* (Albuquerque: University of New Mexico Press, 1989) and Robert M. Levine, *Brazilian Legacies* (New York: M. E. Sharpe, 1997).

The family is treated by Dain Borges, *The Family in Bahia, Brazil, 1870–1945* (Stanford: Stanford University Press, 1992), and Linda Lewin, *Politics and Parentela in Paraiba: A Case Study of Family-Based Oligarchy in Brazil* (Princeton: Princeton University Press, 1987), and her "Some Historical Implications of Kinship Organization for Family-Based Politics in the Brazilian Northeast," *Comparative Studies in Society and History*, 21:2 (April 1979), 262–292. Also, Emilio Willems, "The Structure of the Brazilian Family," *Social Forces*, 31:4 (1953), 339–345. On Brazil's twentieth-century conservative tradition, see Jeffrey D. Needell, "History, Race, and the State in the Thought of Oliveira Vianna," *Hispanic American Historical Review*, 75:1 (February 1995), 1–30.

Another aspect of Vargas's legacy is discussed in Charles W. Wood and J. A. Magno de Carvalho's *The Demography of Inequality in Brazil* (Cambridge: Cambridge University Press, 1988). A magisterial overview of many aspects of industrial policy and environmental conditions is provided by the late Warren Dean's *With Broadaxe and Firebrand: The Destruction of the Brazilian Atlantic Forest* (Berkeley: University of California Press, 1995).

Book publishing and cultural history is analyzed in detail by Laurence Hallewell's *Books in Brazil: A History of the Publishing Trade* (Metuchen, N.J.: Scarecrow Press, 1982). For brief treatments of Brazilian social and cultural history, see G. Harvey Summ, ed., *Brazilian Mosaic: Portraits of a Diverse People and Culture* (Wilmington, Del.: SR Books, 1995), esp. 100–132.

Orson Welles started to make a movie filmed mostly in Brazil as part of the cultural Good Neighbor Policy but it was only completed posthumously, a half century later. *It's All True* tells the story of the four raft fishermen who journeyed to Rio to win Vargas's ear and also contains scenes of Carnival. Chico Buarque de Holanda's *Opera de Malandro* entertainingly sets Kurt Weill's "Beggar's Opera" in 1950s Rio during Vargas's elected presidency.

INDEX